DISCARD

DATE DUE

DEMCO

THE ROAD TO ARMAGEDDON

THE ROAD TO

THE MARTIAL SPIRIT IN ENGLISH

DUKE UNIVERSITY PRESS *Durham and London*

A R M A G E D D O N

POPULAR LITERATURE, 1870–1914

CECIL DEGROTTE EBY   1987

Permissions
J. M. Barrie letters with the kind permission of the
Walter Beinecke Collection at Yale University.
Rupert Brooke's "My First Was in the Night," from
Rupert Brooke: A Biography (1964), by Christopher
Hassall. Reprinted by permission of the Rupert Brooke
Trustees and Faber & Faber, Ltd.
E. W. Hornung's poems from *Notes of a Camp-
Follower on the Western Front* (1919). Reprinted by
permission of Constable and Company.
Rudyard Kipling poems in *Rudyard Kipling's Verse*
(1943). Reprinted by permission of Doubleday &
Company.
Lines from "Letter to Lord Byron," in W. H. Auden,
Collected Poems, edited by Edward Mendelson,
copyright 1976, Random House, Inc., and Faber &
Faber, Ltd.
"Our Contemporaries," in Ezra Pound, *Personae,*
copyright 1926. Reprinted by permission of New
Directions Publishing Corporation and Faber & Faber,
Ltd.

Frontispiece: How English families amuse themselves
during the Siege of Mafeking. Children chasing a shell.
From Baden-Powell's *Sketches of Mafeking.*

*My argument is that War makes rattling
good history; but Peace is poor reading.*
THOMAS HARDY, *The Dynasts*

Contents

▼

Acknowledgments

▼

My major debts are to the regents of the University of Michigan for authorizing a sabbatical leave for work on this book and to the trustees of the Rackham School of Graduate Studies for two grants allowing research in England. I gratefully acknowledge the assistance of librarians in all quarters of the University of Michigan (particularly those of the Interlibrary Loan Division), and the British Library.

Among those whose contributions have been beyond reasonable call of duty are Alyce DePree, Bruce Zellers, and my daughter Clare, all of whom had countless suggestions or supplied materials that would otherwise have eluded me. Peter Bauland, Thomas Garbaty, and Robert Super—colleagues at the University of Michigan—provided invaluable assistance with arcane matters. Others who deserve special mention are Jean A. Diekoff and Roland Stromberg, specialists in their respective fields of Latin literature and modern cultural history. K. A. Fowler of the British Defence Staff in Washington came forward at the zero hour to supply me with necessary information about the British Army of 1914–18.

From first to last my editor, Reynolds Smith, and Elizabeth Gratch of the Duke University Press offered their assistance and friendship in the finest tradition of American publishing. And finally I am grateful to Pam Morrison for her precision in editing and Mary Mendell for her fine sense of what a book should look like.

1 INTRODUCTION

▼

After all, we're not savages. We're English, and the
English are best at everything.
WILLIAM GOLDING, *Lord of the Flies*

In 1866 John Ruskin delivered a lecture titled "War" at the Royal
Military Academy in Woolwich. In retrospect the occasion seems like
an incongruous combination of an improbable speaker at an improbable
place. Anemic and neurasthenic, a less warlike figure than Ruskin
could hardly be imagined. What could he, an authority on Victorian
aesthetics and Venetian architecture, communicate to an audience composed mainly of young military bloods unless it were to chastise them
for embarking on careers dealing in war and destruction? A listener
might well have suspected him of irony as he warmed to his theme: "All
the pure and noble arts of peace are founded on war; no great art ever
yet rose on earth, but among a nation of soldiers."[1] But no irony was
intended, as he went on to argue that peace was actually inimical to
what he called the "virtues of civil life." Better to ride warhorses than
racehorses. War, by eliminating the unfit, determined who were the
best—those highest bred, most fearless, coolest of nerve, swiftest of eye
and hand. "All healthy men like fighting, and like the sense of danger;
all brave women like to hear of their fighting, and of their facing
danger."[2] Ruskins's arguments in support of war were wholly theoretical. They had nothing to do with diplomatic exigencies of the moment; except for the Crimean venture, England had not been involved
in a major war since the days of Napoleon. If she had few close friends
abroad, the Royal Navy saw to it that she had no formidable enemies
near home.

On first reflection Ruskin's views seem strangely bellicose for a
wealthy cosmopolitan and intellectual in that age of Pax Britannica.

What they resemble, of course, is that loose aggregation of ideas which later came to be lumped under the heading of "social Darwinism"—that is, the principle of biological evolution wrenched into the dominion of moral and social affairs. In opposition to the teachings of Jesus, social Darwinism posited that war was neither unnatural nor malignant. Rather, it functioned like well-managed pruning shears, eliminating the weak and undesirable shoots and allowing the development of luxuriant blooms.

The point here is not to file a claim for Ruskin as a founding father of social Darwinist ideas but to note that a theory arguing in favor of war could be publicly expounded by a respected scholar, not a bloodthirsty madman. Ruskin originated nothing, for these ideas lay at saturation density throughout nearly all layers of Victorian society. He merely recorded attitudes that others, bound by Christian inhibition, were less likely to air publicly.

From acceptance of war on purely theoretical grounds as a primary catalyst in evolutionary growth, it was but a short step to the belief that war was necessary as an anodyne to prevent actual degeneracy within the social body. To adherents of this philosophy, healthy organisms were unrelentingly at war with competitors in their environment—whether on the battlefield, the stock exchange, or the playing field. In former days war had been one of the decorative arts with its professional marionettes gaily decked out in extravagant but nonfunctional uniforms festooned with bright buttons, plumes, and braid. It had been fought in theaters of operation conveniently distant from the general public. Under the impress of social Darwinist theories, however, war became a primary testing ground for national character rather than just a remote game conducted by a caste of professionals. Moreover, radical developments in military technology—telegraphy, nitroglycerine, breech-loading artillery, armor-plated vessels, submarines, steel-and-concrete fortifications, machine guns, and so on—spelled the end of war as a parade ground exercise. Modern warfare had become a serious business indeed.

One measure of its rigor was that by the end of the Great War of 1914–18 soldiers in uniforms of khaki (Britain), field gray (Germany), or horizon blue (France) looked more like factory workers and less like cockatoos or other exotic birds on display in an aviary. Perhaps the most awesome problem confronting commanders of future wars was the sheer size of mobilized armies, which would consist of millions of soldiers, not mere thousands, whose movements would resemble "the most stupendous emigration of peoples."[3] The fiscal problems involved in staging such a gargantuan operation as modern war were beyond known calculation, although a common view of the period was that long wars were impossible because the belligerent powers would quickly run out of money. Spend now—save later seemed to be the prevailing financial policy; between 1860 and 1900 German arms expenditure quintupled, British and Russian trebled, and French doubled.[4] The ability to appropriate money for armaments gave the major powers a certain cachet which the secondary powers lacked and envied. Sir Henry Howarth, an English spokesman, doubtless registered the attitude of many others of the European upper classes when he observed, "The expense of modern war is what makes it a *luxury,* and the poorer nations who cannot *afford* it should desist from the *competition* [my italics]."[5] For a second-class nation to aspire to the luxury of engaging in an all-out modern war was presumably as outrageous as a coal miner or navvy aspiring to caviar and champagne.

In dramatically bringing home to the British public the possibility of future war, the key event was the lightning victory of Prussia over France in 1870. Nothing in Britain or in Europe was ever quite the same afterward, for in social Darwinist terms Germany had overnight become the most dangerous beast in the jungle. British imperial historians have pointed out that henceforth it brought into being a new type of patriotism derived from imperial mission. Formerly the average Englishman wasted few thoughts on the empire, but after 1870 it loomed large as a reservoir of potential power, whether conceived as a source of raw materials or manpower. Essential to the existence of empire was the presence of a unifying monarch. Gushing reverence for the monarch dates from the late 1870s. Between Prince Albert's death in 1861 and 1876, Queen Victoria made few public appearances. In the latter year, when she emerged to be proclaimed Empress of India, her ceremonial role grew thereafter, almost in direct proportion to the deterioration of good relations among the major powers.[6] Her Jubilees of 1887 and 1897 brought for the first time to England a collective array of Indian princes and colonial premiers in exotic and splendid uniforms which publicly displayed the existence of an empire on which the sun never set. The Jubilee celebrations were "invented traditions" which attempted to inject a spirit of national unity into a society already badly fragmented by urbanization and industrialization.[7]

For an English youth growing up in the late Victorian period, infatuation with empire, with its inevitable corollaries—the vision and paraphernalia of war—was as natural as breathing. As a boy Arnold Toynbee succumbed to the toy soldier craze (which boomed when hollow casting lowered the price dramatically), while Clement Attlee has confessed that at the time of the second Jubilee "most of us boys were imperialists" and few had any doubt that "other people were not so good at the game as we were."[8] (*Game* in this context is particularly telling, as I will show later.) There were solid reasons for English complacency during the reign of Victoria. The rapid expansion of industrialism between 1850 and 1914 brought with it a doubling of population, a rise in living standards, a nearly universal literacy, and an increase in leisure time. With these came an explosion in printing technology—steam power, rotary presses, mechanical typesetting, wood-pulp paper. Because of a drop in the unit cost of books and newspapers, accompanied by an increase in the number of readers and more time for literary consumption, the printed word assumed a paramount role in molding opinion. The age of mass media and propaganda (both as commercial advertising and as manipulation of political opinion) had arrived. Increasingly what mattered was no longer what one wanted to buy or to believe, but what some obscure daemon wanted one to buy or to believe.

The printing revolution arrived at a time when values and attitudes, formerly inculcated by primary agencies like the family and church, were coming into question. In the beginning was the Word, but by century's end there seemed to be only words. The printed word and visual image became ubiquitous, escaping from newspapers and books and reappearing on billboards, vacant walls, trams, balloons, food containers, and railway cuttings. With paper production in England up sixfold between 1860 and 1900, with posters running off presses at 10,000 copies per hour, with the cost of a pulp-paper book dropping to as low as one penny, only a blind man or an illiterate could escape the bombardment of words.[9] Adding to these, as John Mackenzie has so conclusively shown, were the proliferation of "cigarette cards" (a generic name for colored cards distributed by companies marketing tobacco, tea, confectionery, biscuits, and other products), most of which fostered the imperial spirit by featuring royalty, generals, admirals, and war heroes. Even the names of cigarettes—Flagship, Invader, HMS, Victory, British Pluck (this one showing Boers being put to the sword)—reeked of military or naval prowess. This strategy of using patriotism to sell a product reached its apogee during the Boer War when a famous ad showed how Lord Roberts' route across the Orange Free State had spelled out the word *Bovril*.[10]

Patriotic messages were not only visible, they were audible. Easier printing meant more sheet music which, in turn, spread the word by song. Composers wrote on the Indian Mutiny, the Death of Gordon, the Boer War, for this was the golden age of music halls, which numbered about five hundred in London alone during the 1880s and could count on a nightly audience estimated at 45,000.[11] In 1901 the sociologist, J. A. Hobson, convinced that music halls had become a more powerful agency for popular education than church, school, or press, warned that they were encouraging jingoism and aggression among the population at large.[12] Perhaps even more blatantly militant were the brass bands formed during these years by mechanical institutes, temperance societies, and paramilitary units. Bandstands sprouted in parks like mushrooms, small boys gawked at the uniforms and marched to the oompah music, while their parents lolled nearby in lawn chairs. By 1889 there were 40,000 such bands in Britain. Initially the Royal Navy spurned them as plebeian, but finally realizing the salutary effect which such music had on recruitment, it founded its own bands in 1903 and five years later was sponsoring more than fifty.[13] It was a sign of the times when a marginal organization originally called the East London Mission Society restructured itself on military lines in 1878, declared "warfare against evil," and launched a successful campaign under its new name, the Salvation Army. Its officers had military titles, its soldiers wore uniforms, and they campaigned throughout the British Isles behind the drums and cornets of a thousand bands. "Onward, Christian Soldier," perhaps the most popular hymn of that generation, captures the prevailing mood of aggressive, militant Christianity. Written by S. Baring-Gould for a children's festival in Yorkshire in 1864 and set to music by Sir Arthur Sullivan in 1871, it revealed a religious faith less inclined to turn the other cheek than to bombard the enemy with Bibles and bullets.[14]

The connection between literacy and religious indoctrination is evident in George III's pronouncement of 1805: "It is my wish that every poor child in my dominions should be taught to read the Bible."[15] Up to this time responsibility for children's education rested with parents, but during the first three-quarters of the nineteenth century the Sunday school movement carried the principal load. Since most children of laborers worked six days each week, only Sunday remained for instruction in reading the Bible. This makeshift denominational monopoly was finally broken by the Elementary Education Act of 1870, which set up free schools on a secular basis. Soon most children could read, and they began to abandon the pious tracts provided by the Sunday schools for more red-blooded fare—lurid accounts of crime, historical novels like those of G. A. Henty (1832–1902) in which young boys rode with Clive in India or shot down Chinese at Peking, and the proliferating genre of boys' magazines like *Boys' Own Paper,* which eventually reached a circulation figure of a million copies per issue. Of Henty's eighty-two boys' stories, one-third treated imperial subjects and conformed to a pro-imperial ideology. Henty made no effort to hide his belief in English superiority—which was bred in the bone—or his distaste for polluting the English gene. He was pleased when recruiting officers reported that his books had been instrumental in attracting young men into the army, particularly into the officer class. As he said, "To inculcate patriotism in my books has been one of my main objects, and so far as it is possible to know, I have not been unsuccessful in that respect."[16] Boys' magazines were perhaps even more jingoist. A writer for Amalgamated Press glowingly reported that they had "done more to provide recruits for our Navy and Army and to keep up the esteem of the sister services than anything else," while a contemporary scholar of the genre has claimed that nearly every story carried some patriotic message in the form of reverence for royalty and respect for existing authority, especially in its military forms.[17]

Typical of anthologies designed for "high-spirited lads" imbued with "the spirit of courage or adventure" was Frederick Langbridge's *Ballads of the Brave* (1890), redundantly subtitled *Poems of Chivalry, Enterprise, Courage and Constancy.* Langbridge, an Anglican clergyman of Limerick, ransacked the literature of the English-speaking world in his hunt for heroic narratives from "The Burial of Moses" to "Ode on the Death of General Gordon." Although his preface claims that "quiet devotion to duty [is] no whit lower as expression of courage than the most splendid dash or the most romantic chivalry,"[18] the compiler professes better than he delivers, for warfare is the warp and woof of the book. The youthful reader would presumably be uplifted and toughened by exposure to the Arming of Achilles, the Destruction of Sennacherib, the Battle of Marathon, the Death of Roland, the Fight at Maldon, the Burial of William the Conqueror, the Last of the Redmen, and on and on. Unlike the boys' magazines, the quality of selection is high (Shakespeare, Longfellow, Byron, and Scott are included), and the tone is "elevated" rather than jingoistic. Langbridge was a gentleman compiling his poems for the benefit of gentlemen-to-be, which required that his scenes of carnage conform to chaste ideals of chivalrous behavior and uphold the ideal of monarchy, even when England fights another monarchy. (In view of the hate campaign soon to be mounted by publicists and poets against Kaiser Wilhelm II only a decade later, it is ironical that the concluding poem in Langbridge's miscellany treats the burial of Wilhelm I, who is eulogized for unifying Germany and for having "kindred blood" shared with the English queen.)[19]

In this epidemic of martial feeling nearly all young Englishmen were exposed to the contagion, and there is little reason to believe that other Western powers were quarantined from the disease. This almost loving infatuation with war appeared to result less from fear of a particular foreign power than from a sense of generalized xenophobia—although boredom no doubt played a major part. If the specific lineup of belligerents in some future war posed a conundrum for propagandists and scaremongers (for at one time or another England during this period had recourse to saber rattling with Russia, France, Germany, and Turkey), few of them doubted that the conflict, when it came, would be a "great war." At the heart of this expectation lay the flotsam of certain Christian beliefs, specifically those prophecies calling for the end of the world. From the Revelation of Saint John (16:16) came a tantalizing reference to Armageddon (*Har-Magedon*), the site of the final battle between the cohorts of God and Satan, at the end of which evil would be overthrown and destroyed.* Increasingly, in England "Armageddon" became a popular catchphrase referring to an apocalyptic war that would be fought at some time in the future. Thus, when war finally broke out with Germany in 1914, H. G. Wells' famous phrase "the war that will end war" caught the public fancy because it appeared to fulfill St. John's prophecy of the war between the legions of God and Satan—conveniently identified as England and Germany, respectively.

Unfortunately there is no way to measure precisely, then as now, the effect of militant literary outpourings upon actual historical events. Do writers shape public attitudes toward war and peace, or do they merely reflect opinions already lodged in the public mind? In most cases we suspect that the writer, like a sensitive radar apparatus, responds to

---

*Biblical scholars have never been able to pinpoint the specific location of Armageddon, though most believe that it is in Palestine, near the town Megiddo, which lay on a major route from Egypt to Syria and Mesopotamia. Others believe that the word is a corruption of "his fruitful mountain" (Mt. Zion) or merely "the desirable city." In any case, it came to denote the final apocalyptic battle preceding the end of the world. See *The Interpreter's Bible* (New York, 1957), XII, 486.

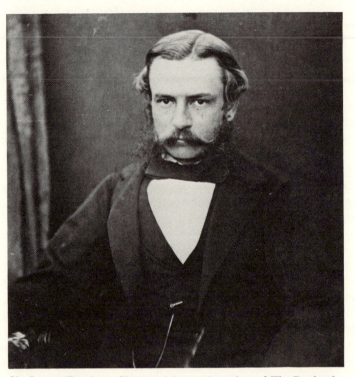

Sir George Tomkyns Chesney (1830–95), author of *The Battle of Dorking*. Reproduced by permission of the India Office Library (British Library).

frequencies already pulsating in the ether. When he is able to convert these signals into coherent and convincing literary discourse, he is subsequently credited with genius. We know that successful writers often capture and imprison that particular prismatic angle by which an historical event or an entire epoch will be viewed—often with such power that the angle may distort historical fact—but we do not know whether the writer created that angle or merely borrowed it.

A case in point is Erich Maria Remarque's *All Quiet on the Western Front* (1928), the most widely read novel about the First World War. We infer that it profoundly influenced antiwar sentiment during the 1930s because the plot and characters of the novel repeatedly demonstrate the futility and waste of war, it sold millions of copies, which indicates that a large and diversified readership found it meaningful, and the novel was regarded as sufficiently subversive to be banned and burned by the Third Reich because of its "degenerate" antiwar theme and tone. So it would seem self-evident that the novel made converts to pacifism, appearing at a time when Europe was again arming itself for war. The problem lies in proving it. Did it make converts to pacifism or merely fortify attitudes already present? If converts were made, how many and what political power did they wield? Did these converts become backsliders as political realities hardened and political choices narrowed during the late 1930s? Does a reader's acceptance of a literary text require his acceptance of the ideas within it? Intriguing though these questions are, they permanently elude historical quantification. Nonetheless, we continue to use literary texts and literary analysis as artifacts in the interpretation and illumination of history, for they are probably as valid and useful as the drier bones excavated from newspaper files, state archives, church registers, institutional minutes, and other "official" repositories of historical record.

This book examines some selected areas of popular literature in Great Britain between 1870 and 1914 in order to isolate and interpret the tides of militarism and xenophobia which prepared the public for the Great War of 1914–18. By "popular literature" is meant those works which circulated among the population almost as freely as common coin—the writings of such figures as Wells, Le Queux, Newbolt, Barrie, Kipling, Doyle, and Brooke. An underlying assumption is that the values expressed or implied in popular literature are more relevant to the study of social and political history than those of "great books." Ephemera being ground out in music halls or being scribbled for the popular press had a greater influence on the way Britons thought and behaved during the prewar years than the work of canonical writers. Throughout this period, popular literature was so steeped in militant nationalism that the Great War, when it finally arrived, came like an ancient prophecy at last fulfilled.

2 PAPER INVASIONS

▼

By the Great Ruler of the Earth and Heaven
This Island from a Continent was riven;
Where mountains could not shield from spoil and slaughter
He—for a national Bulwark—gave the WATER.
MUSIC HALL SONG, *c.1910*

Some eight thousand years ago water from melting glaciers raised the ocean level and flooded the narrow strip of land that had once connected Britain to the mainland of Europe. Had this land bridge remained, the whole course of English history, along with the collective psyche of its present inhabitants, would have been radically different. Twenty miles of treacherous open water provided a formidable first shield of defense against invasion by tribe or nation on the continent that cast curious or covetous eyes upon the chalky cliffs "beyond the dog-day haze."[1] To invade that island required something more than club and spear; it required deliberate intention, superior logistical intelligence, and—most importantly—a naval force. During the thousands of years in which migratory tribes from the east and north swarmed across continental Europe, inhabitants of Britain enjoyed some degree of immunity because of that geological accident.

The Romans, the Anglo-Saxons, and the Normans succeeded in their invasions largely because of the prevailing apathy or factionalism among the islanders. Like them, the Danes splashed ashore almost wherever or whenever they liked, but for the most part they were absorbed or moved elsewhere. By the sixteenth century, however, the islanders had devised a defensive strategy which would serve them well until the advent of aerial warfare in the twentieth: Britannia must rule the waves and thereby give the attackers no opportunity to land on the beaches. This strategy was vindicated when the fledgling English navy—assisted handily by tempest, fog, and freebooters—repelled the mighty Spanish Armada. A greater test might have come from Napoleon's well-laid plans for invasion, but the Corsican became preoccupied elsewhere and broke up his fleet.

With the consolidation of the British Empire in the nineteenth century, accompanied by the protective screen of the world's most puissant navy, further invasions seemed impossible. It is therefore curious to record that during the four decades immediately prior to the outbreak of the Great War of 1914–18 the Impossible Event was described so many times by such an array of military experts (official as well as self-appointed), journalists, and popular writers that it clearly reflected a grave national psychosis. It seemed that countless centuries of looking out to sea, on close watch for signs of hostile invaders, had sunk such deep roots in the collective consciousness of Englishmen that it could not—or would not—be grubbed out by appeals to logic, common sense, or statistics relating to naval tonnage. An examination of popular literature during this period provides a means of measuring the impact of this public wave of xenophobia disguised as invasion neurosis.

Between the conclusion of the Franco-Prussian War in 1871 and the opening guns of the Great War of 1914, English writers of popular fiction—that is to say, fiction prepared for wide circulation to a mass audience—churned out more than sixty narratives describing invasion (or attempted invasion) of their sceptered isle.* In these accounts Germany strikes forty-one times; France occupies second place with eighteen; Russia (usually allied with Germany or France) follows with eight; while China, Japan, the United States, Mars, and others each have at least one go. The stories range from twenty-page pamphlets to a five-hundred-page novel illustrated with campaign maps and facsimile proclamations of occupation army commanders. The subject is handled with ponderous solemnity; less than half a dozen narratives employ invasion as a vehicle for humor.[2] Imbedded in most are strident warnings that the price for beating invaders away from English shores is increased appropriations for national defense, along with a general stiffening of moral fiber. These stories accurately mirror the instability of Great Power diplomacy during the prewar years; the particular invader

---

*This tabulation includes only invasion narratives published as pamphlets or books for adult readers. No attempt has been made to read or to catalog narratives which appeared as short stories in periodicals. By "invasion narrative" I refer only to fictive pieces professing to describe a future war, not to narratives treating actual invasions of the historical past.

at any given time is usually the enemy nation being chastised by the Foreign Office and reviled by the press. Considered as literature most of these stories richly deserve oblivion, but as historical records they are valuable for registering public response to the gyrations of British foreign policy during that volatile period. Moreover, they contributed to the popular notion that sooner or later England would be forced into a major war. In these stories Britain was never the aggressor. Always on the defensive, she aimed at nothing more than to beat back a host of bullies threatening her shores.

The galvanic shock which brought to life the proliferating literature of invasion can be traced specifically to the humiliating defeat of France at the hands of Germany during the fall of 1870, followed by the installation of Wilhelm I as German emperor in the halls of Versailles in January 1871. While in some English circles there was a certain satisfaction in learning that the military legacy of their hereditary enemy was nothing more than a pock-rotten myth, the explosive and unexpected power of imperial Germany raised long-term fears. If what had been regarded since the era of Napoleon as the finest army on the continent could be so decisively outmaneuvered and outfought, how would England fare in the event of a military confrontation with Germany? Very poorly, indeed, considering that the small volunteer English army was designed and trained not for campaigns against major powers but for policing far-flung colonies. Von Moltke's plan of troop mobilization and invasion, which in just six weeks had trapped two French armies—at Metz and Sedan—was regarded as a miracle of organization by English military authorities accustomed to solving transportation problems calculated in months, not hours. (Not until 1875 did the British army prepare a definitive mobilization plan.)[3] To be sure, the German navy was infantile by English standards. But if the Kaiser's Army succeeded in landing on English beaches—what then? During the next forty years Englishmen of all rank and condition would mull over this unsettling question.*

*Throughout this period the assumption that British defense depended on maintaining naval superiority was rarely questioned. Public officials had acquired a singsong litany that naval defeat would be followed automatically by enemy invasion. In 1888 Lord Wolseley told the House of Lords, "If our Navy continues weak, our military forces cannot guarantee the safety of the capital at this moment"; and in 1911 Sir Edward Grey warned the Committee of Imperial Defense that if the Germans obtained a superior fleet, they "could not only defeat us at sea, but could be in London in a very short time with her army." See John Gooch, *The Prospect of War: Studies in British Defense Policy* (London, 1981), 38.

Even as Paris was being starved into surrender, an obscure army officer in the Royal Indian Civil Engineering College at Staines was at work on the prototypal invasion story, *The Battle of Dorking*. Lieutenant Colonel George Tomkyns Chesney (1830–95) submitted his cautionary tale to *Blackwood's Magazine,* where it appeared anonymously in the issue of May 1871. Demand proved so great that within a month it had been reprinted as a sixpenny pamphlet of sixty-four pages, of which 80,000 copies were sold. In his maiden attempt at fiction, Chesney had twisted the lion's tale till it hurt and succeeded in establishing a formulaic narrative that a host of other writers would build on.

In *The Battle of Dorking* the narrator is a gentleman volunteer who recalls, fifty years later, how a German army landed on the South Coast, quickly brushed aside the feeble English forces, and conquered the country. Germany declares war without provocation while the English army is putting down a Fenian uprising in Ireland and its navy is scattered throughout the globe protecting the colonies. In the absence of the Royal Navy, the Germans have no difficulty in landing near Brighton and in pushing back poorly trained militia to the ridge between Guilford and Dorking. Here, in pitched battle, advancing lines of Germans in spiked helmets convert the thin English line into a "mere mob" scuttling back toward London. (The spiked helmet will in time be joined in the English popular imagination by the goose step, the sawtooth bayonet, and poison gas as heinous accoutrements of the Hun.) The narrator watches helplessly as civilians are turned out of their domestic sanctums and forced to hold lanterns to illuminate the march of the invaders, two of whom gloat over their victory:

> "Sind wackere Soldaten, diese Englischen Freiwilligen" [They're decent soldiers, these English volunteers], said a broad-shouldered brute, stuffing a great hunch of beef into his mouth with a silver fork, an implement I should think he must have been using for the first time in his life.
>
> "Ja, ja," replied a comrade, who was lolling back in his chair with a pair of very dirty legs on the table. . . . "Sie so gut laufen können" [Yes, they can run pretty well].
>
> "Ja wohl," responded the first speaker; "aber sind nicht eben so schnell wie die Französischen Mobloten [*sic*]" [That's right, but not nearly as fast as the French draftees [?]].[4]

Showing more grit than the French is one of the few bright spots for an English reader of Chesney's grim narrative.

From his woebegone perspective of 1921, the *Dorking* narrator summarizes the legacy of defeat—occupation, taxation, pauperization. Because of its rich agricultural base, France can recover rapidly from a military disaster, but poor England, dependent for its wealth on trade and finance, is drained of resources and initiative. The cause of this catastrophe? Political power had passed from the traditional ruling class to the "lower classes, uneducated, untrained to use of political rights, and swayed by demagogues."[5] In Chesney's Tory catechism, "demagogue" stood for any politician unwilling to beef up the English military and naval establishments. The lesson taught by this story conformed to the prevailing conservative policies for use of public funds—invest in national defense, not in quixotic educational reform designed to raise the populace to a level where it could exercise its franchise intelligently. (Twenty years after writing *Dorking*, General Sir George Chesney was elected to Parliament on the Conservative ticket.) His conclusion employs social Darwinist rhetoric: "A nation too selfish to defend its liberty could not have been *fit* [my italics] to retain it."[6] In the struggle for life only the fittest will survive, and if England has become a diseased organism, it deserves to die. In Chesney's parable the end product of the debacle at Dorking is the ultimate collapse of the British Empire, the fountainhead of national wealth.

At best *The Battle of Dorking* is a stilted performance, the sort of narrative that Daniel Defoe could have written left-handed while simultaneously engaged in his *Journal of the Plague Year*. Its battle scenes resemble movements of sandbox soldiers rather than the blitzkrieg of a Prussian juggernaut. Yet by voicing a deeply felt public anxiety and by dramatizing it within a fictional model, Chesney fashioned a matrix which scores of writers would soon adopt. The impact of his story on the popular imagination was jolting. Within a year nine anonymous or pseudonymous writers would rally to the defense of the English lion, all of them demonstrating how the Royal Navy would decimate the invaders before they got ashore or how the English army would trounce them when they moved inland. The sanguine nature of these rebuttals is conveyed by titles like *After the Battle of Dorking: or, What Became of the Invaders* (1871); *The Other Side at the Battle of Dorking* (1871); and *What Happened After the Battle of Dorking: or, The Victory of Tunbridge Wells* (1871). Pooh-poohing the ideas of a foreign power daring to invade England, a music hall rhyme-slinger wrote:

England invaded, what a strange idea!
She, the invincible, has nought to fear.

> John Bull in his sleep one day got talking,
> And dreamt about a battle fought at Dorking![7]

For years afterward in army circles we may assume that any officer with a bandaged arm or gouty leg was in danger of being hailed with the query, "I say, weren't you wounded at the Battle of Dorking?"

Despite these assurances that an invasion of England was out of the question, a thoughtful reader might have wondered why—if England were so invincible—there was so much fuss over the Dorking script. The truth was that Chesney's little pamphlet struck a mighty blow at English complacency, although the full effects would not be felt for some time. Within three months of its initial publication the book leaped the Channel to appear in a French translation, *Bataille de Dorking, Invasion des Prussiens en Angleterre,* which included a thirty-page introduction and a lurid frontispiece depicting a German eagle straddling a bedraggled British lion and ripping his heart out.[8] The success of the novel in France suggests that readers there took particular pleasure in imagining England being forced to take a healthy dose of Prussian medicine. Translations into German, Dutch, and Italian swiftly followed.* In September Prime Minister William Gladstone, disturbed by the *Dorking* controversy, denounced the story for exposing the so-called folly of high command. He warned that stories in this defeatist vein "make us ridiculous in the eyes of the whole world" and urged loyal Englishmen to "be on your guard against alarmism."[9] As it happened, military maneuvers that autumn were planned to test cooperation between the regulars and the militia. The results were proclaimed—at least in official communiques—to be highly satisfactory. But the specter of the militia in full flight was not entirely dissipated; *Punch* featured a full-page drawing of Mr. Punch reviewing the army with the caption "All's (Pretty) Well!"[10] For the moment it was.

Colonel Chesney only tapped, he did not construct, the great reservoir of invasion fears that had always lain dormant in the consciousness of Britons. These fears had a kind of tidal flow dependent on imagined strengths or weaknesses of England's position with respect to outside powers. The last flood tide had been experienced during the Napoleon-

---

*The first systematic study of English invasion narratives was prepared by a Frenchman, C. Louis, in 1910. In *Fictions guerrieres anglaises* he concluded that fear of invasion is "endemic in England." It might also be noted that prior to their projected invasion of England in 1940 the Nazis brought out a fresh edition of *Dorking* under the title *Was England erwartet* [*What England Can Expect*]. These translations are ably discussed in I. F. Clarke, *Voices Prophesying War, 1763–1984* (London, 1966), 41–46.

ic period when the French actually had planned a full-fledged invasion. Then in 1848 the Duke of Wellington launched what has been called the "bolt-from-the-blue" approach to national defense when he fired off a public letter claiming that, except under the forts at Dover, "there is no spot on the coast in which infantry might not be thrown on shore at any time of tide."[11] Aroused by French construction of steam-powered ships, which could cross the Channel in a single night, the Duke called for reestablishment of the militia system for home defense, a paid force which had been disbanded as useless after the Napoleonic crisis. The Louis-Napoléon coup of 1851 and the development of Cherbourg as a major port (seen in England as a possible invasion depot), followed by French annexation of Savoy and Nice in 1860, led in England to the establishment of the Volunteer Force designed exclusively to repel invaders. Tennyson, the incumbent poet laureate, contributed stanzas to the cause with "Riflemen Form," which had urged readers of the *Times* to postpone domestic reforms in order to beef up national defense:

> Let your reforms for a moment go!
> Look to your butts, and take good aim.
> Better a rotten borough or so
> Than a rotten fleet and a city in flames!
> Storm, Storm, Riflemen form![12]

Liberals fretted because they feared that the covert purpose of the Volunteers was to control urban masses and thereby squelch necessary reforms; Conservatives, on the other hand, worried about the possibility of revolution if the workers received arms and military instruction. In point of fact, the V.F. was such a toothless lion that sometimes regular soldiers had to be rushed to city parks to protect volunteers at drill from abusive spectators. (A favorite cry of street urchins on seeing a volunteer in uniform was "Who shot the dog?"—an ignominious allusion to the only recorded "kill" in the fifty-year history of the force.)* Volunteers were recruited from a segment of the working and clerical classes eager to escape their monotonous routine by playing soldier in uniforms, firing rifles (which were replacing muskets), and camping out once each year. Since each volunteer had to supply his own arms and equipment, this guaranteed that no "riffraff" would be en-

---

*On another occasion the Volunteers were called out to fire a volley at an escaped elephant near Bursley and were afterward "borne off as heroes to different inns," but it is not clear whether they succeeded in killing the elephant in question.

rolled. Being a "gentleman" was the most important qualification for officer rank. (A draper's son was once rejected as ensign because he would not be able to associate off duty with squires and gentlemen.) The regular army despised them. Discipline was nearly nonexistent; the volunteers smoked in ranks, were exempt from military law except during periods of emergency—none of which occurred—and had the right to quit altogether by giving fourteen days' notice.[13] By the 1870s the force numbered more than 100,000 amateur warriors.

Climaxing the martial displays among the Volunteers were the annual rallies and sham battles like the fiasco in Derbyshire where nearly a quarter of a million holiday trippers swarmed across the battleground where ten thousand volunteers engaged in combat maneuvers. In the south, the Easter Monday rallies at Brighton were notorious exercises in military chaos, though they richly entertained the crowds. The *Times* scathingly noted of the 1871 affair, "If England were about to be invaded, no wise man would think of putting the Volunteers in the front line of the defending Army."[14] The scenes of military disaster so vividly described in his novel suggest that Colonel Chesney had officiated at, or at least suffered through, his share of these ignominious paramilitary spectacles. Others might be amused, but he sounded the alarm. The regular army never lost its contempt for the v.f., and succeeded eventually in having it abolished in 1908, when the Territorials were formed.[15]

Despite official demurrers, the seeds of doubt planted by Colonel Chesney countinued to sprout. In their zeal to prove that an invasion of England was impossible, writers with army or navy credentials betrayed their inward anxieties. Complacency had a setback in 1884 when W. T. Stead, the distinguished editor of the *Pall Mall Gazette*, jolted the defense establishment with his series, "The Truth about the Navy." Though by nature a pacifist, Stead accepted the premises of the pseudo-Darwinists of the Admiralty, who believed that a "scramble for the world" was inevitable among the major powers. According to the "blue water" school, as it came to be called in opposition to the bolt-from-the-blue theorists, England was safe because its navy was omnipotent.* Stead's report conclusively showed that the Royal Navy was in

*The apotheosis of the blue water school was Gladstone's formula: "The strength of England is not to be found in alliances with great military powers, but is to be found henceforth, in the sufficiency and supremacy of her navy—a navy as powerful now as the navies of all Europe" (1878). See Frederic Whyte, *The Life of W. T. Stead* (New York, n.d.), 147.

trouble. During the past fifteen years, expenditure on naval armaments had actually declined. While England held the lead in first-class iron-clads, France was building second- and third-class vessels at a faster rate and arming them more effectively. At present, English trade routes could not be protected in the event of a major war. The "truth about the Navy," Stead warned, was that "our naval supremacy has almost ceased to exist."[16] The ensuing clamor in the public press refueled invasion anxieties and gave scribblers another opportunity to disseminate bolt-from-the-blue screeds.

As an example of how other writers picked over the dry bones of the *Dorking* prototype, a ninety-six page novella by an anonymous "Captain of the Royal Navy," titled *The Battle Off Worthing: Why the Invaders Never Got To Dorking* (1887), may be worth a brief summary. In his introduction the writer recalls how Chesney's fable, while condemned by the press as visionary and improbable, nevertheless had instilled in the populace "a latent feeling of insecurity." It was that pamphlet which "first stirred the national pulse. Everybody read it, and everybody spoke of it."[17] What the army colonel failed to take into account and the naval captain wished to show was the genius of the English race in nautical improvisation.

The narrator, a retired naval officer, looks back on the German invasion attempt of 1871. The conflict had been brought about by paralysis of the national will. Following the glorious epoch of the Napoleonic Wars, England sank into an "apathy toward all but the commercial interests."[18] In the mad pursuit of individual wealth, effective leadership vanished, treaties were broken, and national defense was neglected. Seeing her chance, Germany joined with France and Russia to partition the tottering British Empire. As with *Dorking* and most other invasion stories, this scenario is derived from simplistic renderings of social Darwinism calling for the weak inevitably to succumb to the strong. However, our Captain did not agree with Chesney that the English lion had lost all his teeth, for his narrative vindicates the resourcefulness of the English when pressed to the wall not by one, but by three powerful antagonists.

The power game in *Worthing* begins when Germany consolidates its Atlantic position by overrunning Holland and Denmark. Then its army, in concert with the French, pours into Belgium and forces England to declare war.* The Royal Navy, hoodwinked by a Russian feint

---

*So far so good. The captain accurately foresaw England's official reasons for entering the 1914 war. In his speech to the Commons on August 3, 1914, Sir Edward Grey explained

toward the Dardanelles, steams off in hot haste, leaving the English coast unprotected. Seizing this providential moment, the Germans assemble a vast invasion fleet. But all is not lost. The First Lord of the Admiralty knows that the unarmed enemy transports must be destroyed before they land, for recent maneuvers have demonstrated that if any invaders ever reached the beaches the English army would be "annihilated in a few minutes."[19] To meet the threat, three hundred steam launches are outfitted with guns firing shot and grape. Placed at three-mile intervals along the coast, they wait to blow the invaders out of the water.

Our narrator is assigned to a launch patrolling off the coast of Sussex, near Worthing. Armed octogenarians, who remember when Boney was coming, patrol country lanes. ("An Englishman's house is his castle, as all the world knew; no jury would convict him for defending it.")[20] The supreme moment arrives when German barges, pulled by tugs, attempt their landing, and the English boats inflict a "terrible carnage." German casualties number 50,000, and only 15,000 soldiers reach shore, where without support or supplies they hoist the white flag within twenty-four hours. At Worthing (as at Dunkirk seventy years later) England is saved from disaster by amateur mariners with hearts of oak. And what happens to the sinister alliance between Germany, France, and Russia? It dissolves as they quarrel over their continental spoils, and in time England herself becomes the arbiter of European affairs.

Worthing is, of course, a preposterous narrative—a kind of *Dorking* warmed over and supplied with a happy ending. In its breezy simple-mindedness it is typical of that spate of invasion stories designed to allay or to exacerbate the fears of readers who had been jarred to the marrow by Chesney's doomsday vision. Almost without exception these stories hammer upon one theme: the price for averting invasion is preparedness, which entails financial sacrifice in shoring up army and navy. Many of these invasion stories were written by officers of the Crown who understood that scaremongering was an efficacious means of wringing larger defense appropriations from apathetic parliamentarians. Meanwhile the public acquired an appetite for disaster stories which writers in the years ahead would do their best to satisfy.

---

that England must fight Germany because, one, the treaty of 1839 guaranteed Belgian neutrality and, two, Germany might seize the Channel ports. See Sir Edward Grey, *Speeches on Foreign Affairs, 1904–1914*, edited by Paul Knaplund (London, 1931), 297–315.

Because they responded to winds of change blowing across diplomatic frontiers, invasion narratives serve as convenient weather vanes pointing toward three storm centers publicized by the Foreign Office. While the fear of invasion seems to be a constant, the imagined enemy shifts according to diplomatic storms. During the 1870s the winds blew from the northeast; between 1882 and 1904 they were variable easterlies; and after 1904 they swung back northeast at gale force. Because of their blitzkrieg in the Franco-Prussian War, invasion by Germans occupied writers' attention during the seventies. In the second period the invasion genre became almost the exclusive preserve of Francophobes, for this was an era when Anglo-French relations deteriorated. In Siam, Morocco, Niger, and Egypt there were imperial collisions that brushed dangerously close to war. Moreover, when the French were allied to the Russians in a defensive coalition after 1894, alarms sounded in Whitehall, for Russia had long been feared as the major threat to India, the keystone of the British Empire.* A rapprochement with Germany ensued. In 1899 the Kaiser paid a state visit to Windsor, and Prime Minister Joseph Chamberlain talked about a new Triple Alliance of the future that would weld together the three major limbs of the Anglo-Saxon race—England, Germany, and the United States. By 1901 hope of an Anglo-German alliance (the United States having repudiated the idea altogether) evaporated in mutual distrust. Finally, after the Second Hague Peace Conference in 1907 failed to reach an agreement on limitations in naval construction, rivalry between Germany and England became the dominating factor in European geopolitics. Henceforth, *all* English invasion narratives dealt with attacks from Germany.

But before the Germanophobic phase got under way, writers and publicists occupied themselves with the French threat. Symptomatic of the suspicion with which the average Englishman viewed France was the popular outcry in opposition to the English Channel tunnel scheme. In 1882 debate over the plan in Parliament spilled over into the streets

---

*The contemporary meaning of "jingo" as superpatriot originated in 1878 with G. W. Hunt's music hall composition (popularized by G. H. McDermott) in response to a possible intervention in the Russo-Turkish War of that year. At a mass rally in the Corn Exchange, the crowds sang:

We don't want to fight, but by Jingo if we do,
We've got the men, we've got the ships, we've got the money too,
We've fought the Bear before, and while we're Britons true,
The Russians shall not have Constantinople.

See J. S. Bratton, *The Victorian Popular Ballad* (Totowa, N.J., 1975), 54.

as a mob of irate Londoners smashed the windows of the Channel
Tunnel Company in protest. A petition opposing construction collected
the signatures of Tennyson, Browning, Newman, the Archbishop of
Canterbury, along with a parcel of ten earls, seventeen admirals, fifty-
nine generals, and a host of smaller fry.[21] The memorandum of Lord
Wolseley, adjutant general, reflected the common fear that "a couple of
thousand armed men might easily come through the tunnel in a train at
night, avoiding all suspicion by being dressed as ordinary passengers,
or . . . with the blinds down, in their uniforms and fully armed." Once
the English terminus of the tunnel were seized, "then England would
be at the mercy of the invader."[22] Is it possible that Wolseley and his
fifty-nine generals really believed that England could be overrun by a
French army disgorged from the mouth of a tunnel? Or that a single
explosive charge, properly placed, could not quash the invasion handily? It seems unlikely. The paramount issue seems to have been psychological; a Channel tunnel would annex England to the continent of
Europe and end her insularity forever.

Nowhere is *isleophilia* among the English seen more clearly than in
the hubbub occasioned by the tunnel scheme. Writers of popular fiction leaped into the fray with pens drawn and sharpened, putting the
cause célèbre to good use by preparing a spate of sensational tales that
rivaled in implausibility the dire predictions of the War Office. Foreign
soldiers in their national regalia—or craftily disguised as tourists or
waiters—pop out from the nether regions in such tales as *How John
Bull Lost London, or The Capture of the Channel Tunnel* (1882); *The
Surprise of the Channel Tunnel* (1883); and *The Capture of London*
(1887). The magnum opus of this phylum of invasion literature is Max
Pemberton's *Pro Patria* (1901), a 316-page tome which appeared nearly
two decades after the white heat phase of the tunnel excitement. This
author thickens his somewhat thin gruel by introducing a renegade
Englishman who bores from within while the French invaders bore
from underground. In Wessex, Thomas Hardy made use of the uproar
over the tunnel scheme to write "A Tradition of Eighteen Hundred and
Four" (1882), a tale told by an old shepherd about an encounter he had
with Napoleon in a secluded cove during the year when England was
steeling itself against an invasion led by "the Corsican tyrant."[23] Two
years earlier Hardy had written *The Trumpet Major*, an historical novel
treating the period of the anticipated Napoleonic invasion. While the
writing of these books was perhaps influenced by the invasion furor, by
casting his events in a distant period, Hardy distanced himself from the

mainstream company of scaremongers. (Hardy's wife did not share her husband's sangfroid. The panic over the tunnel scheme convinced her that the French were coming and kept her in a condition of near hysteria with a packed suitcase ready to take to the fields.)[24]

In the halcyon days of Colonel Chesney an invasion was an invasion was an invasion. Enemy troops were somehow ferried to Albion and engaged in a battle that was fought on relatively honorable terms. But by 1900 the fictive invasion had become a dirty business indeed. Foreign spies began their insidious work often in collusion with renegade Englishmen willing to betray their country. As early as 1888, Horace F. Lester's *The Taking of Dover* described how France had conquered England through trickery. The narrator is a Frenchman assigned to the occupational army who explains how he infiltrated the famous fortifications at Dover by carousing with the local officers. They are so trusting of him and so convinced of England's invulnerability that they obligingly conduct him on tours of the underground galleries. Meanwhile France sends over five regiments of men disguised as civilians—accompanied by an equal number of Russians—and scatters them about in local lodging houses. (For reasons nowhere made clear, this sudden bulge in foreign tourism passes unnoticed among the locals.) At the signal the narrator leads the attack and secures the fortifications without the loss of a man. Within twenty-four hours 150,000 men land at Dover unopposed and England surrenders. Writing to his son at St. Cyr, the narrator reiterates Napoleon's critique of the English as a nation of shopkeepers as he explains that the will to fight was gone because "the pedlar spirit pervades everything here."[25] It is a familiar refrain; England is in danger only because her population selfishly refuses to spend what is necessary for defense.

After France forged her alliance with Russia in 1894, the old one-on-one balances which had formerly characterized diplomacy among the major powers began to be replaced by a dangerous teeter-totter game involving complicated networks of alliances—all the more dangerous because many of them were secret—which could tumble a number of players into universal war by some seemingly insignificant incident at some far-flung corner of the world. It is hardly coincidence that in 1893 there appeared *The Great War of 189–: A Forecast,* an ambitious attempt by Whitehall to show how England would fare in the event of a world war in the future. Written by a committee of seven military and naval experts, headed by Rear Admiral Philip H. Colomb, this futurist narrative undoubtedly reflected the sober ruminations of leaders at the

Admiralty and War Office. It systematically chronicled the events of a world war which the compilers believe "will probably occur in the immediate future." Admiral Colomb confessed that he was an admirer of *The Battle at Dorking,* which he called "a wonderful and stirring romance,"[26] but his geopolitical vision of universal war looks forward to the twentieth century rather than backward to the nineteenth. Anyone who read the Colomb book in 1893 would have had a sharp sense of déjà vu on experiencing the events of July and August 1914. Even the designation "Great War" seems to have been invented by the Colomb book.

In the strictest sense, *The Great War of 189–* is not an invasion narrative, for the army and navy of Great Britain execute their requisite maneuvers with such staff college precision that the final issue is never in much doubt. But it conforms to the others in showing a simon-pure England going to war only as a last resort—in this instance because *France* invades Belgium. The authors are knowledgeable about the festering areas on the body politic of Europe: Alsace-Lorraine, Italy's "unredeemed territory," Serbia's hatred of Bulgaria, the Triple Alliance (Germany, Austria, and Italy), and—most importantly for the English—the pernicious Franco-Russian connection.

The Great War of the future erupts in a remote Balkan village with the attempted assassination of a Bulgarian prince by a Russian spy disguised as a priest. The Serbs, having been thrashed by the Bulgarians in 1885, seize this opportunity to provoke a border incident, only to be surprised by a lightning attack from the Austrians, who occupy Belgrade. Outraged by this violation of Serbian sovereignty, the Tsar lands troops in Bulgaria and demands the evacuation of Belgrade. Construing the Russian move as a threat upon Austria, Germany mobilizes and rolls eastward upon Russia with the Kaiser in personal command. At this, Paris explodes "in maddest ferment" as the press urges war against Germany in support of Russia, France's ally. Convinced that the Germans plan an attack through Belgium, the French beat them to the draw, thereby forcing England to declare war on France for her dastardly violation of Belgian neutrality. The first month of the Great War of 189– concludes with England, Germany, Belgium, Austria, and Bulgaria pitted against France, Russia, and Serbia. In spotting the Balkans as the tinder box of Europe and in hypothesizing that the Great War would result not from an overt invasion but from the policy of interlocking treaties, the predictions of the Colomb committee were borne out by the events of 1914. Granted, the committee got its bellig-

erent parties wrong, but their lineup was no more unlikely than the
friend-foe alignments of 1914, which for the casual reader sometimes
requires a program to determine who fought whom.

To head off a Russian move toward the Mediterranean, Britain dis-
patches an expeditionary force to support Turkey and Bulgaria, and
then, in a bold logistical stroke, reinforces the Afghanistan frontier by
transporting troops across Canada. The Royal Navy saves the German
fleet from destruction at Kiel by intercepting a pincer movement by the
French and Russian navies. Meanwhile another English fleet whips the
French off Sardinia and clears the Mediterranean. In land operations
the Anglo-German combination is victorious. After a night battle under
gigantic electric lights ("which modern Science had thus hung up to
facilitate the work of slaughter, as if the very sun refused to look any
longer upon the human carnage")[27] the Russians fall back to Warsaw,
their much vaunted numerical superiority having been neutralized by
German long-range guns and defensive barbed wire. Encouraged by
French reverses the timid Italians edge into the war by invading the
Riviera and taking Monte Carlo (where gamblers continue to frequent
the tables despite the battle raging about them). Meanwhile on the
French front the Germans invest Verdun and push their juggernaut
rapidly toward Paris. And way down in Bulgaria the English army
experiences little difficulty against the Russians in spite of the arrival of
a secret French invention—a power-driven balloon which the Russians
use to bomb Varna.

After three months of fighting, the Great War of 189– enters a
stalemate. A brilliant charge of French cavalry near Paris halts the
German advance. Intimidated by this reverse, the Italians check their
campaign in the south of France. In turn, the Germans call off their
Russian campaign and create the state of Poland as permanent buffer
against invasion from the east. The war ends as abruptly as it began.
Disenchanted with the Russians, the French abandon their alliance.
Russia renounces its claim to Afghanistan, thereby strengthening the
English position in India. France resigns itself to the loss of Alsace-
Lorraine but regains the territory snatched by Italy.

The Great War of 189– became a best-seller in Germany, where a
translation went through five editions within a year. In his introduction
to the book, General von Below differentiated it from the usual scaremongering tale: "This work has a higher aim. It concerns itself with the
subject of international politics in Europe."[28] Like his counterparts in
Whitehall, von Below was intrigued by the prospect of a military al-

liance between Germany and England. The English navy linked to the
German army would be omnipotent. But Admiral Colomb and his
committee realized that an Anglo-German arrangement would be un-
palatable to Parliament, for in their conclusion they lament that the
grand opportunity for world peace is lost because politicians order
immediate reduction of the fleet and army. Their final query, "How far
the future will justify our omission to secure the peace of the world by
taking proper steps for it, it is for the future generations to determine,"[29] would be answered by the Generation of 1914 destined for
slaughter in the real Great War.

The most notable achievement of the Colomb book lies in its thesis
that war among the major powers would inevitably become world war,
and that an insignificant spark could be fanned into holocaust by random diplomatic winds. The authors accurately fingered the danger
spots, Belgium and the Balkans, and predicted that war would come
becuase of the vagaries of interlocking alliances. In matters bearing
upon logistics, tactics, and weaponry, they were less prescient. Their
prediction of a three-month war looked backward to the Franco-Prussian War and reflected a commonly voiced opinion among military
statisticians that long wars had become obsolete through the inability of
the industrial base of a nation to support them. Moreover, the committee's faith in bold offensive movements, especially the cavalry charge
and amphibious landing, did not take into account the fact that military
technology had tipped the scales in favor of defensive warfare. Although searchlights, protozeppelins, and barbed wire figure in their
narrative, more awesome paraphernalia of future wars—machine guns,
gas, submarines—proved to be well beyond their imagination. Yet,
placed against the common run of invasion stories existing up to that
time, *The Great War of 189–* passes as a respectable transcript of modern war. One important side effect of the book appears to have been
George Bernard Shaw's *Arms and the Man* (1894), which took advantage
of the hubbub to satirize the romantic notion of war.

▼

Invasion narratives discussed thus far have been productions of what
might be termed a professional cadre of writers housed within the
military or naval establishment of Great Britain. The purpose of the
narrative, in each case, was to warn the public about the dangers attending lack of preparedness, especially in view of massive military
expenditures by other European powers. By the mid-nineties, however,

the invasion genre became itself invaded by amateurs less concerned with selling defense than books. Moreover, the Chesney formula of a straight-from-the-shoulder attack had become stale and vaguely old fashioned. This was a period marked by internal disruption throughout Europe. The Dreyfus case, which came to a head in 1894, crystallized fears that spies and traitors were peddling state secrets with impunity. This was the period when Bakunin's strategy of "propaganda by the deed"—resorting to direct violent action as a means of fomenting revolution—unleashed what appeared to be a sinister international conspiracy that culminated in bombings (the Paris stock exchange, the Chamber of Deputies, Chicago's Haymarket) and assassinations (Tsar Alexander II, President McKinley, the Empress of Austria, Prime Minister Canovas del Castillo of Spain, President Carnot of France).* The seeds of this new genre—the fiction of international intrigue—would reach fruition years later in the spy novels of John Buchan, Ian Fleming, and John Le Carré. These posited that the nation was endangered less by outside adversary than by a Judas figure betraying from within.

As doomsday prophecy the Dorking model was tepid indeed when placed beside the work of William Le Queux (1864–1927), an opportunistic panicmonger who pioneered the new mode of invasion story. His novel *The Great War in England in 1897*, published serially in 1893 and brought out in a 330-page book the following year, went through sixteen editions after Lord Roberts (England's foremost advocate of preparedness) endorsed it in a prefatory note. Inspired by the visit of the Russian fleet to Toulon in 1893, Le Queux's novel meticulously documented the invasion of England by the combined forces of Russia and France. In his introduction he warned that those who think that the Franco-Russian alliance is designed to neutralize Germany are deluded: the French, while fearing Germans, despise the English and thirst for their humiliation.

Central to the plot is the villain, Count von Beilstein, a suave German Jew who agrees to spy for the Tsar in order to avoid prosecution for gambling debts contracted at Monte Carlo. In London he easily gains access to the Foreign Office, where pretending to wait for companions,

---

*There were also attempted assassinations of King Umberto of Italy, King Alfonso XII of Spain, and the German Emperor. In *The Princess Casamassima* (1886) Henry James wondered if revolutionary movements would "set the world on fire" or be "dissipated in sterile heroisms and abortive isolated movements." According to Joseph Conrad, the later alternative was more probable; *The Secret Agent* (1907) treated the farcical attempt to blow up the Greenwich Observatory in 1894.

he reads state secrets through a hole in his newspaper. His discovery of a secret Anglo-German alliance provides the excuse France and Russia need for launching their invasion. "It was our policy of *laissez faire*, a weak Navy and an Army bound up with red tape, that caused this disastrous invasion," intones the author.[30]

After the French land on the South Coast and the Russians strike though the Midlands, public order in England collapses. In London anarchists raise liberty caps and enlist lumpenproles in a wave of looting and murder that spills out of the East End into Trafalgar Square. At the National Gallery a mob screams, "What do we want with Art? Burn it!" Singing the bloodcurdling "Marseillaise," these "denizens of the slums" make a bonfire of paintings and conduct "wild reckless orgies" (the nature of which is unexplained) amid smoke and flames.[31] These scenes match with horror accounts coming in of Russian troops impaling babies on their bayonets, a detail which would resurface in 1914 when stories circulated in England that German soldiers in Belgium amused themselves with this activity. But good news arrives from the Continent, where the "brave, well-drilled legions of the Emperor William" attack France. As Germans come to the rescue "a feeling of thankfulness spread through the land."[32] Moreover, Britons take comfort in the news that Italy has attacked the south of France and that 25,000 Irishmen of all creeds have put aside their political bickering in order to join their English comrades. Still, the issue on the home front is in doubt. The Russians fan across the Midlands, fly the Tsar's standard over the Council House in Birmingham, and attack Edinburgh. They plan to bomb the city with a giant inflatable airship, but a British spy learns of the plan and arranges to pick off this "Demon of War" with dynamite shells. On the London front, the French commence the bombardment of the city from Crystal Palace Parade. Westminster Abbey burns to the ground, Victoria Tower collapses, and Londoners starve in Hyde Park and Kensington Gardens.

The tide of battle turns abruptly when the British fleet annihilates the French off Dungeness, the Germans invest Paris, and the Indian army reinforces the citizens' militia at London. In a pitched battle near Dorking the English finally oust the enemy that had for weeks "overrun our smiling land like packs of hungry wolves."[33] Then, in the north, the Russians are thrashed at Glasgow and Manchester. Just three months after the first shot (confirming the theory that long modern wars were financially impossible) a treaty is ratified: England takes Algiers from the French and territory bordering on India from the

Russians. In the final chapter Le Queux returns to the melodrama
which had opened his tale (and presumably been forgotten during the
excitement of Armageddon), the execution of the villain von Beilstein
on Horse Guards Parade. Thereafter a period of prosperity and power
dawns for Britain, sealed by the dream of Admiral Colomb and Prime
Minister Chamberlain—joint operations of the Royal Navy and the
Imperial German Army. The Anglo-Saxon Century had truly arrived.

Although Le Queux's *The Great War in England in 1897* made a great
stir, the diplomatic alignments among the major powers which it described were soon rendered archaic by developments during the first
decade of the new century. As a result of the Boer War (1899–1902),
England encountered such hostile reactions from her neighboring
powers that a kind of paranoia seized the national mood. While the
Royal Navy had not been tested in that war, the army had been so
thoroughly humiliated by its long-suffering attempts to deal with what
at first was called by the press "a tea-time war"[34] that Whitehall feared
that some essential élan had disappeared from the English race and that
some weaknesses had been exposed which other countries were eager to
exploit. When the Reichstag passed its Navy Bill of 1900, which fore-
shadowed the development of a German navy comparable to its awesome army, all possibility of an Anglo-German accord abruptly ended.
Thereafter, the Admiralty and War Office substituted their Franco-
Russian fears for an implacably anti-German policy. In 1903 the Committee of Imperial Defence (CID) was created to coordinate efforts to
overhaul the entire military and naval establishments. Their delibera-
tions raised fears as rapidly as they allayed them. It was reassuring to
discover that any successful invasion would require 70,000 men in 200
boats, but unnerving to learn that while it took 35,000,000 pounds to
mobilize the German army for a war against either France or Russia, a
raid on the Essex coast would cost only a fraction of that sum.[35] (It was
axiomatic in these calculations that the Kaiser's possession of a great
army meant that he intended to use it.) Recognizing that scaremongering in the press was probably as dangerous to the future security of
England as the Germans, the CID debated the issue of muzzling newspapers but dared show no teeth in the matter.* Writers of invasion tales

*The *Daily Mail*, founded by Lord Northcliffe, regularly featured lurid spy stories and
disseminated as gospel that "every German officer has his own bit of England marked off
on which he has been examined." In November 1914 Northcliffe published a booklet
Scaremongerings from the Daily Mail, 1896–1914, which proudly summarized his role in
exposing German hostility. When Northcliffe purchased the *Times* in 1908, he promised

continued to clang the tocsin, although they had to adapt to the new "enemy" over the horizon. Between 1900 and 1914, for example, they ground out thirty-one invasion narratives, only five of which did *not* feature Germany as the attacker. And like a well-greased weather vane, William Le Queux swung toward the North Sea to accommodate to the Teutonic menace. But before examining his most lurid achievements in this genre, it is appropriate first to discuss the contribution of Erskine Childers.

Certainly as early as 1900 German strategists like Baron Colmar von Goltz had begun to theorize in print about the possibility of Germany acquiring command of the North Sea, the weak spot in English naval operations. Then in 1903 Erskine Childers (1870–1922), a Cambridge-educated clerk in the House of Commons, published *The Riddle of the Sands: A Record of Secret Service*, one of the most successful spy and counterspy novels of the twentieth century. (By 1976 sales figures were approaching the two-million mark.)[36] Based on six voyages which the author made into the narrow, sand-choked channels of the Frisian Islands aboard his seven-ton sloop, his novel achieved such verisimilitude that it was endorsed (privately) by the first sea lord, Sir John Fisher, and fooled many readers, including ex-Prime Minister Lord Rosebery, who believed that Childers had uncovered a real invasion scheme.

Childers consciously sought to make his readers think his account was *record*, not fiction. While at work on it he wrote a friend: "It's a yachting story, with a purpose, suggested by a cruise I once took in German waters. I discovered a scheme of invasion directed against England. I'm finding it terribly difficult as being in the nature of a detective story. . . . I was weak enough to 'spatchcock' a girl into it and now find her a horrible nuisance."[37] Childers uncovered no such plot, but seems to have convinced himself that he had. He fought his publisher's decision to advertise the book as "a novel," and some years later told another friend that although he had invented the story, he had subsequently learned that the Germans had actually worked out an invasion plan along the lines of his fantasy.[38] The matter is entangled further by Childers' draft of a plan during the Great War, while serving as a lieutenant in the naval reserve, which would have had England invade Germany by a flanking attack across the Frisian sands, thereby

---

not to interfere with editorial policy *unless* the editor failed to warn of the German peril. See A. J. A. Morris, *The Scaremongers: The Advocacy of War and Rearmament, 1896–1914* (London, 1984), 6.

reversing their devilish scheme.[39] Had this been executed, Childers would have succeeded in making life, on a truly grand scale, imitate art.

The Riddle of the Sands purports to be the true story of one Carruthers, a minor functionary of the Foreign Office, who stumbles on the German plan while yachting in the Frisians. After British authorities summarily reject his report, his friend Childers comes forth and edits the manuscript as patriotic duty. Under this elaborately woven blanket of spurious nonfiction, Childers combines the ingredients of nautical adventure, spy tale, and love story. The result was what John Buchan, himself a master at this buccaneering genre, called "the best story of adventure published in the last quarter of a century,"[40] a best-seller so widely acclaimed that its reception "stunned" the author.

Following three decades of invasion stories which had chronicled the failure of public officials to head off an impending national disaster, Childers' novel restores the private hero to his rightful place as defender of the realm. The narrator Carruthers receives a letter from one Arthur Davis, an eccentric friend of his Oxford years, inviting him to cruise in his sloop *Dulcibella* from Flensburg. Having nothing better to do in a dull summer, he joins Davis on his dingy boat—light years away from the spotless yachts of the Cowes Regatta that he is accustomed to—and learns of an incredible invasion scheme. Split in half by Denmark, Germany is building secret bases in the shoals of the Frisian Islands, which the Royal Navy does not subject to surveillance because they are too shallow for conventional warships. Davis suspects the complicity of a renegade English Jew named Dollman—Jews figuring prominently in spy literature after the Dreyfus case—with headquarters on the island of Memmert Sand. Carruthers eagerly joins this counterspy expedition which pits two lone Englishmen against the German empire. Love of country and a zest for danger quickly purge Carruthers of any lingering club-and-regatta decadence exacerbated by consorting with the "pseudo-Bohemians of Soho."[41]

Davis is portrayed as a kind of T. E. Lawrence before his time, an English eccentric and *Übermensch*, who works outside the establishment in order to save it. Like earlier freebooters who arose when England was imperiled, Davis embodies "a devotion to the sea, wedded to a fire of pent-up patriotism struggling incessantly for an outlet in strenuous physical expression."[42] He does not blame Germany for wanting to expand at England's expense—far from it. Expansion is a symptom of national health, just as contraction is of national disease. "We've been safe so long, grown so rich that we've forgotten what we owe it to," he exclaims to Carruthers. "By Jove, we want a man like the Kaiser, who doesn't wait to be kicked, but works like a nigger for his country and sees ahead." For reading matter, he carries a well-thumbed copy of Mahan's *The Influence of Sea Power*. In his simple geopolitical catechism, German aggression is a positive benefit to England, because "It'll teach us to buck up, and that's what really matters."[43] Davis is the lineal descendant of Tom Brown of Rugby, ferocious in his love of country but without enmity toward a gentlemanly enemy also intent upon "playing the game." His loathing is reserved for Dollman, the English traitor, and it is no less keen for his having fallen in love with the villain's beautiful daughter.

Closely watched by German patrols, the two patriots penetrate and chart the tangled network of channels, rivers, and canals until they unlock the secret plan. The Germans will equip seven fleets with seagoing, shallow-draft lighters. At zero hour these will issue simultaneously from their island cover and make a full-scale, surprise attack on the beaches of East Anglia. The Frisian Islands, viewed as nothing more than landlocked tidal marshes by British intelligence, would thus provide major sea lanes leading back to Hamburg, Bremen, and Wilhelmshaven—the heart of industrial Germany. The traitor Dollman would supply precise information concerning the disposition of English troops and the strategic areas to be seized. The issue is never in much doubt, of course. In the end the English stalwarts capture Dollman (who conveniently commits suicide), and Davis wins the love of the traitor's daughter (whose patriotism outshines her paternal affection). Childers broke new ground by introducing a sexual dimension in a genre that had formerly been infested by superpatriotic male achievers, but his real achievement lay in his vivid accounts of tricky seamanship among the Frisian shoals, details which still intrigue fans of nautical literature. Moreover, English readers could not fail to be pleased by the portrait of a lounge lizard like Carruthers—a kind of first-stage Dorian Gray—evolving into a stalwart man of action. Underneath their foppish mannerisms, the young men of Oxbridge were quite all right.

Although Childers claimed that his book brought about changes in naval policy through strengthening the North Sea fleet, the claim has been disputed by professionals like Prince Louis of Battenberg, a future first sea lord: "As a novel it is excellent, as a war plan it is rubbish."[44] But there is no question that it brought the precarious invasion issue to a host of English readers just at the time when self-confidence was at a low ebb. (The Committee of Imperial Defence was established that same year.) Childers soon abandoned fiction in order to take a more authoritative role in military affairs. Encouraged by Lord Roberts, retired commander in chief of the British army, he wrote two prescient books, *War and the Arme Blanche* (1910) and *German Influence on British Cavalry* (1911), designed to prove the obsolescence of both massed formations and cavalry in modern war. Had they been heeded, the British would have been spared many mistakes in early campaigns of the Great War, but Childers' views were heretical to the cavalrymen who assumed control of the war. Disenchanted with the military establishment, Childers became an activist in the movement for Irish independence. In July 1914 he smuggled into the port of Hawth one thousand 9mm Mausers which he purchased in Hamburg—the first large shipment of contraband rifles ever received by the Irish revolutionaries. In 1919 he settled in Dublin to write propaganda for the Irish Republican Army, was captured by forces of the Irish Free State in 1922, and was sentenced to be executed. He went out in fine style; after shaking hands with each member of the firing squad, he instructed them, "Take a step or two forward, lads. It will be easier that way."[45] Childers achieved the distinction of becoming the only known spy novelist to be shot as a spy. His novel has lived on, weathering many editions and translations.*

With the launching of the first dreadnought in 1906, a battleship that rendered all navies of the world obsolescent—including England's own—the momentum of the armaments race accelerated, culminating in the Great War. Taking advantage of the latest hue and cry and seduced by the success of Childers' novel in reaching a nongeneralized market, William Le Queux again entered the lists. During the decade that had elapsed since his *The Great War in England in 1897*, he had been busy pummeling editors and officials with his revelations of plots in high places. Since Germany had replaced France as England's nemesis, Le Queux adapted quickly to the winds of change. His book *Spies of the Kaiser* showed how Germans were fanning out in England, where they had been detected crouching under railway bridges, asking questions about public reservoirs, and taking suspicious bicycle rides in Epping Forest. Bigger game lay ahead. Somehow he became intimate

*The first American edition appeared in 1915, when Anglophiles were urging the United States to enter the war. In 1940, during the battle of Britain, when the Nazis threatened a real invasion, the novel was again published in the United States, once more to drum up support for Great Britain.

with Lieutenant Colonel James Edmonds, who in 1906 had been placed in charge of ferreting out German spies in England. Le Queux was able to sell Edmonds a bogus invasion plan worked out by a ring of forgers in Belgium, but the CID wisely refused to act upon it.[46] Le Queux then carried his discovery to the *Daily Mail,* a major scaremongering news sheet regularly featuring stories of spies and traitors, and obtained a commission to write a serial based on his notes. Le Queux found the financial support and publicity offered by the *Daily Mail* a godsend, for his more recent scribblings in the sensational line, works like *The Hunchback of Westminster* (1904), had sold poorly.

Fortified with an expense account, Le Queux reconnoitered the by-ways of East Anglia for four months, covering ten thousand miles by automobile as he studied weak spots in Albion's defense. Editors of the *Daily Mail* at first rejected the route he prescribed for the German juggernaut on grounds that he had picked "remote one-eyed villages where there was no possibility of large *Daily Mail* sales,"[47] but the author obligingly diverted his invading hordes to pass through larger towns in order to boost circulation figures. When the invasion story was finally published serially by the *Mail* in March 1906, Londoners were astonished by the appearance of men walking the streets wearing Prussian helmets and sandwichboards which announced the daily progress of the Germans. In the House, Prime Minister Campbell-Bannerman urged suppression of the story because it "might conceivably alarm the more ignorant public at home"—a critique which Le Queux triumphantly printed in the preface of his book.[48]

Bolstered by Lord Roberts' introductory note (". . . History tells us in the plainest terms that an Empire which cannot defend its own possessions must inevitably perish . . ."), Le Queux's potboiler, *The Invasion of 1910* (1906), was an instantaneous success. Translated into twenty-seven languages—including Urdu and Chinese—it sold a million copies, according to Le Queux's tally. (A German edition, rewritten to depict a Kaiser victory and illustrated with pictures showing the sacking of London, was gilt-bound and offered as a prize for schoolboys.)[49] Jam-packed with black-white stereotypes and lurid details of mayhem, this book more than any other prepared the English public for their showdown war with Germany.

The Invasion of 1910 is an amalgam of stock devices which Le Queux, like a clever magpie, plucked from three decades of invasion stories. From the Colomb committee he took the fictitious on-the-spot journalistic report; from H. G. Wells' *War of the Worlds* scenes of universal panic and moral collapse; from Childers the sortie from behind the Frisian Islands. Added to these was Le Queux's grab bag collection of spies and anarchists popping from their secret lairs. More than any other writer Le Queux can take credit for the spy scare that seized England during the decade preceding the Great War and resulted in jail terms and near-lynchings of German nationals in 1914. In this novel German waiters, bakers, hairdressers, and servants are all bound by oaths to serve the fatherland; moreover, each has a special lapel button by which he can be identified by the invading armies as a loyal subject of the Kaiser. A summary of this novel reveals the quintessential Le Queux.

It is September 1910 when five German army corps, totalling nearly 200,000 men, debouch from the Frisians and land without opposition on the east coast of England. Their surprise is complete, for it is Sunday and no one remains on duty at the War Office or the Admiralty. Nearly ten hours elapse before an enterprising journalist, suspicious about the interruption of communications with East Anglia, discovers the invasion. All this while General von Kronhelm, observed lethargically by local fisherman, puts his men on shore and launches a two-pronged invasion toward London and Sheffield. He publishes a proclamation (a facsimile of which is printed in the book) demanding the death penalty for any Briton harming a German soldier, destroying roads or canals, or disseminating misleading directions. The Royal Navy is no match for German gunners, because shortsighted parliamentarians have skimped on ammunition for practice shooting.

In London the stock exchange collapses, Parliament ignominiously flees to Bristol, and Whitechapel mobs storm into the West End and lynch some German waiters. Mobilization for defense is out of the question, because order and leadership have vanished. Repeatedly Le Queux, as stalking horse for the Lord Roberts get-tough faction, hammers home his thesis—the real criminals are British demagogues who have left the country unprepared. Meanwhile the Kaiser lands at Scarborough, Sheffield falls, and the Germans converge on London. From artillery positions at Hampstead, they shell the city. The British Museum goes up in smoke and gaping ruins mark the destruction of Bloomsbury. A tower of Westminster Abbey crashes down upon the shrine of Edward the Confessor. Refugees cram into the tube stations, trampling one another to death on the stairways. "London—the proud capital of the world, the 'home' of the Englishmen—was at last ground beneath the iron heel of Germany."[50]

Yet all is not lost. Far to the west, in that region sacred to King Arthur, the seeds of resistance are sprouting. In the Commons at Bristol, Gerald Graham, scion of a noble house, rallies the defense. Elsewhere, Leagues of Defense spring up and counterattack, utilizing paramilitary groups recruited from neighborhoods and bearing names like the "Kensington Cowboys" and the "Southwark Scalp-hunters." As the invaders advance down Harrow Road, the populace attacks with saloon pistols and hatchets. A captured German diary reads, "The British are dull and apathetic, but once aroused, they fight like fiends."[51] At St. Pancras Station the enemy retaliates by massacring civilians, even women, but they have rough going in the tortuous streets of the inner city. While the Germans are masters of open-country maneuvering, they are baffled and outclassed by the English genius for guerrilla warfare. As thousands of reinforcements pour into London, the Kaiser, sniffing disaster, repairs to Berlin. Gerald Graham's name is now on the lips of every English patriot, and the German offensive withers away. Just two months after invading England, the Germans request a truce.

The end of the war finds the British Empire outwardly intact but weakened inwardly, while Germany, having grabbed Denmark and Holland en route, remains perched for a future attack. Runaway socialists, with their creed "Thou shalt have no other god but thyself," have undermined the English spirit. High rates of taxation for the rich have driven into exile many of the most productive capitalists. "There were few rich left, but the consequences to the poor, instead of being beneficial, were utterly disastrous."[52] It is to be hoped that Gerald Graham (whose bulldog tenacity at a time of peril anticipates the role of Winston Churchill in 1940), will trim throwaway social programs from the budget in favor of defense appropriations, but the future of England lies in doubt as Le Queux concludes his cautionary tale.

Germanophobia in popular literature reached its apogee with *The Invasion of 1910,* which brought within reach of every English fireside a frightening outline of enemy perfidy and destruction. Scaremongering had been a regular feature of the yellow press for many years, but Le Queux became its high priest. Even serious journals began to succumb to panic; in July 1908 the *Quarterly Review* addressed the problem of German espionage in Britian and solemnly warned that there were some 50,000 German waiters in the country.[53] M.P.s lined up on either the blue water or the bolt-from-the-blue side of the issue and ground the question into a fine powder. After one such inconclusive debate in Parliament, a writer noted sardonically in the *National Review*, "No one seems to have a clear conception whether a dinghy with five men, or a Fleet with an Army Corps is the minimum which the inhabitants of Clacton may have to entertain one day with tea and shrimps."[54] The problem was compounded by French intelligence operations which manufactured German invasion schemes and attempted to pawn them off on the British in order to cement the loose Anglo-French alliance. Lord Esher, a member of the CID, wrote in his journal in 1909, "Spy catchers get espionage on the brain. Rats are everywhere—behind every arras."[55] In the same year a Somerset M.P. reported that Germanophiles had sequestered 50,000 Mauser rifles and seven million rounds of ammunition within a quarter-mile radius of Charing Cross.[56] The German Naval Bill of 1908 added to the panic, and the Kaiser did not allay fears when he boasted, "Now that Germany is in the saddle we can ride down our enemies."[57]

Although Le Queux tried many times to repeat his success—in his career he wrote over a hundred novels, most of them treating espionage—his work plummeted in quality and plausibility from its original basement level. No English peers rushed in to endorse such potboilers as *The German Spy* (1914) or *The Bomb-Makers* (1916), because with the arrival of a bona fide war there was catastrophe galore in any daily newspaper to make his fictions a trifle stale. Like Erskine Childers, William Le Queux came to believe that his fantasies were fact. According to his biographer, Norman Sladen, who swallowed whole whatever Le Queux told him, royalties from his books were used to finance secret service operations on the continent, where he bribed his way into German gun factories, infiltrated the Kaiser's own spy bureau, and fraternized with such notables as Tsar Nicholas, Peter of Serbia, and the King of Montenegro.[58] When the Great War (which he had done his part in bringing about) finally arrived, he served his country by delivering 228 lectures, some of them on a platform shared with Horatio Bottomley, editor of the jingoist sheet *John Bull*. Even after the war Le Queux refused to give up his invasion scribblings. In *Hidden Hands* (1925), one of his last novels, the Germans (surprisingly resilient after their 1918 defeat) plot to blow up the Forth Bridge, thereby trapping the Royal fleet inside, and to invade England. Unlike Childers, Le Queux was not eventually shot by a firing squad for political or literary crimes.

In Graham Greene's *The Ministry of Fear* (1943), a spy thriller set in London during the blitz, Arthur Rowe has a nightmare. Pursued by a Nazi ring, he falls asleep in a tube station and dreams of taking tea with his mother in Cambridge on the eve of the First World War. Her world had been defined by tea on the lawn, evensong, and croquet—"lady novelists describe it over and over again in books of the month, but it's not there any more."[59] In his dream he tells her, "You used to laugh at the books Miss Savage read—about spies, and murders, and violence, and wild motor-car chases, but dear, that's real life: it's what we've all made of the world since you died. . . . The world has been remade by William Le Queux."[60] Rowe then imagines a compilation called "The History of Contemporary Society" consisting of hundreds of volumes, "most of them sold in cheap editions." His imaginary list reads like William Le Queux's bibliography: *Death in Piccadilly, The Theft of the Naval Papers, Seven Days' Leave*. Le Queux was symptom, not cause, of the modern disease. He and other writers of invasion narratives, as Greene suggests, not only prophesied the war of the future but created a climate of political paranoia that encouraged the acting out of fears in order to purge them. In this sense Oscar Wilde was right: life can imitate art. History itself becomes at last a tawdry tale written for a sixpenny cheap edition.

3 THE COLLIDING WORLDS
OF H. G. WELLS

▼

The Germans are frightfully efficient and will
invade us too. We must have a levée en masse. *We*
must get out our shot guns and man the hedges and
ditches, but it will be the end of civilization.
H. G. WELLS *in conversation (August 4, 1914)*

In his eighteenth year H. G. Wells (1866–1946) began an appren-
ticeship in biology at the Normal School of Science in South Kensington under the tutelage of Thomas H. Huxley. One of three
scientists whom Charles Darwin had asked to read *The Origin of Species*
prior to its publication in 1859, Huxley had been dubbed "Darwin's
Bulldog" for his aggressive defense of organic evolution. By the time
Wells arrived at the Normal School the concept of evolution had already won its major battles among scientists and was engaged in mop-
ping up operations among theologians and sociologists. The former
aspired to enlist it under the banner of Christian meliorism, while the
latter, under the leadership of Herbert Spencer, were prepared to argue
that social "organisms" also evolved from simpler, undifferentiated
hordes into complex and invariably "higher" civilizations. Thomas
Huxley shared neither of these benign views of the evolutionary process
with their optimistic assumptions of infinite improvement in human
conditions. His interpretation was pessimistic; so far as mankind was
concerned, retrogression was just as likely as progression. It was his
view that society and nature worked at cross-purposes. He compared
the course of human development to the trajectory of a shot fired from a
mortar with the "sinking half of that course as much a part of the
general process of evolution as the rising."[1] The youthful Wells, who
many years later wrote that his exposure to Huxley had been "beyond
question the most educational year of my life,"[2] absorbed the lessons of

his master, even though his own scientific writing would vacillate between Huxley's grim pessimism and the prevailing millennialism of the later Victorians.

Wells found the invasion genre irresistible. For nearly three decades such stories had been a staple in the popular literary diet and he sensed the bizarre appeal which apocalyptic literature had for an audience raised on the Bible. A contemporary historian has summarized the mood of the English public at this time: "One word could send a *frisson* of terror coursing down the middle class spine—invasion."[3] Gifted with a more inventive intelligence than Colonel Chesney and his followers, he entered the field by projecting an invasion not by humanoids wearing Zouave trousers or spiked helmets but by extraterrestrial creatures looking like boilers on stilts. The arrival of hostile Martians in *The War of the Worlds* (1897) provided him with a fictive opportunity to describe the sociological consequences of invasion upon the collective psyche of the English people while they were engaged in a life-and-death struggle with beings coming from a more technologically advanced civilization. Whereas most invasion writers up to this time had focused upon causes and results of war, Wells devoted the bulk of his narrative to the inward reactions of a noncombatant trapped inside the zone of destruction, and he treated these reactions as though from the perspective of a frenzied and impotent insect whose nest has been wrecked by an indifferent and all-powerful attacker. Unlike his predecessors in the invasion genre, Wells had no military "lesson" to convey, no homily about the terrible price of unpreparedness. On the contrary, the Martians are nearly immune to human weaponry as they stalk the countryside, fueling themselves with human blood. In the end they are destroyed by microorganisms and disease picked up from a contaminated planet. Bacteria from a poisoned Earth destroys the enemy, without help from the Admiralty or War Office.

Like the literary naturalists, who approached literature through a maze of data collection and quasi-scientific measurement which were somehow to lead to the discovery of fundamental laws of human behavior, Wells was intrigued by the possibility of reducing civilized man to a level of what a proper Victorian might have called "animal" behavior. In this view man was less "God in ruins," as Emerson had said, than mere aggregation of assorted atomic particles basic to all organic life. This principle of reductionism appears in the opening paragraph of *The War of the Worlds* and is central to Wells' theme: "With infinite complacency men went to and fro over the globe about their little affairs, serene in the assurance of their empire over matter. It is possible that the infusoria under the microscope do the same."[4] This passage yields both biological and historical interpretations. On the one hand, the Martians, seeing Earthlings as the infusoria and having depleted the resources of their own planet, ruthlessly invade the domain of "lower" creatures with a logic that Herbert Spencer (author of the phrase "survival of the fittest") would have applauded—unless he were willing to be convicted of special pleading. As an older and therefore expiring planet, Mars serves as a preview of conditions that may evolve on Earth. (In a sketch four years earlier, "The Man of the Year Million," Wells had described future human beings as pulpy, nearly immobile creatures consisting mainly of brain.)[5] His Martian fable lodges squarely within the frame of Huxley's dire predictions about the future of species in an evolutionary process. Wells even uses Huxley's trajectory metaphor in conveying the Martians to the Earth and in destroying them, for they are literally fired from mortars and collapse into protoplasmic jelly at the final point on their trajecting arc.

Yet this opening paragraph, with words like *complacency, globe,* and *empire* suggests that Wells was also alluding to specifically English conditions at century's end. At this period the British Empire occupied one-quarter of the land mass of the globe and accounted for one-quarter of its population. Despite these proofs of Britannia's rule, there were deep undercurrents of hesitation and doubt about the permanence of the status quo. As we have seen, the sudden rise and proliferation of invasion narratives testified to national insecurity. Wells' minutely chronicled account of collective panic in *The War of the Worlds* reflected his own war against English complacency. From his home at Woking he wrote a friend about his novel: "I'm doing the dearest little serial for Pearson's new magazine, in which I completely wreck and destroy Woking—killing my neighbors in painful and eccentric ways, then proceed . . . to London, which I sack, selecting South Kensington for feats of peculiar atrocity."[6] In a sense Wells was writing a covert anti-imperialist tract in which the colonial experience is turned inside out with the English population as helpless as Tasmanians or Zulus when overrun by invaders with superior weaponry. The Martians, who land only a few miles from Dorking, use their heat rays and black smoke (a precursor of poison gas) to scatter the civilian population, which clogs the highways to the north in its pell-mell flight. In effect, civilized Englishmen are forced to descend several rungs in the evolutionary ladder as they react like terrified animals intent on saving their own skins—nation and community be damned. The appearance of Wells' novel during the year of Victoria's Second Jubilee, when national amour propre reached its apogee, provided a harsh emetic for banqueters celebrating Britannia's rule. At about this same time, not far from Woking, Rudyard Kipling was writing "The Recessional," the poem which would sound the last trumpet for the British Empire so far as its evolution and growth were concerned.

Wells dramatized, if he did not invent, the concept of "total war" that would characterize global conflict of the twentieth century. Traditional morality with its noblesse oblige and rules of civilized warfare simply has no place in the Martian scheme for world conquest. When the first cylinders crash in Surrey, the Earthlings naively attempt to establish communication with the creatures, but this is abandoned precipitously after the Martians reveal that Earth people are to them "as alien and lowly as are the monkeys and lemurs to us." What follows is a wholly amoral scenario derived from Spencer's "life is an incessant struggle for existence." Just as the English exterminated the Tasmanians, so it is natural that the Martians wish to do the same with Earthlings. The Martians have a superior technology, they embody the work ethic with a vengeance, they labor without periods of sleep, and they are "absolutely without sex, and therefore without any of the tumultuous emotions that arise from that difference among men."[7] It is as if their remote ancestors were workaholic Puritans.

During his flight from these hideous creatures, the anonymous narrator finds himself trapped in a cellar with a curate, who wails like a mad prophet proclaiming the end of England for following the road to Sodom and Gomorrah. "This must be the beginning of the end," he cries. "The great and terrible day of the Lord! When men shall call upon the mountains and the rocks to fall upon them and hide them— hide them from the face of Him that sitteth upon the throne."[8] Yet instead of greeting the Martians as agents of the Apocalypse, the curate collapses into a pool of abject terror when a Martian outside nuzzles against their hiding place. The level-headed narrator rebukes him: "Be a man. You are scared out of your wits. What good is religion if it collapses at calamity."[9] Eventually the cleric, who functions as a stalking-horse for Wells' gibes at the failure of institutionalized religion, has to be killed by the narrator to prevent his sniveling cries from being heard by the Martians.

Having disposed of the clergyman, Wells moves on to another agent of protection, the soldier. Our narrator briefly allies himself with an artilleryman who plans to occupy the sewers of London and mobilize guerrilla sorties against the invaders.* A better companion than the curate, he proves ineffectual in the end. His formula—the tame will perish and the savage will prevail—is rigorously Spencerian. Women will be admitted to their elite band, but only as mothers and teachers— "no lackadaisical ladies—no blasted rolling eyes."[10] The social detritus of the old culture must be stripped away in order to return to those streamlined fundamentals absolutely necessary for survival. They must develop their minds to surpass the Martians by raiding libraries and committing themselves to intensive study programs—"not novels and poetry swipes, but ideas, science books."[11] The soldier, characterized by one Wells critic as "a clownish version of the Nietzschean super-man,"[12] while filled with grandiose schemes, utterly lacks the will to implement them. Ultimately he proves to be more diligent at scavenging cigars and wine than in defeating the Martians. Obviously, in singling out the curate and the soldier for lengthy treatment, Wells was suggesting that Victorian alternatives—whether empty lamentations from the priesthood or braggadocio from the military caste—were equally useless in the face of unknowns which threatened mankind from the twentieth century and beyond. In his later work Wells would salvage the soldier for his managerial elite, but with the clergyman there was nothing to do except leave him to heaven.

In concluding *The War of the Worlds*, Wells sweetened the bitter pill of evolutionary determinism by suggesting that the Martian invasion had brought together the bickering nations of Earth into a unity heretofore unknown: "It has robbed us of that serene confidence in the future which is the most fruitful source of decadence . . . and it has done much to promote the conception of the commonweal of mankind."[13] But having said this, Wells drops the subject, and the reader remains unconvinced. Far more powerful and plausible is the paragraph at the end of the novel, where the narrator reflects on the busy multitudes in Fleet Street and the Strand who have forgotten their brush with extermination: "It comes across my mind that they are but ghosts of the past, haunting the streets that I have seen silent and

*For Wells the future was often associated with chthonian refuge for survivors, as in his earlier futurist romance *The Time Machine* (1895) and in his account of trench warfare in *Anticipations* (1901). His biographers, Norman and Jeanne Mackenzie, suggest that this may have resulted from his "downstairs" status at Up Park, where his mother had been a servant. See Norman and Jeanne Mackenzie, *The Time Traveler: The Life of H. G. Wells* (London, 1973), 118.

wretched, going to and fro, phantoms in a dead city, the mockery of life in a galvanized body."[14] Two decades later T. S. Eliot would employ similar imagery in *The Waste Land* to convey, within the frame of another postwar London, the empty panorama of death-in-life following a war that had nearly destroyed Western civilization.

While *The War of the Worlds* was being serialized, Wells, in a review of George Gissing's novels, referred to "a change that is sweeping over the minds of thousands of educated men. It is a discovery of the insufficiency of the cultivated life and its necessary insincerities; it is a return to the essential, to honourable struggle as the epic factor in life."[15] The implication was that a major upheaval like an invasion by Martians—or by one of the Great Powers, if the Martians failed to materialize promptly—would invigorate lives grown stale and complacent after decades of money-grubbing self-absorption. Bernard Bergonzi has traced this *fin du globe* mood of Wells' early fiction to the sensibility summarized in Max Nordau's sweepingly popular *Degeneration* (1895) with its world-weary thesis of "a Dusk of the Nations, in which all suns and all stars are gradually waning, and mankind with all its institutions and creations is perishing in the midst of a dying world."[16] This interpretation is, of course, in accord with Huxley's regressive vision of the evolutionary process, but it is also not far removed from traditional Christian predictions about the end of the world, the stuff of countless sermons which had afflicted Wells before his conversion to scientific positivism. Christians envisioned at least three ways in which the world might end—by cosmic collision, by a blinding explosion, and by the arrival of a host of angels; in a sense, Wells' novel had fused the second and third. At one swoop *The War of the Worlds* had embraced a gamut of growing intellectual preoccupations of the nineties—eschatology, evolution, and entropy.

More than any other English writer of the age, Wells was haunted by the specter of mass destruction. The narrator of *The War of the Worlds* is introduced as a rationalist engaged in writing a book about the moral progress of civilization. Ironically the Martians appear just as he has written the line, "In about two hundred years we may expect———,"[17] and at the conclusion of the novel he returns to his manuscript but fails to complete the sentence. Like Kurtz of Joseph Conrad's *Heart of Darkness*, published the same year, he has looked into the depths and found his meliorist assumptions, bred by civilization, displaced by scenes of unforgettable horror. In his headlong flight from the Martians, his instinct for self-preservation took full control, but he also found himself responding to an antithetical impulse as well, a joyous anticipation of the killer instinct. When he first heard of the developing war, he put into words what thousands of Europeans would feel just seventeen years later when the real, not fictive, Great War began: "I had been feverishly excited all day. Something very like the war-fever, that occasionally runs through a civilised community, had got into my blood. . . . I was even afraid that last fusillade I had heard might mean the extermination of our invaders from Mars. I can best express my state of mind by saying that I wanted to be in at the death."[18] There is no cant here about defense of homeland, family, or suburban villa. Instead, Wells foresaw the lemming impulse that would carry over the brink, without benefit of reason, millions of acquiescent European lives in the Armageddon lying a few years in the future. "To be in at the death"—never mind whose.

▼

With the death of Queen Victoria in 1901, England lost a symbol of progress, stability, and empire—an icon that no longer bore resemblance to the real senescent dowager occupying her hive at Windsor as the nineteenth century waned and expired. With her passing, things seemed to fall apart. Wells compared her to "a great paper-weight that for half a century sat upon men's minds, and when she was removed their ideas began to blow all over the place haphazardly."[19] In the same year he published his own idea book, *Anticipations of the Reaction of Mechanical and Scientific Progress upon Human Life and Thought* (1901), a remarkable futurist tract which spelled out the agenda for the new century and devoted one entire chapter to the subject "War." Serialized in the prestigious *Fortnightly Review*, it reached a body of readers among the ruling elite of Europe and brought its author from the back to the front door of the intellectual establishment. Henceforth Wells would be regarded as something more than a "master in the art of producing creepy sensations," the verdict of one reviewer.[20] Even the top-heavy title of his new work, which sounded like an English translation of a ponderous scientific tome emanating from Heidelberg or Göttingen, underscored the author's profound seriousness.

In a self-important moment Wells called *Anticipations* "the keystone to the main arch of my work," but in a jocular vein he wrote a friend that his design was "to undermine and destroy the monarch monogamy and respectability—and the British Empire, all under the guise of a speculation about motor cars and electrical heating."[21] As might be expected, prognostications about future war occupied a large segment of this work, his thesis being that "war is being drawn into the field of the exact sciences" and that a nation must develop "educated efficient classes or be beaten in war and give way upon all points where its interests conflict with the interests of more capable people."[22] The days of "muddling through" under the command of gentlemen amateurs had ended. In the war of the future, God would not be on the side of the largest battalions but on those better organized, supplied, and trained. As Wells saw it, the Darwinian struggle had left the jungle and entered the laboratories.

As prophetic book *Anticipations* shows that Wells understood intuitively what a succession of generals on the Western Front in 1914–18 would learn only by trial and error (when learned at all): that existing technology had tipped the scales in favor of the defensive position in warfare. Machine guns had rendered superior marksmanship irrelevant; smokeless powder had made massed frontal attacks under sulphur clouds obsolete. Wells envisioned a static front line consisting of a network of trenches eight miles deep in which troops would dig toward one another more like moles than men. (This was another of his underground survival ideas). Cavalry would cease to exist, replaced by armored vehicles of enormous size. The Great General of old-fashioned wars would be superseded by a "central organiser at a telephonic centre far in the rear." Lighter-than-air machines would patrol the skies, bombing the enemy's rear camps and fighting each other to establish aerial supremacy. "Once command of the air is obtained the war must become a conflict between a seeing beast and one that is blind."[23]

In the great wars of the future victory belonged to the side which created a soldiery linked "in sympathy and organisation with the engineer and the doctor and all the continually developing mass of scientific educated men that the advance of science and mechanism is producing."[24] As for the vanquished, led by generals whose knowledge of war had been gained in the vanished nineteenth century,

> It will be more like herding sheep than actual fighting. Yet the bitterest and cruelest things will have to happen, thousands and thousands of poor boys will be smashed in all sorts of dreadful ways . . . before the obvious fact that war is no longer a business for half-trained lads in uniform, led by parson-bred sixth-form boys and men of pleasure and old men, but an exhaustive demand upon very carefully-educated adults for the most strenuous best that is in them, will get its practical recognition.[25]

Anyone could have written this in 1918; the measure of Wells' genius at divination is that it dates from 1901. It was as though he had entered one of his own time machines and been wafted forward to witness the carnage of Loos, the Somme, and Passchendaele—all of them failures of vision and command. Yet while he accurately foresaw the demise of war as romantic activity, he failed to predict the incapacity of military leadership to adjust to the new technology. These were more ignorant and obstinate than even Wells could conceive. The events of the Great War would show that the new weapons of destruction—gas, tanks, airplanes—would be deployed too niggardly or too late to give either side the decisive edge. Technology simply would outrun the capacity of army staffs to absorb it, but that was no fault of Wells.

Central to Wells' thought at this period was the idea of rule by a managerial and scientific elite which—borrowing from Plato—he called the New Republic. This entailed a rigorous program of eugenics that would "pick over, educate, sterilize, export, or poison its People of the Abyss," defined as that segment of the population which had been shown to be worthless in both peace and war.[26] Slovenly democracy would be replaced by efficient technocracy. The existing economic system, which honored vendors of pork more than men of intellect, would become a major casualty of change. Essentially, Wells envisioned a state which would tolerate only those institutions—or individuals— regarded as useful in the struggle for survival against the random forces of nature.

Unlike the earlier spate of invasion tales, or Wells' own scientific romances of the nineties, *Anticipations* was written from a millenialist point of view. After a transitional period of national rivalry—particu- larly a struggle between France and Germany for linguistic domination in Europe—all nations would reach a plateau of cooperation through a "Larger Synthesis." New Republicans would constitute an informal and open freemasonry of kindred intellects who would control the apparatus of their respective governments, taking as their goal the welfare of the whole human race. Revolution along Marxist lines would be quite unnecessary because science would be harnessed to the mecha- nisms propelling social evolution.

Arriving at a time when the privileged classes, defined by wealth or birth, were coming under the guns of the reformers, Wells' formula for a gradualist, nonviolent reconstruction of contemporary society had enormous appeal for progressives aware of England's eroding power (especially vis-à-vis Germany) but with no stomach for revolution. William Archer, a leading literary journalist, went so far as to recommend that Wells be publically endowed as a prophet.[27] Overtures soon arrived from the Fabian Society in the form of Sidney and Beatrice Webb in riding togs "riding very rapidly upon bicycles from the direction of London" to enlist Wells into their society.[28] Invitations came from the circle clustered about Herbert Asquith, who later served as prime minister during the Great War. Wells became a charter member of the Co-Efficients, a coterie of intellectuals and politicians modeled on the elite he had described in *Anticipations*—a kind of Edwardian think tank consisting of such notables as Richard B. Haldane (minister for war after the Liberal landslide of 1906), Sir Edward Grey (foreign secretary during the opening years of the Great War), and Lord Milner (former high commissioner for South Africa).[29] Although the Co-Efficients soon collapsed, Wells' presence testified to his newly gained reputation for social prophecy and to a brief, but apparently unhappy marriage between intellect and politics. In time Wells would gain access to even greater power brokers like Lenin, Churchill, and Stalin—but with no more effect in imposing logic upon politics.

How to cope with a stalemate between two massive armies is the subject of Wells' story "The Land Ironclads" (1903). After observing that invaders are unable to advance against the well-dug trenches of defenders, the central character, a correspondent, mulls over his dispatch captioned, "Is War Played Out?" An exultant defender boasts that the enemy consists of "devitalised townsmen" who are no match for his "rowdy-dowdy cow-punchers and nigger-whackers" for whom fighting is a natural instinct. But at dawn the invaders attack with ironclads, "something between a big blockhouse and a giant's dish cover." Moving at six miles per hour, the machine is safe from artillery and quickly overruns the defenders' trenches and forces them to flee in panic. Inside the ironclads soldier-engineers fire their automatic rifles by means of a camera obscura picture projected into a box, and they provide no targets for the sharpshooting "louts" on the other side. A defending cavalry colonel who had perfected "shooting from the saddle charge" has nothing to show for his pains except "truncated Paladins." To the technicians belong the spoils. The correspondent reflects that "as long as their science keeps going they will necessarily be ahead of open-country men."[30] Not until the panzer divisions of the Third Reich overran Poland and France during the Second World War would

Wells' vision of blitzkrieg be realized.* Far more important than Wells' "invention" of the tank—which is what this story is famous for—was his recognition that technology, not physical prowess or courage, would win the war of the future. The training of the English army, which considered its cavalry and sharpshooters the best in the world, had become in Wells' view hopelessly irrelevant.

Having shown how to break a static front, Wells next showed how fronts could be bypassed altogether in his scientific romance *The War in the Air* (1908), which was inspired by ominous reports that Germany was forging ahead in zeppelin technology at a time when England was putting its money into naval dreadnoughts. Once again Colonel Chesney's influence worked upon Wells, who in describing his plan wrote that he envisioned "a sort of aerial Battle of Dorking."[31] Here Wells clearly showed the irrelevance of Britannia ruling the waves if the imperial eagle could soar far above unmolested. While this forecast of zeppelin invasion unleashing worldwide war was a brilliant idea, as a novel it is little more than a slapdash application of feckless characterization, preposterous plot, and authorial harangue.

In his novel Wells addresses two grave social problems, the rootlessness and mindlessness of the laboring classes engaged in the economic struggle for existence, and the unleashing of a world war because moral organization within the Great Powers has been outstripped by technological developments. Unfortunately the low-mimetic presence of his hero, Bert Smallways, tends to trivialize the impact of a world at war. Bert, a small-time motorbike mechanic, is carried off by a runaway balloon which lands in a German zeppelin park just as Germany launches an attack on the United States. Mistaken for a British airplane inventor, he is carried along by Prince Karl Albert, who plans to extract his secrets. Only a "vulgar little creature," Bert exemplifies the undereducated, misinformed Englishman "with no sense of the State, no habitual loyalty, no devotion, no code of honour, no code even of courage," who has "blundered into the hot forces of welt-politik."[32] He witnesses the attack upon the American fleet and the aerial bombing of New York. After the zeppelin is disabled by bushwhackers and crashes above Niagara Falls, Bert kills the evil prince and escapes with

---

*Published originally in *Strand Magazine*, Wells' story was reprinted by that magazine in November 1916, just after British tanks made their debut on the Somme. Actually the idea of a tank came from the Aldershot inventor and aeronaut, J. W. Dunne, who also gave the author his first flight in an airplane as well as technical details for his novel, *The War in the Air*. See Mackenzie, *Time Traveler*, 221.

secret plans for an airplane, which he turns over to United States authorities so that they can continue the war, which has spread world-wide with a coalition of Japan and China pitted against the West. The outcome of the war is never decisive—at the end of the novel it is rumored to be still in progress.

Embalmed in this thin plot, which reads like a fabrication by Le Queux, are Wells' prescient observations on the march of civilization toward Armageddon. Unlike the run of invasion stories written to spark military defense, Wells' novel preaches the reverse. Because the major powers have become obsessed with prospects of war, money that should have been spent in developing intellectual and educational resources has been squandered on conventional weaponry, which is invariably made obsolescent by scientific breakthroughs like zeppelins and air-planes. New York represented for Wells the "supreme type of the city of the Scientific Commercial Age" with palaces of marble inhabited by the very rich juxtaposed against the dingy warrens of "a black and sinister polyglot population . . . beyond the power and knowledge of government."[33] The fault lay in inequality of opportunity, rapacious economic competition, and the absence of social planning. The novel concludes in a mood of bleak despair about the future of humanity, as though Malthus, Huxley, and Gibbon had pooled their doomsday prophecies:

> Could mankind have prevented this disaster . . . ? As idle as to ask could mankind have prevented the decay that turned Assyria and Babylon to empty deserts or the slow decline and fall, the gradual social disorganisation, phase by phase, that closed the chapter of the Empire of the West! They could not, because they did not, they had not the will to arrest it.[34]

In the ten years between *The War of the Worlds* and *The War in the Air*, Wells had shifted his apocalyptic concerns from ultimate biological possibilities to immediate political dangers. When he named Germans instead of Martians as the major threat, he precisely echoed the fears of a host of scaremongers writing in the decade that preceded the Great War. Wells was beginning to look more like a weather vane than a prophet. In a jingoist article, "The Common-Sense of Warfare" (1913), he blamed "German truculence" for the erosion of international rela-tions and compared Germany with "a boxer with mailed fist as big as and rather heavier than its body."[35] Conveniently he forgot that not too long before he had argued for an Aryan political union and had rejoiced that Prussia's victory in the Franco-Prussian War marked a "final defeat" for Latin peoples and Roman Catholicism.[36] In his view the best that England might hope for was to delay a war with Germany for twenty years, for it was inevitable that the Germanic population increases would expand eastward. When this happened "the Western European Armageddon" would be "off," and England might even consider sending troops to side with France and Germany against Russia.[37]

Even though Wells' writing, with its warnings of holocaust, was formally enlisted in the cause of peace, within the unconscious levels of his psyche he shared with many others of his generation a mysterious craving for war. Years later he confessed in his autobiography that as a schoolboy he dreamed of becoming a great military dictator like Cromwell, and on solitary walks he worked out imaginary battles in which the enemy were "mown down by the thousand." Looking back on his early life, he acknowledged (in 1934) that he had grown up at a time when the idea of a blond, blue-eyed Nordic was "the best make of human being known," and he had a vision of the Aryan people "driving the inferior breeds into the mountains" as a "picturesque background to the duller facts of history." His ideas about radical eugenics as a means of eliminating undesirables and perfecting society had been a prominent feature of *Anticipations,* and he confessed that the mind of Adolf Hitler was "almost the twin of my thirteen year old mind in 1879."[38] (This, of course, before he had any knowledge of death camps.) Even as a grown man Wells was fascinated by war games using tin soldiers and accurate miniature cannon. Weekend guests at his house were recruited for parlor campaigns that lasted all day and were fought with such ferocity that visitors arriving at teatime might be greeted by Wells with a brusque "Sit down and keep your mouth shut!" as the game continued until the last toy soldier had been downed.[39] Stranger still was his book of 1913, *Little Wars: A Game for Boys,* which he called "a homeopathic remedy for the imaginative strategists." It outlined proper rules for campaigning with toys and contained a picture of Wells in white duck trousers crawling on all fours among his tin soldiers and cardboard houses. Although Wells claimed that the purpose of the book was to neutralize a boy's lust for war— "You have only to play at Little Wars three or four times to realize just what a blundering thing a Great War must be"—it is absurd to think that collecting and manipulating toy soldiers induced dovelike feelings in normal youths.[40] For adolescents, the glory of war and conquest were natural correctives to monotonous middle-class existence.

Time was running out for the West, as Wells knew, and early in 1914 he published *The World Set Free: A Story of Mankind,* an omnibus novel recounting the destruction of the existing world order by proliferating atomic warfare. Civilization had evolved because of man's unceasing pursuit of energy—wood, coal, electricity, and oil. Finally, in the 1950s, scientists develop the first engine for harnessing the internal energy of the atom, and immediately automobiles, airplanes, and industrial machinery switch to atomic fission because it is cheap and its supply is infinite. But economic dislocations follow; coal mines are abandoned, railroads become obsolete, monetary standards collapse (gold can be made cheaply in laboratories), massive unemployment plagues the industrial nations, and the gap widens between rich and poor. Suddenly, without warning, the Central Powers attack the Slav confederation; England and France join forces to assist the Slavs.

The grand paroxysm arrives when the Germans drop an atomic bomb on Paris. The Allies retaliate by obliterating Berlin. By 1959 two hundred world cities, from the United States to Japan, have been destroyed by nuclear attacks. Manufactured of carolinium, these bombs cause continuous explosions lasting for years as they ignite other fissionable materials. (Only the explosions are destructive; Wells had no inkling of nuclear fallout.) Finally, representatives from ninety-three nations, under the moral leadership of King Egbert of England, gather at Lake Maggiore and agree that the only way to end world war is to devise a single government for all mankind. The way to salvation is pointed by Egbert, who renounces his throne and expatiates to his shocked political advisor: "For the first time in my life I am going to be a king. I am going to lead, and lead by my own authority. For a dozen generations my family has been a set of dummies in the hands of their advisers. Now I am going to be a real king—and I am going to—to abolish, dispose of, finish, the crown to which I have been a slave."[41] Science, he explains, will be the new king of the world. Atomic power comes under rigid controls and is employed for the elimination of poverty. With cheap fuel available to all regions of the earth, decentralization of populations becomes possible. Capitalism disappears along with man the warrior and man the lawyer. As a special sop to Britons, Wells makes English the official world language and saves English literature for posterity! (Why the countrymen of Dante, Goethe, and Flaubert acquiesce in this, Wells does not say.) In this peaceable kingdom where the lion lies down with the lamb, the old conflict between science and religion is resolved when the scientist, confronting the moral problems of collective life, "comes inevitably upon the words of Christ."[42]

In all of Wells' prophetic books his vision of destruction carries more authority than his recipes for reconstruction. While writing his autobiography, he recalled that as a boy he was "scared by Hell," and the residue of this "furious old hell-and-heaven Thunder God of my childish years" remains as the clay out of which he modeled his versions of apocalypse.[43] Like the biblical prophets, Wells had less trouble with imagining the end of the world than the reign of peace in a new Jerusalem. Whenever he reflected on his ideas of an intelligent elite who would arise to lead mankind into the World State, one senses that his emotions have leaped far ahead of his reason. Thoroughly bourgeois in his attitudes toward political transformation, he rejected radical solutions like Marxism because of its "mystical and dangerous ideas of reconstituting the world on a basis of mere resentment and education: the Class War."[44] Letting the people rule was equivalent to turning back the clock of evolution. Democracy, at least in its present form, was little more than a convention of Bert Smallways, hopelessly ignorant and ill prepared to make decisions pertaining to world affairs. During the prewar period, Wells' various schemes to save humanity involved withdrawing from them the sources of political power. During the Great War, as he watched a vast political demonstration in London more intent upon hanging the Kaiser than in mourning the mountains of English dead, Wells reflected on the limitations of democracy: "And this, thought I, is the reality of democracy; this is the proletariat of dear old Marx. . . . This seething multitude of vague kindly uncritical brains is the stuff that old dogmatist counted upon for his dictatorship of the proletariat, to direct the novel and complex organization of a better world."[45] A mob was a mob, and it made little difference whether it celebrated an illusory victory in Flanders or streamed up the Great North Road ahead of the Martians.

Despite his uncanny prophesying, the Great War caught Wells off guard, as he afterward confessed: "The world disaster . . . so overwhelmed me that I was obliged to thrust a false interpretation upon it."[46] While the German army was pouring into Belgium and Parliament was preparing to enter the war, Wells was attending a flower show near his country house in East Anglia. When another guest, George Bernard Shaw, complained that diplomatic bungling had drawn England into an unnecessary war, Wells became angry. His world-state facade shattered as he launched a tirade against quietism: "The Germans are frightfully efficient and will invade us too. We must have a *levée en masse*. We must get out our shot guns and man the hedges and ditches, but it will be the end of civilization."[47] This recruiting of literary weekenders garbed in plus fours and armed with bird guns holding the German juggernaut at bay must surely rank as one of the great comic visions of the war. That same night Wells began writing his pamphlet *The War That Will End War*, the title of which became a national slogan (and later an embarrassment to the author).*

In the emotion-charged atmosphere of 1914 Wells had got it into his head that Germany alone was responsible for the war, and his pamphlet reads like an exhibit of Orwellian doublethink. All swords drawn against Germany are drawn for peace, because the role of England is to destroy "an evil system of government and the mental and material corruption that has got hold of the German imagination and taken possession of German life." According to this argument, England's holy mission was to destroy Germany so that Germans could be restored to their rightful German heritage. The defeat of Germany would bring to an end "all the blood and iron superstition of Krupp, flag-waving Kiplingism, and all that criminal sham efficiency that centers in Berlin."[48] (Wells seems to have conveniently forgotten that he had pushed efficiency for years and that Kipling had been waving the English, not the German flag.)† Although he does not use the word *Armageddon* in his pamphlet, clearly Wells had in mind that final battle in the Book of Revelation which marked the final victory of the Lord's minions, for he proclaimed that a struggle against Germany was nothing less than "a war to exorcize a world-madness and end an age," and that "every soldier who fights against Germany now is a crusader against war."[49] In this jingoist treatise Wells stops just short of calling the Kaiser the Antichrist and fitting the Allied soldiers with wings.

Imbedded in all this hysteria lay Wells' hope for a world state on the

*In *Experiment in Autobiography* (1934) Wells wrote a retraction: "My pro-war zeal was inconsistent with my pre-war utterances and against my profounder convictions." This retraction came too late. For many, his credibility as prophet had been permanently damaged.
†In 1941 George Orwell observed that much of what Wells admired in government had come true in Nazi Germany—"the order, the planning, the State encouragement of science"—but that paradoxically science was "fighting on the side of superstition." See "Wells, Hitler and World State," in *The Collected Essays, Journalism and Letters of George Orwell* (New York, 1968), II, 143.

order of the one described at the end of the great war in *The World Set Free*. It took two years of carnage, culminating in the casualty lists from the Battle of the Somme, before he could accept the fact that nations at war pursued the same selfish interests as those at peace. In the meantime he bombarded newspapers proposing inventive schemes for winning the war, alienated intellectuals like Clive Bell and Bertrand Russell by his attacks on supporters of peace movements, and shocked the conservatives by his "bolshie" talk about nationalization of basic industries. H. L. Mencken echoed the opinion of many others during this phase when he called Wells a "merchant of banal pedagogies . . . a hawker of sociological liver pills."[50]

Wells had reached intellectual maturity during a Victorian interlude when it was accepted as an article of writ that the problems of mankind could be solved by reflective, sensible men and when the prospect of apocalypse had been the special preserve of a minority of theologians and scientists speculating on remote cosmic disorders. His early scientific romances brought into popular currency the notion that all was not right with the world, and that the *fin du globe* sensibility, which many had felt but few had understood, could be supported by existing scientific observation. As writer of fiction, Wells was most successful when he treated catastrophe beyond the scope of man's capacity to counteract it because this allowed him to play a Cassandra role without being expected to devise an antidote for the calamity. However, with the deterioration of international relations after the Boer War, Wells began to realize that human beings themselves were entirely capable of destroying the world order, whether by aerial warfare in *The War in the Air* or by atomic war in *The World Set Free*. The prophet changed his mission from predicting the future to preventing it from happening. The result was that he was, as a critic has said, "dragooned into the didactic service of his sociological ideas,"[51] all of them incapable of realization because they required qualities which the world had no intention of adopting—moderation, sacrifice, and reason. Orwell charged that Wells was "too sane to understand the modern world," and that he failed to comprehend that "the energy that actually shapes the world springs from emotions—racial pride, leader-worship, religious belief, love of war—which liberal intellectuals write off as anachronisms."[52] Therefore, when the Great War of 1914–18 actually arrived, Wells, like other invasion writers we have examined, banged on a jingoist drum, insisting that *his* country must be blameless. In effect, he became just another animated recruiting poster pressed into service against the Germanic hordes (which he now disparaged for their scientific efficiency). It was ironical that the writer who most effectively warned his countrymen about the dangers of world war and whose novels served as an illuminating beacon for a generation of English youths should turn into hawk when the real war came. By that time the novelist was barely visible under his propagandist feathers, and whatever light he threw off lit the pathway into the inferno.

During the Second World War, Wells told a Cambridge friend that he wanted his epitaph to read: "God damn you all—I told you so."[53] From prophesying about the future of the human race, Wells in the end became the writer of its obituary.

▼

The great phylum of invasion stories between 1870 and 1914 contains some mutations which defy neat Linnaean classification. A curious example is *After London; or, Wild England* (1887) by Richard Jefferies (1848–87), a tale about a period so far in the future that the narrator has neither knowledge of nor curiosity about the invaders of England, if indeed there were invaders at all. Some believe that the collapse occurred when the level of the sea sank; others think that perhaps the ports silted up and destroyed commerce. In any event, London reverted to "vast stagnant swamp" and was evacuated.[54] After the unknown "event" occurred, rats swarmed across the countryside from the cities until they were devoured by dogs of an emergent wolf-type (pedigree creatures failed to adapt and perished, like their owners). "Everything quickly fell into barbarism."[55] Albion reverted to a preindustrial country, and developing towns become no more than agricultural centers. Opposed to the sturdy yeomen farmers are a wild band of bushmen resembling outcast Yahoos who inhabit the woods, while tribes of gypsies establish their capital at Stonehenge. The Welsh and Irish raid the country periodically but for the most part fight each other. Among the yeomen a rustic nobility has arisen, an elite whose rank is derived from their ability to read and write, skills which they teach only to their own children.

From this description of a future England one might conclude that Jefferies was just another doomsday writer warning his country about the grim future ahead. Far from it. Like William Blake, he loathed industrialism and envisioned a retrogressive utopia premised upon primitive settlements of the Celtic or pre-Celtic epoch. His ideal England is embalmed in the prehistorical past. Almost alone among writers haunted by apocalypse, Jefferies welcomed the collapse of modern civilization. Therefore his eerie book is less warning of what might happen when "the wars and hatreds sprang up and divided the people" than wish that it might occur in order that "the countryside become universal green."[56] In his Wiltshire ruminations Jefferies is a distant cousin of Thomas Hardy, whose rustic Wessex was similarly a bourn remote from the grosser problems of industrialism.

Unquestionably the laurels for writing the most eccentric and vitriolic invasion narratives of this period belong to Charles M. Doughty (1843–1926), whose verse dramas, *The Cliffs* (1909) and *The Clouds* (1911), were expressly designed to "lay upon the altar of Alma Britannia" offerings that would warn Englishmen of the perfidy of German expansionism.[57] Like Wells, Doughty laid claim to a scientific education, but his Cambridge studies led only to fossil collecting and other antiquarian pursuits, foremost of which was a lifelong absorption in Chaucer and Spenser. What a tutor wrote of his work in science serves as a fair appraisal of his literary work: "a dishevelled mind. If you asked him for a collar he upset his whole wardrobe at your feet."[58] On going down from Cambridge little was expected of him. Therefore it came as a surprise when, after vanishing for two years in the depths of Arabia, he resurfaced and wrote *Travels in Arabia Deserta* (1888), a cult book which in time acquired "classic" status as a work of travel and exploration.*

Doughty appears to have regarded his Arabian adventure as only an interruption of his major plan, announced as early as 1865, the writing of a "patriotic work" setting forth the origins and development of the English nation for the edification of present-day Englishmen who had fallen away from the heroic ideals of the grandsires. Doughty drew first blood with *The Dawn in Britain* (1906), an epic poem depicting the five-hundred-year struggle between Rome and a British confederacy. Twice the length of the *Iliad*, tangled in archaic syntax and vocabulary, and childishly simple in its exemplifications of Good versus Evil, his magnum opus was a disaster, even his biographer characterizing it as

---

*It was largely ignored until Edward Garnett reduced the original text to only one-third of a million words and arranged for an abridged publication as *Wanderings in the Desert* (1908). T. E. Lawrence was the most famous cultist. As an Oxford undergraduate he made a pilgrimage to the author's home, and after the Great War he set into motion the bureaucratic machinery which supplied Doughty with a small yearly pension from the Crown.

"blood-spattered monotony."[59] Nonetheless, having purged Albion of the foul blood of ancient Rome (and delivered a few ax strokes against the Jewish "Christ-Slayers" en route), Doughty launched his verbal offensive against imperial Germany.

The Cliffs (1909), another verse drama (but mercifully shorter than the last), came directly out of Doughty's alarm about the German zeppelin program and his fear that England might be annexed by the Kaiser. His closet drama reads like a revenger's tragedy composed by Edmund Spenser resurrected for the special benefit of readers of the *Daily Mail*. Within his five acts are two major sections, one featuring the balloon landing in East Anglia of three "Persanian" aeronauts, scouts of an approaching invasion fleet, and the other treating activity at "Britannia's Temple," a kind of English GHQ manned by squires, vicar, hierophants, and elves. On the cliffs the Persanians pause to gloat over the ineptitude of English people—"a moonstruck, woman-ridden race" governed by "loose-brained demagogues"—and to predict an easy victory over their "diseased army of Lilliput."[60] This inventory of English degeneracy (interrupted now and then as they drink and cry, *"Hoch!"*) is overheard by John Hobbe, a crippled Crimean veteran turned shepherd, who personifies the oaken heart of Old England. When, unable to tolerate more vilification, Hobbe bursts from his hiding place and attacks the foreigners with his crook, he is slain by the Persanian baron. ("Die peasant swine!")[61] Hobbe, however is able to raise himself on one shoulder to deliver a patriotic oration before he expires—to the accompaniment of thunder and lightning. The Persanians (who conveniently leave behind a copy of their invasion plan) fly off, but their balloon is struck by a bolt of lightning and all are killed. The dastardly baron meets his end when he is impaled on the very sword he used in dispatching John Hobbe.

Meanwhile, at Britannia's Temple, a "Sacred Band" pledges to lay down their lives for Britain. But first there is a procession of ethereal notables symbolizing the cultural and military heritage of the English race—Oberon, Robin, various elves, King Alfred, Crusaders, Elizabeth, Nelson, and Wellington. A hierophant explains to the throng that before the invaders can be cast out a child must be offered as human sacrifice. Widow Charity yields her babe, the deed is done, and elves prepare to embalm the victim in honey. The Sacred Band moves out against the Persanians, who by this time have inexplicably withdrawn their fleet. The drama concludes with two enemy battleships blown up by their own mines, followed by a songfest among Hobbe's villagers as the vicar embraces the English flag. The work concludes with a pledge to Britannia echoing within the temple: "How sweet it were,/To fall, to die for THEE, an hundred deaths!"[62]

Other than a faint titillation among certain Georgian poets pleased by his affirmation of Elizabethan pastoral motifs, Doughty's poem met only a leaden reception except among those critics expressing outrage at the scene depicting human sacrifice. Some branded him "jingo" and "scaremonger," while the *Times* accused him of having but small acquaintance with actual men and things.[63] Doughty took umbrage when one reviewer suggested he might have plagiarized from Thomas Hardy's *The Dynasts*. His denial throws light upon how remote his interests were from the contemporary scene: "I have never heard of the book or the author and remain in my ignorance till now and shall continue to do so."[64] A recent Doughty scholar dismisses *The Cliffs*, despite its high seriousness, as "an intriguing equivalent of a 1909 comic book."[65]

With a determination born of fanaticism, Doughty next embarked upon a sequel calculated to drive home his invasion message. To a friend he wrote that his new book would rest upon a bedrock of "technical knowledge." The result was *The Clouds* (1911), another verse drama in which his "technical knowledge"—government proclamations, telephone conversations, and mysterious death rays—is incongruously conveyed in Spenserian decasyllables. His thesis is that England has been six times invaded, six times vanquished, and is "ripe and over-ripe" for the seventh wave. The barbarians in this round are "Eastlanders," who burn East Anglia and force the inhabitants to evacuate to the hilltops of Wales. A young Englishman named Carpenter joins this forlorn exodus, and through his eyes Doughty contrasts scenes of famine and chaos with bucolic pictures of pastoral landscapes soon to be violated by the invaders, only one of whom—a drunken major—materializes in the flesh. Visions of faery weddings and encounters with Piscator, who carries a copy of *Compleat Angler* bound in purple velvet and expatiates on fishing in rhetoric of the same color, fail to mesh with garish descriptions of war-ravaged England. Doughty seems not to have considered that the Old England he cherished had already been invaded and sacked, not by outlanders but by his fellow Britons who had conquered in the name of railroads, factories, suburbs, and other paraphernalia of industrialism—all financed by solid English pound notes. The author often shelves his invasion theme altogether to insert rhapsodic asides like this account of a nightingale:

> But hark! 'tis that self gentle bird, whereof
> We newly spake, that gurgles in his trance;
> On some fresh spray, in the moonlight, amidst
> That haythorn grove, which borders nigh this place.
> *Itchu, swat swat;*
> *Chu-chi chu-chi chu-chi, chu-chi:*
> *Occhi, wocchi wocchi wocchi wocchi!*[66]

In the end the invasion peters out without explicit cause, as though Doughty had tired of the whole enterprise and had given up hope of kindling fires in the hearts of his degenerate countrymen. Presumably, England will be saved by her five overseas dominions led by some latter-day Arthurian leader, although this is not entirely clear.

Although Doughty's two verse dramas show a certain prescience in alluding to airships, submarines, and laserlike ray guns, these are little more than gadgets superimposed upon turgid allegories written in a perversely archaic style and reflecting a mind nearly unhinged by his hatred of Germany (and his dissatisfaction with England as well). Nothing short of a return to Elizabethan values, accompanied by a massive scheme for depopulation, would have satisfied Doughty. (A linguistic reactionary, he told T. E. Lawrence that he had made his Arabian journey to redeem the English language from the slough into which it had fallen since the time of Spenser.)[67] While his erudition and fame as Arabian chronicler guaranteed him a reading from the literary establishment, his fanatical dramas attracted few admirers. A reviewer in the *Pall Mall Gazette* accurately stated the case: "The cult of Mr. Doughty is a punishment for the over-cultured and hyper-refined, who probably mistake this kind of heavy incompetence for natural simplicity and a return to more primitive art."[68] Even T. E. Lawrence, whose admiration for Doughty was unquestioned, confessed after the war that he was appalled by the anti-German portions of Doughty's work: "They give me the creeps. Such fanatic love and hatred ought not to be."[69] His work shows that a gentlemanly scholar had no more immunity from the German virus than the semiliterate assistant clerk soaking up scaremongery from the *Daily Mail*. As Germanophobe, Doughty was an upper-class equivalent of William Le Queux. If his impact on the public was less persuasive, it was only because few people bothered to read him at all.*

Proof that the English privileged classes were as preoccupied with invasion fears as the common folk is offered by the diaries of William Scawen Blunt (1840–1922), a poet and aristocrat who was exposed to the prevailing atmosphere of hate and hysteria but who, unlike so many of his compatriots, kept his head. His friendships extended into the highest quarters and he was privy to many confidential reports about projected German invasions. In 1908 he recorded in his diary that King Edward was talking seriously about a Kaiser plan to invade England, not in a spirit of conquest, but only "to deliver him from the Socialist gang which is ruining the country."[70] More ominously he recorded four years later that Winston Churchill, at a private dinner, spoke with assurance of "the coming European war and the chances of a German invasion."[71] Churchill was haunted by the fear—confirmed during the naval maneuvers of 1908—that 20,000 German troops could land on the east coast without opposition from the Royal Navy. By this time the fear of invasion had permeated into the highest echelons of government. For nearly everyone, spiked helmets lay just over the horizon.

As *invasiophobia* metamorphosed into war mania on August 4, 1914, it is gratifying to report that not everyone acquiesced in the collective madness. Blunt wrote in his diary one day later: "The real cause of the quarrel with Germany, I well knew, was no more honourable a one than that of our dread of a too powerful commercial rival and the fear of Kaiser Wilhelm's forcing France, if we stood aside, into commercial alliance with him against us in the markets of the world. . . . In this madness I would take no part."[72] With that entry he terminated his diary, and in the years to come he refused to sign war-supporting manifestos or to contribute patriotic verse to anthologies. A crusty realist, he saw the economic issues clearly from behind their welter of high-sounding rationalizations. The irony and the pity lay in the statistics shortly to accumulate—nearly one million British soldiers dead, few of them comprehending the cause of the war and most of them saturated with the same *pro patria* sensationalism that had been dunned into them by four decades of alarmist writers.

*In September 1916 two zeppelins were downed in Essex not far from Doughty's domicile, and the twenty-two scorched bodies of the German crewmen were buried with military honors by the Royal Flying Corps in the Great Burstead churchyard. See Michael MacDonagh, *In London During the War* (London, 1935), 133. These and similar burials of airmen are the closest that German "invaders" came to occupying English soil during the Great War.

4 BOY SCOUTS TO THE RESCUE

▼

War is only authorised murder, and ought in these
civilized times to be put a stop to; but so long as
war remains possible, it is the duty of every man
and boy to prepare himself to defend his country in
case it should unfortunately become necessary.
SCOUTING FOR BOYS (*1908*) *[deleted passage]*

Two hundred days into the siege of Mafeking, Colonel Robert Baden-Powell, British commander of the garrison, received a note from his Boer adversary suggesting a temporary suspension of hostilities in order to compete in a Sunday game of cricket. (The Boers normally refrained from shelling the British outpost on the Sabbath because of religious scruples.) Baden-Powell ("B-P"), whose initials also stood for "British Public"—a detail not lost upon the people back home—declined the invitation: "Just now we are having our innings and have so far scored 200 days, not out, against the bowling of Cronje, Snijman, Botha [names of a succession of unsuccessful Boer attackers] . . . and we are having a very enjoyable game."[1] This was how a gentleman played the game of war—with style, with British phlegm, with cool condescension.

In an otherwise dreary and ignominious South African War (1899–1902), B-P transformed the defense of an obscure railway village at the northeastern tip of Cape Colony into a symbol of imperial grit. Even his first message from beleaguered Mafeking showed the stuff from which heroes are cut: "All well. Four hours bombardment. One dog killed."[2] Back in England the public rejoiced in reports of B-P's theatrics: how he built a gun from a four-inch steel pipe mounted on a threshing machine which could throw an eighteen-inch shell some 4,000 yards; how he issued postage stamps printed with his own likeness instead of the Queen's; how he made a portable searchlight out of a biscuit tin nailed to a pole, which he moved about to make the loutish Boers abandon night attacks; how he armed 300 "Niggers" with rifles to patrol his outer perimeter and facetiously called them his "Black Watch."[3] Good show! B-P turned a traumatic war for the British into jolly fun and frolic. Over the caption "Children Chasing a Shell," an illustration in *Graphic* showed bonnetted mothers and beaming tots in an eager holiday race to capture a Boer projectile about to fall in the veldt—an illustration which B-P later inserted in his *Sketches of Mafeking and East Africa* (1907).[4] Outnumbered six to one, B-P held on to Mafeking like a traditional English bulldog for 217 days until relieved. When news of the relief reached London, the public demonstrations lasted three days and eclipsed, in riotous celebration, those days marking the termination of the Great War and World War II. From East End to West End enormous crowds packed the streets, cheering, singing, and carousing. (As a result of this saturnalia, the word *maffick* entered the English language, defined as "extravagant demonstrations of national rejoicing.") B-P found himself the youngest major general in the British army and the most illustrious British hero since Gordon of Khartoum.

Only later did there leak through the public adulation scraps of information which faintly blemished the record, at least among liberals. It was said that whites of the Mafeking garrison appropriated rations of blacks to encourage them to desert through the lines. Moreover, B-P had ordered the execution, for stealing food, of an indeterminate number of starving blacks and had another 115 publicly flogged. Jogged memories of old hands in South Africa recalled how B-P had once been charged with murdering an unruly African chief and how he jocularly referred to local wars as the "sport of nigger hunts."[5] Others in the army belittled his achievement. An officer of the Mafeking relief column wrote in a private letter: "To me the whole affair of the siege . . . was an enigma. What in the world was the use of defending this wretched railway-siding and these tin-shanties; to burrow underground on the first shot being fired . . . seemed to me the strangest role ever played by a cavalry leader."[6] This officer completely missed the point. The durable results of warfare proceed as much from morale boosting as from military genius. The South African heroics of B-P, standing as they did in such sharp contrast against the inglorious bungling that marked most operations of that war, established the foundation for B-

P's supreme mission in life—creator and chief evangelist of the Boy Scout movement.

B-P's involvement with Scouting was entirely accidental. During his earlier years as a cavalry officer in India he had written *Reconnaissance and Scouting* (1884), a handbook explaining how to infiltrate enemy territory to obtain vital military information. In India and later in South Africa the term "scouting" for B-P had only military connotations; the trefoil later adopted as the international symbol for Boy Scouts was originally designed for his army scouts. Moreover, his popular book *Pig-Sticking or Hog-Hunting* (1889), illustrated with his own clever drawings, went through several editions during his lifetime and became the authoritative textbook on that sport for a generation of English officers posted to India. B-P traces the origin of pig-sticking back to St. George—"the patron saint of cavalry, of chivalry, of scouts, of England"—and defined its rules to fit the tradition. St. George might have destroyed the dragon with a piece of poisoned meat, but he chose to meet the monster head-on, with his lance.[7] Subsequently, Boy Scouts would carry six-foot staves, blunted versions of the dragon-killing lance.

After his triumphal return from South Africa, B-P was made inspector general of cavalry. As an observer of German military maneuvers in 1903, he told the Kaiser that the lances of the fearsome Uhlans were "too long for practical use" and recommended that the Germans "go in for pig-sticking," but His Imperial Majesty replied that wild pigs were not abundant in Germany.[8] During the year following he was a guest at the French maneuvers and detected symptoms of decay in French morale. Thereafter, B-P became convinced that in the event of a continental war the Germans had the edge, despite their ungainly lances.

The turning point in his career came in 1904 when he attended a review in Glasgow of the Boys' Brigade, an organization founded in 1883 by Sir William Alexander Smith, a local merchant-prince seeking a method of controlling rowdy working-class boys at his Sunday school. Smith had never been a soldier, but he peppered his Bible classes with social Darwinist remarks like "No nation ever yet attained true greatness or influence without going through the training and discipline of war."[9] With their pillbox caps, military belts and haversacks, and close-order drill, the Boys' Brigade conformed to the model of the Christian-soldier. Smith had no difficulty in raising funds for his organization, which was credited with neutralizing dangerous anarchistic tendencies among urban boys; he had only to remind middle-class donors that it was cheaper to give a few guineas now to the brigade than to pay for a larger police force in the future. His organization had burgeoned until it numbered some 50,000 youths, most of them denizens of large congested cities.* Seven thousand of them swelled the Glasgow rally—some of them, B-P recalled, "hardly as tall as the toy guns they carried."[10] They wore uniforms, drilled, and paraded like martinets to the music of brass bands. B-P was appalled by the spectacle. Ruefully he contrasted the degenerate-looking boys of an English city, their narrow chests clogged with cigarette smoke, with the manly youths he had observed among the Boers, an outdoor race at home in the saddle, camp, and field. The youth of Britain needed a program not to become knee-jerk drill field soldiers but to develop their independent powers of observation like "noting and remembering details of strangers, contents of shop windows, appearances of new streets."[11]

Meanwhile Lord Roberts (1832–1914), commonly known as "Bobs" but officially first earl of Kandahar, who had served as the popular commander in chief of the British army during the Boer War, was stumping the country in behalf of the National Service League with a series of lectures warning against the national failure to prepare for war. His principal theme was the necessity for a system of national service— a doomed enterprise, as it proved. Denouncing the blue water school (those who relied solely upon the navy as a deterrent to invasion), Lord Roberts called for an army of a million men, including both regulars and reserves, and warned that Britain had been lucky during the Boer War in dealing only with a minor power. Conditions had changed: "We could not have hoped to have been successful against an army of anything like equal strength, trained and organized as are the armies of the great military powers."[12] As we have seen, Lord Roberts had already endorsed the scaremongery of William Le Queux, and his own lectures drilled home the thesis that "in case of invasion, every Briton should be liable to serve in person against the enemy, and that that obligation ought to be recognized and enforced by law."[13] (England would enact

*Total alumni membership is estimated at two million. In addition there were offshoots such as the Church Lads' Brigade (Anglican), the Jewish Lads' Brigade (London Jewish), and the Catholic Boys' Brigade (London Anglo-Irish), all of them with strong religious affiliations. John Springhall, historian of English youth movements, estimates that by 1967 three out of every five adult males in England had belonged when young to some uniformed group. See John Springhall, *Youth, Empire and Society: British Youth Movements, 1883–1940* (London, 1977), 13.

such a law, but not until 1916, when total mobilization rather than repelling invasion would be the object.) Like B-P, Bobs had been impressed by the Boers' guerrilla tactics—particularly their splendid marksmanship—and he called for compulsory programs to develop martial arts in schools, universities, and units of the various Boys' Brigades. He even went so far as to urge that rifle shooting be elevated into a national sport rivaling football or cricket. "In many schools," he wrote, "cricket is made compulsory, and I have never heard that it suffers in popularity on this account, except with the incorrigible loafer."[14] His alarmist writings, collected as *A Nation in Arms* (1907), did not refer to Germany by name, but few readers could doubt that in that direction lay the future threat to England.

Undoubtedly influenced by his former commander's grave concerns, B-P in the same year adapted his text on military scouting as a booklet for distribution among the Boys' Brigades. Then, during the summer of 1907, he collected twenty youths, obtained the use of Brownsea Island off Dorset, and set up an experimental camp. Near his headquarters tent he plunged a pig-sticker into the ground, attached the flag that had waved over Mafeking, and launched what eventually became the Boy Scout movement. Organizing his boys into four patrols with names from the animal kingdom—Curlews, Ravens, Wolves, and Bulls—he taught them first aid, mat weaving, and jujitsu.* In the morning he roused them with the weird notes of an African Kudo horn; in the evening he taught them Zulu marching chants. In one game B-P explained that he was going to "invade" the island and their object was to stop him; he reported delightedly that the scouts successfully captured him as he crawled under a tree. In their zealous hunt for additional quarry, the boys "arrested" a party of ladies and gentlemen visiting Brownsea Castle. On a game-playing level these boys were subconsciously engaged in exercises designed to save their island—England—from invasion.[15]

B-P spoke a boy's language. The one-week camp was an instant success. After breaking camp, B-P wrote a report and sent a copy to R. B. Haldane, the minister for war, inquiring if the army would object to

---

*During the preceding year B-P had struck up a friendship with Ernest Thompson Seton, an American whose book, *The Birch-Bark Book of the Woodcraft Indians*, had provided the basis for a boys' organization which contained a merit system based upon winning feathers and badges for various activities. B-P subsequently borrowed ideas from Seton but drew back from linking white youths to Red Indian customs, which he thought were archaic.

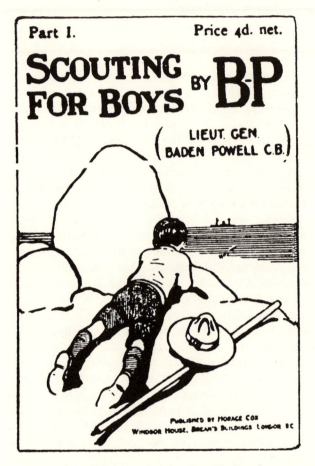

From the first number of Baden-Powell's Boy Scout magazine: a young Scout carefully watches an enemy landing party.

his boy scout project. Far from objecting, Haldane saw the scout concept as an ideal breeding ground for his pet project, the Territorial Army of 300,000 men which the government planned as a supplement to the regulars and reserves. In January 1908 B-P's *Scouting for Boys* appeared, a fourpenny best-seller which the *Times* discussed in two columns on its editorial page. The invasion motif appeared on the cover drawing, which featured a small boy lying behind a large rock along the shore where he watched the landing of a mysterious party of men (Germans?) from an offshore ship. This vigilant youth wore the short trousers of the future Boy Scout uniform; nearby lay his broadbrimmed hat and stout wooden staff. Inside the book were articles describing secret signs, details on how to raise a patrol by enlisting five other boys, and as a sugar pill, some excerpts from Rudyard Kipling, whom B-P especially admired. Immensely popular throughout this century, *Scouting for Boys* may rank third among best-sellers in English—behind the Bible and Shakespeare.[16]

Four months later the first issue of *The Scout*, a weekly newspaper, came out. It sold 110,000 copies the first week and later attained a circulation of 1,700,000. There was a tidal wave of boyish enthusiasm. White tents and red campfires sprouted all over England as boys built rustic huts and bridges and stalked animal tracks or one another's. Oblivious to the irony that the life of pioneers and Red Indians had largely been forever obliterated from the world by the steel armies of civilization, boys eagerly clutched at this primitivist, once-upon-a-time vision of Baden-Powell.

There was as yet no official boy scout organization, only a mass movement of exuberant youths without head or coordination. B-P was still an army officer and early in 1908 assumed a new position as commander of the Northumbrian Division of Haldane's fledgling Territorial Army. Transferring his headquarters into an oversized motorcar, the Hero of Mafeking recruited his "Terriers" (his term for them recalling the animal nomenclature of Boy Scout patrols) in the mining districts. In his patriotic speeches he stressed that the Territorials had been formed to "resist invasion"; a century ago the enemy had been France—now it was Germany. Never one to hedge, B-P proclaimed that "Germany wants to develop her trade and commerce and must, therefore, get rid of England."[18] Liberal M.P.s and pressmen attacked him for the "alarmist character" of his recruiting effort, fearing that such inflammatory talk would raise the hawks in Germany.

Liberals became more uneasy during the summer of 1908 when B-P, though still a general of the British army, called for a second boys camp, this one in Northumberland fittingly within sight of the Roman Wall—that crumbling reminder of ancient invasion. By this time the scouting movement was ballooning out of control; hundreds of boys had to be turned away. B-P's expectation that the program which he had extemporized would be taken over by the Boys' Brigade failed to materialize. Having tasted the pleasures of Red Indian life, the boys wanted nothing to do with close-order drill, while Sir William Smith withdrew his cooperation because he regarded the religious aims of the Boys' Brigade as paramount. It is likely that he also feared that B-P intended to seize control. That autumn the Boy Scouts officially came into existence as B-P began to enlist adults as scoutmasters and outlined training programs.* Since no details for a uniform were spelled out, scoutmasters decked out their troops in costumes ranging from North-western Mounted Policemen to Sioux Indians. In time a directive from headquarters banned spurs, swords, riding crops, and revolvers.

At the first national rally, held at the Crystal Palace in 1909 and attended by 11,000 scouts, B-P read a telegram from the King, which clearly showed that higher powers of the realm acknowledged a martial role for the movement: "Tell them that if he [the King] should call upon them later in life, the sense of patriotic responsibility and the habits of discipline which they are now acquiring as boys will enable them to do their duty as men, should any danger threaten the Empire."[19] At this rally B-P was temporarily nonplussed to find seven little girls who, among the ocean of boys, identified themselves as "girl" scouts. Initially he feared that their presence might demoralize his boys. But later his sister Agnes came forth to organize them as Girl Guides—the name "Scouts" remaining, in England, the exclusive designation for males. Significantly, when the *Handbook for Girl Guides* was published, it bore the subtitle *or How Girls Can Help Build the Empire*.[20]

The Crystal Palace rally brought Scouting into a crossfire from two extremist positions, the pacifists and the ultrapatriots. The former expressed horror that among the trophies competed for was a model machine gun. They accused B-P of fomenting a dangerous crypto-

---

*The provenance of "Boy Scout" falls into debatable ground. During the Boer War the editor of *Boys of the Empire* serialized portions of B-P's book on military scouting under the heading "The Boy Scout." But by this time, in Mafeking, B-P had mobilized boys of the village into an ancillary militia group which he employed as orderlies and scouts.

militarist order and denounced *Scouting for Boys* as "the cloven hoof of the military alarmist seeking to embroil the British nation in the bloody war with her neighbors."[21] (There was in fact cause for wonder when in 1910 out of 250 Boy Scout commissioners, 140 were military officers, many of them supporters of Lord Roberts' National Service League.)[22] On the other side, the ultraists blamed him for instilling in British youth a mindless hankering after silly games and idle vagabondage. To counteract B-P's baleful influence, pacifists founded the National Peace Scouts and the ultraists launched the Empire Scouts—but both quickly collapsed through inanition. Trade unionists and socialists saw the Scouts less as a pubescent paramilitary order than as an anti-labor conspiracy. Seizing upon a line of the Scout law, "A Scout is loyal to the King, and to his country and to his employers. He must stick to them through thick and thin against anyone who is their enemy, or who even talks badly of them,"[23] they argued that B-P planned to turn English youths into scabs and wage slaves. In some cities hooligans jeered at passing Scout patrols: "Here come the Brussels Sprouts / The stinking, blinking louts. . . ." or shouted, "Go 'ome and wash your knees."[24]* Sometimes scouts retaliated by attacking blasphemers with their staves.

Within a month of the great rally, the King knighted B-P at Balmoral. Thereafter he was "Sir Robert," rallies were staged at Windsor, and he was granted a lieutenant general's pension by special intercession of King George V. In 1910 he resigned from the Territorials to devote all his time to the burgeoning Scout movement. Speaking for others in the government who saw the military potential in a national youth organization, Haldane wrote: "I feel that this organisation of yours has so important a bearing upon the future that probably the greatest service you can render your country is to devote yourself to it."[25] Haldane hoped for a "second line" of national defense by absorbing all uniformed youth groups into a giant hopper that would feed the Territorials. Others in the government welcomed his retirement. Because he evoked great enthusiasm from the man (or boy) in the street, he was regarded by many in the military establishment as too "theatrical" and "unprofessional"—altogether a tough act to follow. Old

---

*During this period boys' knees were regarded in some quarters as erotic objects, and the short pants worn by Boy Scouts were as shocking as the short skirts for women somewhat later. During the late Victorian era a Rugby headmaster required that his boys in football games wear trousers tightened at the calf so that they would not become sexually aroused at the sight of each others' knees. See Jonathan Gathorne-Hardy, *The Old School Tie: The Phenomenon of the English Public School* (New York, 1977), 75.

soldiers remembered that as a youth he had been able to bypass Sandhurst because of outstanding performance on examinations; moreover,
they were displeased by his disparaging remarks about orthodox military training in *Scouting for Boys*, in which he urged scoutmasters to
avoid military drill because it destroyed individuality. A story got
around that the Queen had been miffed when he put his face on a
Mafeking stamp—like the presumption of a third-century Roman
legionnaire challenging the authority of his Caesar.[26]

Public confirmation that Boy Scouts would provide a deep reservoir
of potential manpower in the event of war came at the Windsor rally of
1911, attended by 30,000 scouts. This celebration culminated in a review by King George in which there was a carefully staged "Grand
Rush," described by an awed journalist: "A sudden roar filled the air,
and the whole mighty horseshoe of 30,000 boys with one impulse leapt
forward from either side, rushing as only boys can rush, screaming out
the rallying cries of their patrols as they swept, a kaleidoscopic mass of
colour, with flags fluttering, hats waving, knees glinting, into the great
charge toward the king." Howling like wolves, roaring like lions,
cheeping like sandpipers they swooped down like Zulus or Red Indians
on their prey, but instead of tearing the King to gobbets they stopped
dead around him and his retainers: "Up went a forest of staves and
hats, and higher into the sky went the shrill, screaming cheers of the
boys in a cry that gripped the throat of every onlooker—'God Save the
King'—that apogee of patriotic fervour in young Britain, that surge of
enthusiasm to do anything that might be demanded of them in the
name of their country and the king."[27] Little wonder that the presence
of Boy Scouts curdled the blood of pacifists. As patriotic demonstration
it was like the eve of Agincourt in *Henry V*. Let the enemies of king and
country beware!

As Britain drifted almost imperceptibly toward Armageddon, B-P
had rallied thousands of youths to patriotic highs, provided them with
protomartial habits of discipline and organization, and keyed them to
the dangers of foreign invasion. In 1914 he enlarged the pool of future
patriots by founding a junior Scout organization, the Wolf Cubs, borrowing heavily from the *Jungle Books* of Kipling, who was an ardent
supporter of the Scouting movement. When war broke out, B-P mobilized his Scouts for immediate action. They were promptly employed in
patrolling railway lines, guarding bridges and reservoirs, serving as
messengers at war offices. Their counterespionage activities were more
on the order of a South Coast troop which reported to police the where-

abouts of "well-dressed gentlemen speaking good English, but with a distinct guttural accent."[28] In all some 30,000 Boy Scouts served as coastguard auxiliaries, watching eagle-eyed for sight of the German invasion fleet that never came.

Baden-Powell himself added to the glamour of intrigue with his bizarre book *My Adventures of a Spy* (1915), designed as a handbook of instruction in the technique of espionage, illustrated with his own drawings. He claimed that six years before he had obtained the master plan for a German invasion; after submarines and mines had blocked the British fleet at Spithead and Portland, the Germans would embark from nine bases and land ninety thousand men in East Anglia, seize the Midlands industrial region, and after expelling the population, destroy the towns. He does not give the source of his information, but one suspects a crony of William Le Queux. There are anecdotes of his own spy activities: how he ferreted out Germans in Southeast London disguised as a plumber; how he once guessed the inhabitant of a house in South Africa was a "clean Englishman" because he spotted two toothbrushes on a window sill; how he infiltrated an Austrian fort, and so on. For the novice he provides various tricks which every spy should learn: how to draw a "butterfly" in a sketchbook that in reality is a map of a fortification; how to deceive the enemy by feigning intoxication or walking in an odd manner; how to signal confederates with piles of sticks or rocks (clearly more useful in Swaziland than downtown Dusseldorf). He assures his readers it is not unsporting to be spy—only *traitor spies* are wicked. In his finale he even provides a glowing obituary for the noble failure: "Though the 'agent,' if caught, may 'go under,' unhonoured and unsung, he knows in his heart of hearts that he has done as bravely for his country as his comrade who falls in battle."[29] It was this book which led to a rumor, reported by the press during the war, that B-P had left England and was serving as a spy somewhere in Germany or Austria-Hungary.

Lord Kitchener, whose major achievement during the war lay in organization of the New Armies for the carnage of the Western Front, wrote B-P one week after the declaration of war: "What a splendid thing this war is for you!"[30] Swept up in the fervor of the national crusade, few of patriotic stripe would have disagreed. Yet except for inculcating patriotic regard for king and country, the Scout movement was a poor preparation for the real war that youths would find in Flanders or along the Somme. Had the Great War been fought along the lines of the Boer War, or the T. E. Lawrence campaign in Arabia,

then B-P's program for developing individual initiative and bold movement would not have been anachronistic. Against mud and machine
guns imagination would prove to be irrelevant.

One legacy of the Boy Scout movement in the Great War is *The
Scout's Book of Heroes: A Record of Scouts' Work in the Great War*
(1919), a compilation of heroic deeds by ex-scouts in military service. In
his foreword B-P explains that "Play the game" is the creed of a Scout:
"Play in your place; play all out to win; play for your side and not for
yourself."[31] Among the players was Captain G. B. McLean of Alberta.
During the Arras attack of 1918 he hurdled the German wire and fell on
top of a Hun. As another "big Hun"—small Huns seem not to exist in
these stories—"gaily advanced" with poised bayonet, the scout shot
him in the throat. Underneath, the first Hun stirred. The scout pressed
the muzzle of his revolver into him and pulled the trigger. Then the
scout moved down the German trench and shot two more Huns. In
panic, others sought safety in a dugout. The scout tossed down a bomb.
Lest his readers be shocked at this final carnage, the editor modestly
writes, "I leave to the imagination what happened to the Huns."[32] A
dozen years later in Berlin two "Huns," von Ribbentrop and von
Schirach, told B-P about the great debt which the *Hitler Jugend* owed to
his Boy Scout movement.[33] Although B-P spurned all association with
the Nazis, unwittingly he had earned an accolade for nationalism from
two masters at playing that game.

▼

As mass movement the Boy Scouts filled a great emotional vacuum
during the half-decade preceding the Great War. In psychologically
mobilizing the youth of England for the impending crisis, Baden-
Powell was motivated by both a deep loyalty to his country and a desire
to improve the physiques and spirits of his charges. No such altruism
characterized the writers and publishers of a host of boys' magazines
proliferating during this period. Magazines like *Boys' Herald* and *Boys'
Friend* (both Lord Northcliffe publications) were juvenile equivalents
of the *Daily Mail* in raising circulation figures by unleashing scaremongering and xenophobic extravaganzas. To vultures of the yellow
press it made little difference whether the enemy consisted of Boers,
French, Russians, or Germans so long as public events could finger an
outside menace somewhere. A generation of English youths was
weaned on drawings of Boers shooting down English soldiers bearing
flags of truce, and on cartoons captioned "How the French Love Us,"

showing a Frenchman beating an Armenian beggar for presuming to speak to him in English.[34]

Boys' magazines consistently prepared their readers for wars in the future and unflaggingly pumped up their morale by depicting English victories. (For some reason, perhaps because boys had no vote and could not assist in jacking up military budgets, juvenile invasion stories had to have happy endings.) As early as 1897 *Boys' Friend* featured a story, "Britain in Arms," in which England successfully fought a world war and enriched itself by occupying Paris and forcing France to pay an indemnity of a 100 million pounds. The moral of this "tale of loyalty and devotion to the Old Flag" appeared to be that war was a paying proposition for those that truly "play the game."[35] The same magazine in 1903 described how Captain Strange, a prototypal English eccentric, fought a one-man war against the French in a vessel equipped with giant claw which could seize an enemy submarine and shake out a handful of "Froggies."[36] *Magnet*, another such magazine, described how England beat back a war balloon invasion by the Chinese.

As might be expected, after 1904 the diabolic enemy featured in boys' magazines was almost always Germany. In issue after issue of *Union Jack* Sexton Blake, a plagiarized Sherlock Holmes character, uncovers plans by the German High Command to invade and sack England. John Tregallis, perhaps the most kinetic of these juvenile scaremongers, in 1912 had three stories running simultaneously in boys' papers. His literary idol was Le Queux, and his masterwork, "Britain Invaded," was a watered-down version of that already watery *The Invasion of 1910*. Five German corps land on the east coast, occupy London, and massacre starving mobs in the streets. Fortunately the German second wave is wiped out by the brainstorm of cadets who spill petrol on the ocean and toss a match to it—a twist of plot resurrected by Ian Fleming in one of his "Cold War" novels four decades later.[37]

Behind this literature of juvenile belligerency stands the patriarchal figure of G. A. Henty (1832–1902), author of more than eighty historical novels with total sales estimated at 25 million. While his settings ranged from Pax Romana to the Boxer Rebellion, the plot was ever the same: a fledgling protagonist graduates from boy to man through adjustment to and enjoyment of honest combat and conflict. Henty, whose own career as a journalist had carried him to the Crimean War, the Garibaldi anabasis, the Franco-Prussian War (which he reported from both sides), the Carlist insurrection, and the Balkan War of 1876, never doubted that nearly all young boys defined heroic ideals in terms

of physical action and military prowess. Success was always measured
in terms of force. The existence of the British Empire, the seed of
which had been an insignificant island, was for Henty proof of the racial
superiority of the English. He disliked Jews, Niggers (as blacks are
consistently called in his novels), strikers, and threats to the status quo.
(Characteristically, his novel about the American Civil War, *With Lee in
Virginia*, backed the slave states rather than the Union.) Henty made no
secret of the didactic strain of his novels: "To endeavour to inculcate
patriotism in my books has been one of my main objects. . . . Officers
of the Army and Volunteers have assured me that my books have been
influential in bringing young fellows into the Army—not so much into
the rank and file as among the officers."[38] An upwardly mobile youth,
desiring more nourishing literary fare than staples in the boys' magazines, naturally gravitated to Henty novels where heroes were manly,
direct, truthful, and resourceful—all those qualities endorsed subsequently by the Boy Scout movement. The price paid for absorbing the
Henty message was high, according to a Dutch observer who in 1908—
when relationships between England and Germany were dropping to
their nadir—blamed Henty and his imitators with having made the
British nation "the most conceited people on the earth." Because of
such "piffle," a young male Englishman had come to believe that "he,
personally, is equal to two or more Frenchmen, about four Germans,
an indefinite number of Russians, and any quantity you care to mention of the remaining scum of the earth."[39] Whatever his liabilities,
Henty was no scaremonger; he did not write invasion stories. Perhaps he was so secure in his conviction of English superiority that he
never entertained the possibility of lesser beings splashing ashore in
Britain.

Invasion stories had become so pandemic in juvenile magazines by
1908 that *Boys' Herald* addressed the issue in a symposium of famous
military leaders titled "Will There One Day Be a World at War?" Not
surprisingly, the verdict lay in the affirmative, and the editor undertook
to explain why:

> Why? because of our huge possessions and colonies, because of
> our prosperity as a nation, because of our enterprise and grit. . . .
> Foreign spies in Great Britain and our possessions have for years
> been gathering information with regard to our fortifications and
> defences, the weak points on our coast line and a thousand other
> items invaluable to a Power intending one day to strike a blow at
> us.[40]

By using "a Power" rather than "any country" the editor might as well have inserted a fingerpost pointing straight at Germany. Naturally he failed to mention an underlying reason for his belief in imminent invasion—panic sold newspapers. In a retrospective essay on boys' magazines, George Orwell noted that the "moral atmosphere" of these prewar publications has "a great deal in common with the Boy Scout movement, which started at about the same time."[41] Both were instruments, conservative in tone, which prepped boys for war. It is usually overlooked that the Scout motto "Be prepared" originally read "Be prepared to defend your country."[42]

One could enlarge almost indefinitely on the role of the popular press, both adult and juvenile, in preparing the culture into which the war bacteria would be dipped in 1914. Those Britons who expressed shock and surprise at the abruptness with which England involved herself in what was presumed to be a purely continental conflict, underestimated the impact of four decades of xenophobic ravings in books, magazines, and newspapers. Neutral observers, however, had long been appalled by the hawkish drumbeating of English journalism—witness this prophetic admonition in an American newspaper of 1910: "It will be a marvel if relations with Germany are not strained until war becomes inevitable as a direct result of the war-scare campaign inaugurated and carried on with the most reckless ingenuity by the Northcliffe syndicate of newspapers."[43]

Perhaps the most astonishing feature of the invasion genre was its continued health after four decades of hard use by hack writers who had by this time wrung nearly every conceivable plot out of it. The *Zukunftskrieg* (as Germans with their taxonomic thoroughness called these tales of future war, which apparently were as popular there as in England) had become for the English a staple in their literary diet—a verbal counterpart to fish-and-chips coned in newspaper and relished with insatiable appetite. The year 1909 marks the year of greatest suppuration. In London Guy du Maurier's invasion melodrama, *An Englishman's Home*, played to packed houses in three London theaters simultaneously.* The time had perhaps arrived for the whole subject to be aired as a lampoon, and *Punch* led the way with "The Invader," a "terrible story written by a patriotic Briton who resents perpetual invasions." After alluding to Le Queux's "admirable impartiality" in leading both German and Franco-Russian armies into the heart of England

---

*For a discussion of du Maurier's play and its impact on audiences in England and Germany, see Chapter 7.

and to Wells for his Martian and aeronaut attacks, the writer insists on having his own shot at this rich subject. The time is 1912 and the place, Berlin, where Germans drinking lager in beer gardens to music of military bands are totally surprised by an *English* invasion. Five thousand commercial delegates armed with red guidebooks, each containing a bomb, have descended on the German capital and succeeded in destroying public works, railways, and power stations. At Potsdam Leo Maxse (the Germanophobic editor of *National Review*, a right-wing quarterly) and William Le Queux seize the Imperial Palace. Under Le Queux's interminable anecdotes about crowned heads, the Kaiser falls asleep and Le Queux telephones Kiel, truthfully identifies himself as "William," and orders the Canal blown up and the German fleet taken out for collision practice. "English cunning has triumphed."[44]

This refreshing squib appears to have been the stimulus for P. G. Wodehouse's topsy-turvy invasion novella of the same year, *The Swoop! Or How Clarence Saved England: A Tale of the Great Invasion*. The title came from J. Blyth's deadly *The Swoop of the Vulture* (1908), a novel about an attack by forces of the Imperial German Vulture; the military campaign came straight from Le Queux's worst performance (along with scrambled borrowing from du Maurier's play), and the hero came from Baden-Powell's Boy Scout Association. Picking through the rubbish of the English *Zukunftskrieg*, Wodehouse concocted a preposterous plot which, unlike his models, was preposterous by intention.

In his preface, written in a bomb shelter somewhere in London, the narrator of *The Swoop!* announces his purpose: to raise England to a sense of her impending peril. While apologizing for the "too lurid colours" of his chronicle, he assures his readers that his sole motive stems from "patriotism and duty." He will show how Clarence Chugwater, a Boy Scout of fourteen years, became "Boy of Destiny" after he saved England from the grip of an eight-pronged invasion by the Germans, the Russians, the Chinese, the Swiss navy, the Mad Mullah, the Young Turks, the Monacoans, and an assorted band of Moroccan brigands. Using the opening scene of du Maurier's play as springboard, Wodehouse begins his tale in a typical suburban villa on a sultry summer afternoon where "not a single member of that family was practising with the rifle, or drilling, or learning to make bandages." While his father plays diabolo, his brother recites cricket scores, and his sister mends a badminton racket, Clarence tracks the family cat across the carpet by following its footprints. A newspaper arrives: Surry is doing poorly at cricket, and the German army has landed in England.[45]

Led by Prince Otto, the Germans appear at Nasturtium Villa and announce themselves as invaders to the apathetic Chugwater family. The father promptly offers to rent his house to them on easy terms, the son tries to sell them insurance policies, and the daughter makes them buy a ticket for an Old-Age Pensioners' Benefit. Prince Otto remarks lugubriously to a companion, "At last I begin to realize the horrors of an invasion—for the invaders." Meanwhile, at all points from Wales to Scotland, the enemy storms inland without opposition and engages in a mad race to arrive in London first. Bookies give odds of six-to-four in favor of the Germans. The British army no longer exists, because the socialists had seized power during the last election and abolished the army system as unsocial. At Margate the inhabitants momentarily mistake the Moroccans for "a troupe of nigger minstrels on an unusually magnificent scale" until the strangers assert their authority by scalping a small boy. Far away in Wales, the Chinese, baffled by the Welsh language, become hopelessly lost and arrive in London four days later than their allies after finding a cheap excursion train from Chester. The Moroccans are delayed when their leader is arrested for stealing chickens. None of the intruders behave like proper sportsmen: their armies make havoc of golf courses, and near Epping the Russians commit a major faux pas when they shoot a fox.

Prince Otto, obviously a reader and admirer of Le Queux, orders the bombardment of London, but the damage is slight: "Fortunately it was August and there was nobody in town. Otherwise there might have been loss of life." (The chapter titled "Bombardment of London" consists of only three sentences.) The destruction of Albert Hall and the Royal Academy occasions a massive turnout in Trafalgar Square in which Londoners submit a vote of thanks to Prince Otto for removing those architectural monstrosities. Having occupied the capital, the Germans and Russians unite to draw the color line, permitting only the Swiss and Monacoans to remain. The Swiss, however, withdraw voluntarily because they fear inroads into their hotel trade during the high season.

As England is ground under the invaders' heels, only the Scouts effectively resist. As the narrator explains, "With the exception of the Black Hand, the Scouts are perhaps the most carefully organized secret society in the world." At Aldwych Clarence Chugwater rallies his patrol

with its secret cry—the notes of a zebra calling its mate—and selects
the password for the resistance, "Remember Mafeking and Death to
the Injuns." Joined by other patrols like the Chinchilla Kittens and the
Welsh Rabbits, he outlines his masterplan for undermining the conquerors of Albion: they must foment jealousy and dissension among the
Germans and Russians.

Because this is the great age of the music hall in England, the enemy
commanders succumb to the temptation to become popular enter-
tainers—with disastrous results. The general of the Monacoan army,
failing to obtain billing as a card trick specialist, leaves the country in a
huff. Chugwater finds his opportunity when he learns that Jewish theatrical agents have offered Prince Otto 500 pounds per week to appear
on the lecture circuit but have promised the Russian general, the Grand
Duke Vodkakoff, only 450. Disguised as a junior reporter he seeds the
duke's dressing room with this information. The infuriated Vodkakoff
strikes back by placing his cossacks in the theater where Otto is performing. As the Prince attempts to speak, he is drowned out by "the
noise of wild beasts, of exploding boilers, of a music hall audience
giving a performer the bird." Clarence sends a note to the Prince,
fingering the Russians.

The breach is complete as the two allies attack one another. In a
London fog so thick that the armies become entangled, the great war-
within-the-war is joined. In the confused melée the Russians are nearly
annihilated, while most of the Germans perish in a charge near Jack
Straw's Castle. Up to this time the English have done nothing except
employ their crushing Supercilious Stare to work on the invaders' sense
of insecurity by giving them "a perpetual feeling of doing the wrong
thing." Now Clarence, as head of the Boy Scouts, attacks the remnant
of the German army with slingshots and hockey sticks. The greatest
invasion in English history terminates in the frightening gibberish of
scouts signaling to each other with their eerie battle cries—the thin
griffle of tarantulas and the snarls of sandeels bathing.

In the finale the Palace Theatre becomes the setting for a victory
celebration. For liberating his country from the foreign yoke, Clarence
receives 1000 pounds per week. (Lord Roberts was granted a million
pounds for his service as commander during the Boer War.) The audience goes wild at the spectacle of Clarence performing Boy Scout
exercises—twisting his right leg round his neck, hopping on one foot
across the stage, and emitting various animal cries. He is enshrined in
memory as Boy of Destiny and memorialized by the Chugwater Col-

umn in Aldwych and an equestrian statue in Chugwater Road (formerly Piccadilly).

Almost alone during this period of fermenting nationalism, Wodehouse found sources of comedy in the grotesque characters and fantastic plots served up by invasion writers. What Lord Roberts and Baden-Powell thought of his antic comedy—if they read it at all—is not recorded. *The Swoop!* seems to have been largely ignored, for it quickly went out of print and today remains one of the scarcer items in the Wodehouse canon.

It is ironical that the novel which best deflates the ballooning belligerence of the prewar years was the product of a writer devoid of political interests. Wodehouse was not a Clarence Chugwater. In 1940, when the Nazi armies overran France, they captured Wodehouse, who lived in a house at Le Touquet not very different from Nasturtium Villa. Obligingly he agreed to be interviewed by an American journalist, and later he spoke over Radio Berlin. For Wodehouse captivity during a real invasion was not durance vile but another comedy:

> There is a good deal to be said for internment. It keeps you out of saloons and helps you to keep up with your reading. . . . The only concession I want from Germany is that she gives me a loaf of bread, tells the gentlemen with muskets at the main gate to look the other way, and then leaves the rest to me. In return I am prepared to hand over India, an autographed set of my books, and to reveal the secret process of cooking sliced potatoes on a radiator. This offer holds good till Wednesday next.[46]

His countrymen were not amused. As late as 1944 demands were aired in Parliament that he be tried for treason. In the end his "collaboration" with the enemy in time of war was forgiven as the maunderings of someone hopelessly naive and foolish. It was presumed impossible to inculcate patriotism in a man who also wrote as a prisoner of the Germans: "I'm quite unable to work up any kind of belligerent feeling. Just as I'm about to feel belligerent about some country I meet a decent sort of chap. We go out together and lose any fighting thoughts or feelings."[47] The author of *The Swoop!* obviously lacked the right kind of stuff the age required.

If, among writers of social comedy in the Edwardian-Georgian period, P. G. Wodehouse stands as the quintessential dove, H. H. Munro (1870–1916) peers angrily from the crowded aviary of superhawks. Born in Burma, the son of a major in the British military police, Munro (better known by his pen name "Saki"), seems never to have been troubled by doubts about the superiority of Englishmen or the rectitude of the British Empire. At the age of three, when his mother, daughter of an admiral, was killed by shock after a runaway cow pursued her, Munro was deposited by his father in England for rearing by a grandmother and two spinster aunts. After a brief period as a Burma police officer himself—he was retired from service by fever in less than a year—he settled in London as journalist and clubman.

During the Boer War Munro was catapaulted into literary prominence by his *Westminster Alice* sketches, which satirized governmental bunglers charged with conduct of the war. Prime Minister Joseph Chamberlain was "An Ineptitude" encountered by the Cheshire Cat and Alice, who discuss this wizened creature with sagging cranelike neck:

> "What is it, and why is it here?"
> "It hasn't any meaning," said the Cat, "it simply *is*."
> "Can it talk?" asked Alice eagerly.
> "It has never done anything else," chuckled the cat.[48]

Perhaps Munro's most famous target was the marquess of Lansdowne (who briefly headed both the War Office and the Foreign Office), depicted by Munro as the White Knight who rides two horses in case he should fall off one. The Knight, who carries on his saddle a cluster of obsolete weapons, explains to Alice his theory of prosecuting the war:

> "You see I had read a book written by someone to prove that warfare under modern conditions was impossible. . . . You will never guess what I did."
> Alice pondered, "You went to war, of course—"
> "Yes; *but not under modern conditions*. . . . You observe this little short-range gun that I have hanging to my saddle? Why do you suppose I sent guns of that particular kind? Because if they happened to fall into the hands of the enemy they'd be very little use to him. That was my own invention. . . . And then, again, supposing the Basutos had risen, those would have been just the sort of guns to drive them off with. Of course, they *didn't* rise, but they might have done so, you know."[49]

Published with illustrations by F. Carruthers Gould in the style of Sir John Tenniel, the *Westminster Alice* fables sold 25,000 copies and lambasted the indecision and inefficiency which had made the English army the laughing stock of Europe. Not even Lord Roberts escaped Munro's barbs; as Humpty Dumpty he recited to Alice a verse explaining why he failed to utilize the command of Lieutenant General Sir George White:

> "I sent a message to the White
> To tell him—if you *must*, you might.
> But then, I said, you p'rhaps might not.
> (The weather was extremely hot.)[50]

Assignments in the Balkans and in Russia as correspondent for the right-wing *Morning Post* gave Munro an eyrie from which he could observe the unraveling of those gossamer threads that held together the threadbare fabric of European politics. Like Erskine Childers, he came to admire the industrial efficiency and national discipline of imperial Germany, which appeared to be the only major power willing to face the inevitable war of the future and to carefully prepare for it. For Munro, pacifism was just another name for revolution and treason, and he inveighed against those madcaps who "seemed to take a ghoulish pleasure in predicting a not-far-distant moment when Britons shall range themselves in organized conflict . . . against their own kith and kin."[51] He yearned for a resurgence of that English grit and muscle that had forged the Empire, and he was, like Kipling, repelled by evidence of yokiness and self-indulgence which he found in contemporary English life.

Munro's *When William Came: A Story of London under the Hohenzollerns* (1913) was the last of the important invasion novels. It departs from the others of the genre by depicting occupation of the country without showing the war itself. As the novel opens England has been defeated, the King has retired to Delhi, and Britain has become a *Reichsland*. The nation has been betrayed by pleasure-seeking fops unwilling to soil a glove in defense of their country, by cosmopolitans and parvenu Jews deeply resenting the class system, and by gullible Berts and Sids—those householders and voters who danced to the tune played by unscrupulous politicians. Deprived of funds for adequate defense, England has been walked over by the Germans. A Hungarian observer explains how the moral collapse of the English race came about:

> They grew soft. Great world-commerce brings great luxury, and
> luxury brings softness. . . . They had come to look on Christ as a

sort of amiable elder Brother, whose letters from abroad were worth reading. . . . They were tired of their faith, but they were not virile enough to become real Pagans; their dancing fauns were good young men who tripped Morris dances and ate health foods and believed in a sort of Socialism which made for the greatest dullness of the greatest number.[52]

Luxury, sloth, ennui, decadence—Munro's catalog of moral lapses attending twentieth-century existence is a familiar litany earnestly but monotonously recited by a host of writers from H. G. Wells to Rupert Brooke. It comes as no particular surprise, then, that in August 1914 Munro wrote to a friend, without irony, "I have looked forward to the romance of a European war."[53] The shape of the Europe to come would be hammered out on the battleground. Only in this way could England regain her self-respect.

After England's collapse, Murrey Yeovil, the protagonist of *When William Came*, returns home from a bird-collecting expedition in Siberia. He registers shock at finding announcements in Victoria Station written in both English and German and dismay at seeing the imperial German standard flying at Buckingham Palace. His simpering wife, Cicely, the sort of upper-class London woman raised to expect three kinds of red pepper available for caviar at a picnic, accepts the new regime and arranges her building blocks to climb into the new social hierarchy. She drags Murrey to a performance at the Caravansary Theatre, which has adapted its program to the abysmal cultural level of Prussian officers and Hamburg Jews, who now dominate London society. They watch as her friend, Gorla Mustelford, makes her musical debut, performing a dance "suggesting the life of a fern." Her act is preceded by wolves wearing clown caps riding around the stage on bicycles and by coarse American comedians in rags and tatters. Murrey bitterly contrasts this monster show with the elevated taste of London theater before the invasion.

London club life is similarly debased. Murrey finds his old sanctum filled with "Hebraic-looking gentlemen, wearing tartan waistcoats of the clans of their adoption."[54] Former friends peddle family paintings and heirlooms to German immigrants. Here he learns that because the Germans are exempt from taxation they will ultimately displace the English, who will be forced to emigrate to the colonies. Englishmen will be excused from military service in the new Reich, for the intention is to convert them into a caste of harmless shopkeepers with no knowledge of firearms.

Disgusted by conditions in the capital, Murrey entrains for a week-end with Dowager Lady Greymarten at "Torywood," the emblem of a dreamy Georgian estate. With its ducks in the horsepond and lazy roan dairy cattle, "Torywood" evokes the England of used-to be, "a land where it seemed as if it must always be summer and generally after-noon, a land where bees hummed among the wild thyme and the mill-race flowed cool and silent through water-weeds."[55] The Dowager Lady, who has lost her son in the recent war, personifies the spirit of the English past. In contrast with Cicely's round of iced mulberry salads with the horrid Germans in London, she urges Murrey to fight against the new regime. She warns him that time is on the side of the invaders because the rising generation will soon forget their glorious heritage.

How to restore the memory of the English past is the problem. The German policy of gradualism, which gives Britons the illusion that their living standards are unchanged, erodes the will to resist. Murrey has sporadic encounters with verbal guerrillas, like the Anglican clergyman who exclaims, "Beat your sword into ploughshares if you like, but beat your enemy into smithereens first,"[56] but this amounts only to idle chatter. The lesson propounded in Munro's novel is that once invaders have a cultural foothold in the island it is nearly impossible to dislodge them.

Racked by guilt and impotence in being unable to do anything to free his country from the Teutonic yoke, Murrey attends a grand review of the Boy Scouts in Hyde Park. Already the Germans have boasted that the Scouts will become the janissaries of their empire. In the final lines of the novel a mixed crowd of German officers and their English lackeys await the parade of Baden-Powell's Boys of Destiny:

> And in the pleasant May sunshine the Eagle standards floated and flapped, the black and yellow pennons shifted restlessly. Em-peror and Princes, Generals and guards, sat stiffly in their saddles, and waited.
> And waited. . . .[57]

Deliverance from the invader's bootheel lies with the youth of En-gland, who will mobilize not as German mercenaries but as English guerrillas. Unlike Wodehouse, Munro found nothing amusing about the patriotic extravaganzas of the Boy Scout Association. Nor did Lord Roberts, who acknowledged his complimentary copy of *When William Came* with a note saying that he "thoroughly approved" of the novel.[58]

It was as if two generations of adults (Lord Roberts was eighty, Munro was forty-three), through default and exasperation, had turned over the job of saving England to a children's crusade. The betrayal and slaughter of innocents was now less than a year in the future.

One of Munro's favorite subjects in his short stories was the absolute separation that existed between the world of children and the world of adults. In March 1914 he read with devilish glee that a peace council, objecting to the proliferation of war toys among children, had urged parents to substitute "peace toys" as a corrective—things like lead casts of civilians, ploughs, and industrial tools. This news item inspired his sardonic story, "Toys of Peace," in which an idealistic young man named Harvey distributes among his nephews a set of toys which include a model of a municipal dustbin, a YWCA collection, a ballot box, a public library, and figures of notables like John Stuart Mill. Retiring to his library, Harvey ponders whether a history could be compiled which makes no mention of massacre, battles, intrigues, or violent deaths. Perhaps children can become as infatuated with the invention of calico printing as the Spanish Armada. When he returns to the nursery, however, he finds to his dismay the dustbin pierced with holes to accommodate the muzzles of cannon and John Stuart Mill splashed with red ink. The children proceed to attack the YWCA, massacre a hundred girls, and abduct the remainder. Harvey sadly laments, "The Experiment—has failed. We have begun too late."[59]

It was not too late for Munro, for the guns of August provided him with a new beginning. What he most feared about the world situation was that England would fail to join France in her war against Germany. After attending the debates in the house of Commons he wrote in *Outlook:* "There are men in the anti-war party who seem to be obsessed with the idea of snatching commercial advantages out of the situation. . . . There seemed to be some confusion of mind in these circles of political thought between a nation of shopkeepers and a nation of shoplifters."[60]

When England declared war, Munro promptly enlisted as a private in King Edward's Horse. Putting on a trooper's uniform was for him like "a novice assuming the religious habit," a friend remembered.[61] Lacking sufficient strength for the cavalry, he transferred to the Twenty-second Royal Fusiliers and twice refused a commission. The author of *When William Came* was keen to meet Wilhelm halfway.

Shipped over to France in November 1915, Munro continued to

write occasional pieces. One of his last ones lashed out at young men who failed to enlist:

> Boys of the lap-dog breed remain trilling their songs, capering their dances, speaking their lines as complacently as though no war was in progress. . . . After the war let them be treated as something apart; something human and decorative and amusing; but something not altogether British, not exactly masculine, something that one does not treat as an equal.[62]

In June 1916 he came home on leave and inquired of a friend whether it might be possible after the war to buy land in Siberia where he could live, farm, and hunt. At the expiration of his leave, his sister saw him off at Victoria Station, cheerily calling across the barricade, "Kill a good few for me!"[63] In November, near Beaumont Hamel in the Somme fighting, he was shot through the head and killed. His last recorded words: "Put that bloody cigarette out."[64]

In an earlier sketch, "The Cupboard of the Yesterdays," Munro recalled a dullish man in Sofia who had taught him Bulgarian. Later when he was killed in a skirmish of the Balkan War, Munro wrote his epitaph: "After his dullness and his long-winded small-talk it seemed a sort of brilliant *esprit d'escalier* on his part to meet with an end of such ruthlessly planned and executed violence."[65] It might have served as his own.

5 PLAYING THE GAME

▼

We are often told that they taught us nothing at Eton. That may be so, but I think they taught it very well.
GENERAL PLUMER (*1916*)

As the rugged, outdoor model provided by General Baden-Powell served to guide middle-class youths toward ideals appropriate for God, king, and country, so the time-honored mores of the English public school tradition provided directives for sons of the privileged classes. Whether Lord Wellington had really said that the Battle of Waterloo was won on the playing fields of Eton is of less consequence than the fact that it was accepted as true coin by parents determined to enroll their boys into one of the great public schools and thereby assure that their posterity would remain (or become) English gentlemen.

The end product was, more often than not, neither Christian nor gentleman, but rather a hybrid creature trained for no particular purpose yet expected to hold the reins of power because he had undergone, and survived, the rigorous social Darwinist environment of an Eton or a Harrow. What he acquired, other than a smattering of classical phrases drilled into his brain by rote or inflicted as "lines" to be memorized as punishments, was a quality vaguely defined as "character." This often meant little more than the capacity to absorb—and to give—physical punishment.

Public school memoirs and fiction of the prewar period are crammed with accounts of canings by masters and beatings by older boys. In writing of his schoolboy days, General Ian Hamilton, who commanded the Gallipoli expedition, recalled how boys' backs resembled the colors of a peacock—blues of a previous week's beating turning gradually green, then yellow, with recent stripes a vivid purple. On revisiting his old school after service in the Boer War, Hamilton recorded, "My blood went cold," for he remembered how his headmaster had altered the text "Suffer little children . . ." to "Make little children suffer."[1] John Betjeman, who attended Marlborough half a century later, tells a similar story. Corporal punishment was indispensable for building "character." After beating him, a master congratulated him. "I liked the way you took that beating, John / Reckon yourself henceforth a gentleman." Far from resenting such treatment, Betjeman recorded a sensation of triumph: "[Beatings] brought us no disgrace, / Rather a kind of glory."[2]

While the German or French schoolboy labored within a curriculum designed to cope with the conditions of an increasingly scientific age, his English counterpart occupied himself with mastering games. In *The Old School Tie* (1977) Jonathan Gathorne-Hardy argues that between 1900 and 1914 the famous public schools had almost ceased to be academic institutions in order to become places to learn cricket and football.[3] Memoirs make this point repeatedly. Looking back on his years at St. Paul's, Leonard Woolf wrote, "Use of the mind, intellectual curiosity, mental originality . . . all such things, if detected, were violently condemned and persecuted."[4] One entered, as Woolf said, an "educational machine for producing classical pâté de foie gras."[5] Fortunately, Woolf played cricket. At Eton, Lawrence Jones concluded that the famous school prepared one "for a lifetime of hitting balls of different sizes." On one occasion he struck up a friendship with another new boy, but when his friend won most of the events in a junior track meet and became celebrated overnight as a coming athlete, he never spoke to Jones again: "As far as I was concerned, he had died on the day of the sports, and gone to heaven."[6] Although Latin and Greek were the main subjects, few boys knew enough of either to read inscriptions on memorial tablets in chapel, let alone a Greek epigram. Science was confined to chemistry—dubbed "stinks"—while biology, astronomy, and physics were rarely taught at all. French and German were usually examined as dead languages, without conversation. Jones, who had resided in France, was ridiculed because he could speak the language. One Eton master struck a match on the bald head of the French master to show his contempt for the country and the language.[7] This passed as a famous joke.

The object of a public school education seemed not to be the opening of a boy's mind but rather the compaction of it into a rigid mold. "Playing the game," the unofficial canon of the public school youth, meant inflexible and unquestioning adherence to the rules, and it was immaterial if these defied rational explanation. The object was to *do*, not to think. At Eton, for example, taboo was as powerful and as inscrutable as it was in the most primitive African clan. When going into Windsor, a boy had to walk on only one side of the street; to walk on the other side would be "as odd an action as standing on one's head."[8] The secret for survival, wrote an Etonian of this period, was "to look as much alike to everybody else as possible."[9] An eccentric (unless he was titled or very rich) was regarded as a nuisance. The best service a school could perform for the human tertium quid was to hone down his protruding edges and make him conform. Both masters and fellow students declared open warfare upon behavior that departed from, or questioned, the norm. At Harrow, when Winston Churchill asked why he should learn that *mensa* was the vocative case for *table*, he was told by his classics master that it was used in speaking to a table. "But I never do," rejoined Churchill. "If you are impertinent," his master warned, "you will be punished severely."[10] Punishment by one's fellow peers often approximated torture. At Bedales School there was the "pie." An unpopular boy would be thrown into the bath with smaller boys tossed in on top of him and bigger boys jumping in on top, hitting the struggling mass with heels of slippers or topping it off with streams of hot water.[11] Hanging new boys out of tower windows or dropping them into blankets at the bottom of stairwells were other techniques for developing character. Grant Wilson wrote about his first year at Bedales: "I lived in a state of continual fear, and became a cowed and miserable little creature, reduced to lying and skunking, quite abject, without pride, and with very little courage."[12] For Arnold Toynbee the approach of fall term at Winchester was "like execution-day for a prisoner who has been condemned to death."[13] W. H. Auden in later years looked back on his years at Gresham's during the Great War and wrote, "The best reason I have for opposing Fascism is that at school I lived in a Fascist state."[14]

Although the church or Crown originally founded and supported these schools to educate deserving youths of humble birth for whom private instruction was impossible, by the 1830s they had become preserves for sons of aristocrats and rich men. On one occasion, when an investigating committee inquired of the Winchester authorities why so many wealthy students were enrolled, it was told that the charge was untrue: the boys themselves were quite poor—only their parents were rich.[15] Scholarships existed for poor youths of course, but unless they were athletes their social life in the school was marginal at best. A. E.

Housman recalled that the headmaster of his school disliked the "trade element" and contemptuously supplied sons of grocers and farmers with nicknames like "Bacon" and "Carthorse."[16] Insulated from the gasworks of industrial England by stained glass chapel windows, the schoolboy was taught to venerate an archaic vision of English life that was more in tune with the sixteenth century than the twentieth. It was ironical that rich merchants whose gospel of hard work was responsible for their sons' acceptance into the great school hierarchy accepted without question the impractical curriculum. Their sons must become gentlemen, and this accolade the schools alone could give them.

As though in expiation of their sires' wealth, schoolboys often had to live in conditions that would have disgraced a Dickensian workhouse. Some of the houses at Marlborough had been built by the architect of Wormwood Scrubs Prison, with but slight alteration of plan. John Betjeman, who lived in one of them during the 1920s, caught the flavor of the place:

> An eighteen-fifty warehouse smelling strong
> Of bat-oil, biscuits, sweets and rotten fruit.[17]

His allusion to rodents was not a gothic device. Two cartloads of rat bones were removed from under the floorboards of the notorious Long Chamber at Eton during a cleanup in 1858.[18] Sleeping in ancient, draughty dormitories where beds often butted up against one another, boys sniffed and snuffled through the winter term, warmed by adjacent body heat and embers of open wood fires. In many schools fires were not permitted till nightfall, and even in winter servants threw open windows in the morning. House masters claimed that cold weather hardened their young charges and refused to accept the theory that head colds were contracted by exposure—a convenient rationalization for pocketing savings on fuel.[19]

Memorialists vied with one another in describing culinary horrors at preparatory and public schools, but most agree that starvation fare was the rule. Evelyn Waugh recalled that the food at Lancing "would have provoked mutiny in a mid-Victorian poor-house," while A. A. Milne wrote of his school experience, "In all my years at Westminster I never ceased to be hungry."[20] At Cheam, the most expensive preparatory school in England, the boys ate bread and butter at tea while the headmaster and family dined in the same hall on buns and jam. Once each week, according to Ian Hamilton, the pupils received a special treat—leftover jam from the head's table. As a new boy, Hamilton made the mistake of asking for butter at breakfast but was put in his place for this outrageous request when the headmaster wrote on a blackboard, "What is a gorging, guzzling, gobbling cormorant?" and gleefully supplied the answer—"Ian Standish Monteith Hamilton."[21] Yet the prize for describing food at an English school ought to go to George Orwell, who attended St. Cyprian's during the war. His headmaster promulgated the maxim that it was healthy to get up from a meal feeling as hungry as when you sat down. Orwell never forgot the accumulations of sour porridge clinging to the rims of poorly washed bowls, or the porridge itself which "contained more lumps, hairs, unexplained black things than one would have thought possible, unless someone were putting them there on purpose." His headmaster, after a flying visit to Eton, raved about the sybaritic delights that awaited boys fortunate enough to be admitted there—"They give them fried fish for supper." On recalling this incident years later, Orwell exclaimed, "Fried fish! the habitual supper of the poorest of the working class."[22]

Homosexual encounters—estimated by Gathorne-Hardy at twenty-five percent of all boarding students—proliferated at schools despite strict rules and token crackdowns by authorities.[23] Saturated with classical texts lauding homophilic relationships and taught by masters usually conforming to what Cyril Connolly called "that repressed and familiar type, the English male virgin,"[24] schoolboys often found it natural to turn their sexual energies inward upon each other. In defense of what the French called *le vice anglais* there was always the argument that whatever went on at boys' schools was better than illicit relations at coeducational establishments—"At least none of us ever had a baby."[25] Contributing to the problem were unheated rooms so that boys crept like puppies into others' beds for warmth. Because of Victorian reticence about sexual subjects, boys sometimes engaged in love affairs without even knowing their behavior was improper. The first words uttered by Edmond Warre, headmaster at Eton, to new boy Lawrence Jones were an admonition to "beware of filth." Since the doctor did not explain what he meant, Jones deduced that the reference was to dog messes on pavements. Years later he understood: "Sex, although given to us by God, was a dirty little secret."[26] The memoir of a later Eton headmaster devotes only a short paragraph to "vice" (which he never explains) but treats "bad language" at some length.[27] The problem was compounded because the region from waist to knee fell under Victorian taboo, and a young boy easily confused sex with bodily elimination. In his account of St. Cyprian's, Orwell recounts how he was beaten by his headmaster and then ravaged by guilt feelings for nothing more heinous than bed-wetting.

In protecting their charges from immorality, which they defined almost exclusively in sexual terms, authorities found themselves impaled on the horns of a dilemma. On the one hand, if a boy attached himself to older boys regarded as role models (usually athletes), he raised the specter of sodomy; on the other, if he developed solitary habits, he would be suspected of masturbation. "Rings around the eyes," as Orwell tells us, were the telltale symptom of the latter. At some schools boys were required to have their pockets sewn up as a deterrent against self-abuse,[28] which in the Victorian catechism was prelude to insanity, or worse.* Only rarely did schools provide cubicles in lavatories, for fear that these would provide secret places for youths to spill their seeds in solitude or in the company of another depraved boy. In classrooms, in dormitories, and on the athletic field boys lived virtually on top of one another and under a surveillance system that would have done credit to a well-run police state. A favored hiding place for a sensitive boy was the chapel, a refuge when there was no other place to go and especially welcome because it was usually empty.

The rockbound durability of the English public school is best measured by its success in fending off troublesome reformers. By the middle of the nineteenth century the education aims of these schools had become almost ludicrously out of touch with the requirements of modern civilization. A curriculum based almost exclusively on the study of two dead languages persisted because of a logical inversion premised on historical precedent rather than present need. At Westminster School Guy Chapman memorized twenty lines per day of Ovid and Vergil, without context; it was excruciatingly boring but it got him admitted to a prestigious Oxford college.[29] Another public school boy about to begin at Oxford appraised his education: "I could write a passable English sonnet or copy of Latin elegiacs but I could not mend a fuse and the internal combustion engine was a complete mystery to me."[30] Arguments in defense of classical languages went this way: in the past, classics had been the academic pursuit of clever men; therefore, it

---

*Baden-Powell originally planned a section on self-abuse for his Scouting manual. Prior to publication this was dropped, presumably on grounds that it might put ideas into an innocent boy's head. A further note on pockets: as a special privilege at Harrow, footballers of the first Fifteen were allowed to keep their hands in pockets when in football clothes, while the less favored were not. See E. E. Reynolds, *Baden-Powell* (London, 1957), 146.

followed that boys exposed to Latin and Greek would become clever men. Traditionalists doggedly asserted that studying the classics functioned as a kind of muscle builder for the brain, although reformers wondered why German and French could not perform the same exercise and at the same time be more useful. (The latter thought it strange that foreign service examinations evaluated performance in classical languages over German and French by a scale of two to one.) Perhaps the only "modern" education in England at this time was that of the army and navy schools, which emphasized science, geography, and recent history. By way of contrast, at Eton the study of history ended with Marlborough's victory over Napoleon. In the minds of many Englishmen, perhaps this was all a young patriot needed to know. After all, the English beat Napoleon, didn't they? So long as the public schools taught a boy how to pass himself off as a gentleman, that passport allowing entry into positions of power and prestige, adherents of the system showed little disposition for instruction of a utilitarian kind. Two things were demanded for status of gentleman—some sort of bare-boned exposure to the classics and possession of a proper accent. So long as a school could provide these things, it was worth its fees.

The famous "reforms" of Dr. Thomas Arnold at Rugby during the 1830s had been more concerned with spiritual uplift than with curriculum change. To a friend the doctor declared that he would gladly have a youth think that the sun went around the earth so long as he developed the more important attributes of model Christian. "What we must look for here is, first religious and moral principle; secondly, gentlemanly conduct; thirdly, intellectual ability."[31] If the ordering of priorities seems curious, it was distinctly English and conformed to the consensus of that age. For Arnold, as for others, the ugly social and economic problems of industrial England would be solved ultimately by Christian charity and forbearance—certainly not by encouraging trade unionism, which Arnold called "a fearful engine of mischief, ready to riot and assassinate."[32] Always a gentleman should differentiate between the deserving and the undeserving poor—the former being humble, patient, and grateful. To a Cambridge undergraduate Arnold wrote: "I am glad you have made acquaintance with some of the good poor. I quite agree with you that it is most instructive to visit them."[33] Acquaintance and visitation were permissible; friendship and assimilation were not. Although this may strike the modern ear as unbearably smug, it was actually a progressive attitude for the time, since it at least

granted the poor visibility when most English gentleman merely ignored them as a caste apart. A century later George Orwell reflected the
Arnoldian perspective when, in *The Road to Wigan Pier* (1937), he
claimed that the English middle classes were raised to believe that "the
lower classes smell."[34]

Dr. Arnold's Rugby becomes the setting and inspiration for the great
classic of public school literature, Thomas Hughes' *Tom Brown's School
Days* (1857). The novel opens with a glowing tribute to all the
"Browns" of England, those heart-of-oak yeomen who over the centuries have "in their quiet, dogged, homespun way" been doing the
work of empire, and "getting hard knocks and hard work in plenty,
which was on the whole what they looked for, and the best thing for
them," whether in Australia or at Waterloo.[35] Young Tom Brown is
less individual character than cultural synecdoche, an embodiment of
the English race—ordinary, kindly, provincial, commonsensical.
Squire Brown, in assessing his reasons for sending Tom to Rugby, cares
not a whit about intellectual development: "I don't care a straw for
Greek particles, or the digamma. . . . If he'll only turn out a brave,
truth-telling Englishman, and a gentleman, and a Christian, that's all I
want."[36] Ironically, his values are those of the landed gentry, a class
already on the endangered list in any industrialized economy, and nowhere do collieries or belching chimneys intrude in this book. For
Thomas Hughes (1823–97) cosmopolitanism is a minor vice. He has
little use for the modern dandified Englishman who can patter in
French and German, knows the pictures at Dresden or the Louvre, but
has no idea "what the bog-bean and wood-sage are good for."[37]

An overriding theme of this novel is that life equals combat. From
first to last the narrative is crammed with scenes of internecine warfare.
Young Tom rebels against his nurse, battles rustics on his native heath,
and subdues bullies at Rugby. On his first day at Dr. Arnold's school
he undergoes an initiation into violence that would have devastated a
boy with less grit: he is shown the site (appropriately behind the chapel)
reserved for fist fights; he is mauled in a football match; and, as finale,
he is tossed in a blanket so high that his knees brush the ceiling. He
emerges without fear, without complaint.

On Tom's second day at Rugby, Dr. Arnold makes his appearance in
chapel. In characterizing Arnold, whom he reveres, the author lays on
heavy coatings of military imagery: "The true sort of *captain,* for a
boy's *army,* one who had no misgivings and gave no uncertain word of
command [my italics]."[38] An oddity of the book is that while Hughes

treats Arnold with awed reverence, the doctor's influence is more talked about than graphically shown. We catch fleeting glimpses of him at
home in a cozy family circle or wrathfully beating a laggard scholar at
examinations, behavior which in its vacillation between the poles of
love and anger undoubtedly conforms to the Victorian notion of how
God Himself behaves. Dr. Arnold becomes a remote Jovian personage,
a kind of *deus absconditas*, who, having created the world and laid down
its commandments, more or less retires and avoids interfering with the
chaotic social behavior of his creatures. Nominally, Rugby is ruled by
prefects, a group of older boys appointed by the headmaster, but real
authority is vested in those youths strong enough to seize it. Gangs of
bullies tyrannize the weaker boys. After Tom is caught and nearly
roasted at the fire by Flashman, the bully par excellence of English
literature, he gains points from the other boys by not tattling to the
headmaster. Instead he teams with a friend and soundly thrashes his
tormentor. Here is proper retribution at Rugby: justice must be meted
out with fists, not with craven appeals to God or other remote authorities.

For a new boy at school success matters less than mere survival. Tom
Brown, nurtured on field sports and indoctrinated by the mores of "a
fighting family," easily establishes his territorial rights. More sensitive
plants do not sink roots so readily. When Tom is given responsibility
for protecting a fragile boy, George Arthur, he supplies the right formula for survival: "If you're afraid, you'll get bullied. And don't you
say you can sing; and don't you ever talk about home, or your mothers
and sisters."[39] The mushy realm of culture, home, and women must be
eradicated as a first step toward initiation into manhood. As Arnold
Toynbee would write of Winchester half a century later, "It was as
exclusively male as Mount Athos."[40] Fathers and brothers had marginal existence, mothers and sisters did not. In effect, public schools were
as isolated from the influence of women as a military barracks. Moreover, the hierarchy of a public school resembled that of a military
organization with prefects as noncommissioned officers administering
discipline, from which there was no effective appeal. Like the army, the
goal of a public school was to instruct its members how to acquire the
means of survival in a Spencerian universe of unremitting conflict with
fellow human beings. When George Arthur asks Tom Brown what he
expects to gain from his years at Rugby, Tom has a ready answer: " 'I
want to be A1 at cricket and football, and all the other games, and to
make my hands keep my head against any fellow, lout or gentleman. I

want to set into the sixth [form] before I leave, and to please the Doctor; and I want to carry away just as much Latin and Greek as will take me through Oxford respectably.' "[41] No one has characterized the priorities of the public school ethos with more rugged honesty.

A notable peculiarity of *Tom Brown's School Days* is the almost total absence of matter bearing upon the learning process. One has to ransack its pages for evidence that the young rowdies at Rugby enter the classroom at all. Masters exist as dim figures of no consequence barely visible in the penumbra of the sainted Dr. Arnold. They are never characterized because neither their personalities nor their subjects are of enduring importance to Tom Brown or to Thomas Hughes. School life is conveyed in terms of sporting events, poaching sorties, dormitory warfare—all activities which fostered the development of "muscular Christianity" (a term first used in association with Hughes's novel). The book concluded with an episode as revealing as it is extraneous to the work as a whole. Dr. Arnold has died, and Tom Brown, now a grown man, makes a solemn pilgrimage to Rugby Chapel, which houses the relics of the holy man. As he reflects on how he owes everything to his mentor, Tom experiences an epiphany. At Rugby "he had first caught a glimpse of the glory of his birthright, and felt the drawing of the bond which links all living souls together in one brotherhood."[42] On the conscious level Hughes attempted to wrap up his novel in a tidy package of Christian piety, but for a skeptical reader the "brotherhood" and "birthright" might convey something closer to the ideals of warrior cults in the Middle Ages. Hughes' perspective is nostalgic and reactionary. By turning the clock backward he emphatically endorsed, and implanted, a retrogressive ideal which would be idolized, almost as canonized text, by the prewar generation of public school boys.

Criticism has been leveled at Thomas Hughes for bowdlerizing Thomas Arnold's ideals, particularly in emphasizing the importance at Rugby of games, which, in fact, the doctor deplored. Although acclaimed a reformer of and spokesman for the public school, Arnold lamented the ineradicable evils within the system and toward the end of his life insisted he could not recommend sending a boy to any of them. Repeatedly in his writing one finds this theme: "a school shows as undisguisably as any place the corruption of human nature."[43] His was an Old Testament conception of man. If he supported beating and fagging it was less because he thought a boy's nature could be altered than his gloomy view that punishment might subdue a boy's demonic streak and make him respect a more powerful authority. In propagandizing for the public school Thomas Arnold's Rugby of fact was considerably less influential than Thomas Hughes' Rugby of fiction. *Tom Brown's School Days*, with its glorification of brawn and games, acted as a lodestar for Edwardian and Victorian schoolboys and publicists trailing in its wake. It clearly illustrates the paradox implicit in the public school system, which attempted to mediate between two irreconcilable ideologies, Christianity and social Darwinism. As *ideal*, the Christian gentleman prevailed, but in fact the system exemplified those trusty catchphrases "survival of the fittest" and "battle to the strong." (It was hardly coincidental that the favorite hymn for English schoolboys was "Onward, Christian Soldiers," which sounds like a redaction of the Sermon on the Mount by a proselyte of Herbert Spencer.) The problem with this emphasis on strength was that it focused almost exclusively on human muscle and not on development of brain. Englishmen should have known better. They had forged a world empire because their technology had been superior to that of the native populations in territories they wanted. Character and muscle had been secondary.

▼

During the heyday of Arnold and his disciple Hughes, public school life showed little formal organization beyond classroom and chapel. Games were little more than scratch affairs played in old clothes under improvised rules, but by the 1890s this cavalier attitude had been replaced by rigid, intolerant hierarchies which ranked students by their ability at the game and which played according to fixed rules. The introduction of uniforms and team spirit replicated behavior not unlike that on parade ground or even battlefield.* Such lockstep standardization in garb and attitude suggests that public school youths of the 1890s would have been more at home in an army than those of the 1860s. For historical reasons that are still unclear, the late Victorian youth seems to have been less independent than his counterpart a generation earlier. Hughes had seen Rugby as a means toward an end—however murky— but as the century wore on the public school became an end in itself. In 1873 Leslie Stephen sardonically observed: "Neither the British jury,

---

*In his influential work *The Decline of the Aristocracy* (1912) Arthur Ponsonby, a Liberal M.P., noted that photographs of schoolboys taken forty years before revealed a looseness of groupings and a variety of costumes, while boys of the present day stood in arithmetical rows, wore similar clothes, and even looked like one another. See Ponsonby (London, 1912), 220.

nor the House of Lords, nor the Church of England, nay, scarcely the monarchy itself, seems to be so deeply enshrined in the bosoms of our countrymen as our public schools."[44] If this is true—and a great body of evidence can be marshaled in its support—then it can be argued that the English sensibility was shifting from the values traditionally regarded as adult to those of adolescence.

Although there were outcries for reform of the public school system these rarely amounted to anything tangible. As early as 1868 a royal commission recommended that the Prussian model for education be adopted. It was not. In Germany Hegel's conception of the State entailed emphasis upon centralized education in sharp contrast to the English system which followed class lines and made education largely dependent on private initiative. In 1884 another commission was convened and concluded: "The one point in which Germany is overwhelmingly superior to England is in schools, and the education of all classes of the people. The dense ignorance so common among workmen in England is unknown."[45] Despite such warnings, however, during the succeeding decade only one elementary schoolboy out of every 270 advanced to the secondary level.[46] (No state-controlled secondary school system existed in England prior to 1902.) Yet this was a period when German steel production multiplied ten times while that of England only doubled. Meanwhile, ineptly trained classical scholars continued to be the principal export of English public schools.*

Even within the public schools themselves there were sporadic denunciations of the troglodytic curriculum. Perhaps the most powerful voice raised in criticism was that of A.C. Benson (1865–1925), a distinguished classics master at Eton. England's miserable performance in the Boer War had convinced him that her schools had failed to encourage imagination and intelligence, and the heart of the problem lay in the overemphasis on classics and athletics. In *The Schoolmaster* (1902), a collection of essays, Benson charged the public schools with perpetuating an atmosphere in which intellectual pursuit was deliberately suppressed. It was ironical that boys read classics which passionately portrayed the Athenian model of mental development yet imitated in their

---

*On the other hand, among some students the classics succeeded all too well. Arnold Toynbee became so impregnated with Greek and Latin while at Winchester that he became "alienated from my mother-tongue." In later years whenever he felt the need for powerful expression he resorted to Greek or Latin because in using English his "feelings would be bottled up without an outlet." Here was a rare instance of failure through too much success. See Arnold Toynbee, *Experiences* (New York, 1969), 15.

daily lives the mindless Spartan worship of physical prowess as summum bonum. Intellectual standards at public schools were low and were not improving. Schools were producing boys who were not only ignorant but proud of it, because they had somehow come to believe that it was both ridiculous and unmanly to be anything except an athlete. Benson, a former footballer at Cambridge, had no quarrel with sports as a measure for improving health, but he warred with the dangerous notion that success in games was synonymous with success in life. After a game, the boy or master should be willing to turn to books or to an exchange of ideas rather than merely lying down "like a dog curling up in a basket after a vigorous day."[47]

As the eldest son of the Archbishop of Canterbury, Benson was not a woolly radical, but his book unleashed such a stream of obscene and threatening letters that Scotland Yard felt obliged to undertake an investigation. The Eton headmaster Edmond Warre was so infuriated by Benson's book that he invaded his master's classroom and blazed out to the boys that those who proclaimed that Greek had no practical value "were as foolish as people who said that the foundation of a house was no use, because unseen."[48] Warre would have been horrified had he read jottings in Benson's private diaries, which make his observations in *The Schoolmaster* tepid reading indeed. In 1898 Benson had written: "The classics are poor pabulum I fear. I live in dread of the public finding out how bad an education is the only one I can communicate. . . . We do not stimulate. We only make the ordinary boy hate and despise books and knowledge generally, but we make them conscientious—good drudges, I think."[49] Four years later he was more specific: "As for teaching them Herodotus, Livy, Vergil, Horace, Theocritus, and Sophocles—the thing is rot."[50] For Benson the Eton creed had become "Do your work conscientiously—it is dull, but never mind. Then *play* for all you are worth."[51] Finally despairing of the intellectual atmosphere at Eton, Benson moved on to Cambridge in 1904 and in time became Master of Magdalene College.

No such skepticism crept into the work of Henry Newbolt (1862–1938), who has the dubious honor of being the most widely read and quoted of all public school apologists dating from the prewar period. The writing of Newbolt so successfully mirrored the schoolboy sensibility of that era that Patrick Howarth, an English cultural historian, has labeled the product *Homo newboltiensis*, defined as a creature, peculiarly English in origin, who was imbued with the ideals of self-mastery, order, endurance, and self-sacrifice, each of them pursued with determination but not necessarily enthusiasm.[52] The usefulness of inculcating this mind-set in those who were later to be led into the slaughter pens of the Western Front should go without saying. Newbolt, who occupied a time warp that largely blocked out the twentieth century, turned the playing fields of Clifton School into a powerful synecdoche standing for the caparisoned glory of the English past. His blatantly didactic writing, saturated with a glassy-eyed vision of chivalric moonshine, celebrates a sort of Nietzschean *Übermensch* wielding a cricket bat instead of a club.

The son of a Staffordshire vicar, Newbolt came from a social stratum that Orwell was later to define as "lower upper middle class," that is to say a segment of society aware of the higher things in life but lacking the wherewithal to enjoy many of them. As a child he became preoccupied with heraldic devices and genealogical tables. From this sedentary hobby it was but an easy step to tales of knighthood in flower, with their grand but improbable demands upon loyalty, service, and self-sacrifice. War filled his youthful horizon despite (or because of) his timid personality. In preparatory school he learned nearly all of the *Aeneid* by heart, and he was thrilled when his headmaster alternated reports of the English campaign against the Ashanti with accounts of heroic deeds beside the walls of Ilium. He wrote poetry (in the Tennyson vein, of course) and adopted as his motto: "What do I wish for, save that it take fire."[53] Because of his fragility, these fires were fueled primarily by his brain.

His years at Clifton, a public school near Bristol, provided him with a perspective that he never outgrew—or wanted to. He was always haunted by his first sight of the place, which he described with an almost mystical feeling: "A wide green sward, level as a lawn, flooded in low sunlight, and covered in every direction with a multitude of white figures, standing, running, walking, bowling, throwing, batting—in every attitude that can express the energy and expectancy of youth."[54] The "white figures" on the sward are not knights or even monks, but merely cricketeers, who embodied for Newbolt the spirit that was forever England. As something of an outsider desperately longing to get inside, he seized upon this scene, which congealed then froze in his mind, as a kind of divine illumination. Newbolt was fortunate in escaping the usual bullying and fagging inflicted upon a new boy, for his mother rented a house opposite the College Close and came down from Staffordshire to take care of him. Too delicate for cricket and football, he nevertheless became an almost fanatical spectator and

throughout his life equated playing field with battlefield as two manifestations of heroical activity. Among his fellow students he carefully
cultivated martial spirits bound for glory like Douglas Haig. Artists and
the radical sort, like Roger Fry, he left alone.

Newbolt desperately wished to become a poet. He took great pains to
analyze verse plays and poems by counting lines and words per line in
order to penetrate the mystery of how great poets created their effects,
but their secret always eluded him. While at Oxford he wrote a long
Arthurian poem he titled *A Fair Death*, which was inspired by *Idylls of
the King*, only to become bitterly disenchanted when he learned that his
idol Tennyson had bowdlerized Malory's *Morte d'Arthur*. Newbolt fell
back on the study of law. In 1892 he tossed off a short poem inspired by
his nostalgia for Clifton School. "Vitai Lampada" was only a minor
effort, but it became, to Newbolt's great surprise, one of most frequently quoted poems in the English-speaking world. More than any
other single work it embodies, or embalms, the public school ideal of
the prewar years.

"Vitai Lampada" or "Torch of Life" comes from Lucretius' *De
Rerum Natura* and refers to an Athenian relay in which a torch is passed
from one runner to another.[55] In one stroke Newbolt fused those two
staples of the public school tradition—classical lore and athletics. The
first of its three stanzas concerns cricket:

> There's a breathless hush in the Close tonight—
> Ten to make and the match to win—
> A bumping pitch and a blinding light,
> An hour to play and the last man in.
> And it's not for the sake of a ribboned coat,
> Or the selfish hope of a season's fame,
> But his Captain's hand on his shoulder smote—
> "Play up! Play up! and play the game!"[56]

Up to this point the poem reads like an English version of "Casey at the
Bat," except that we never learn whether the batsman connects with the
ball. But homily, not narrative, is Newbolt's suit. In his second stanza
the cricket field is abruptly abandoned for a nameless battlefield:

> The sand of the desert is sodden red,—
> Red with the wreck of a square that broke;—
> The Gatling's jammed and the Colonel dead,
> And the regiment blind with dust and smoke.

> The river of death has brimmed his banks,
> And England's far, and Honour a name,
> But the voice of a schoolboy rallies the ranks:
> "Play up! play up! and play the game!"

The highest purpose served by a public school is to train its youths to serve king and country in an abstract war. Here the philathlete and the patriot are two facets of a single personality, cheerfully accepting defeat or death when duty calls. Lest one miss his point, Newbolt explains in his final stanza that the lesson to be learned at school is how to pass on to future generations, "like a torch in flame," the words "Play up! play up! and play the game!" This tag seemed to lodge like an implant in the brain of a whole generation. Visiting Canada in 1923, Newbolt found crowds roaring "play up!" and saw his words embellishing flags and memorials. The poem had become, as he said sadly, "a kind of Frankenstein monster that I created thirty years ago."[57]*

Having struck the right chord with "Vitaï Lampada," Newbolt wrote *Admirals All* (1897), a collection of poems about English sea power, which went through twenty-one editions of a thousand copies each within one year.[58] Flushed with success, he promptly resigned from the law to devote himself to patriotism and poetry. A fair sample is "Drake's Drum," written when the Kaiser was making another "threatening move" at sea. ("Threatening" for the English meant the launching of any significant warship in Germany.) It would have served as an epigraph for any number of invasion novels of the period, Wodehouse's *The Swoop!* excepted. As the Spanish Armada descends on England, Drake lies in a stupor in his hammock, but when roused to the danger, he proves invincible. Drake embodies the spirit that will infuse Englishmen whenever a crisis arises:

> Call him on the deep sea, call him up the Sound,
> Call him when ye sail to meet the foe;

*In the course of the twentieth century, "Playing the Game" has become perhaps the most familiar and influential cliché in the English-speaking world, assisted by the prefatory lines (a spin-off from the original) "It is not whether you win or lose but etc. . . ." Baden-Powell knew a good slogan when he saw one, for in the 1909 edition of *Scouting for Boys* one finds this advice for apprentice patriots: "Don't be disgraced like the young Romans who lost the Empire of their forefathers by being wishy-washy slackers without any go or patriotism in them. Play up! Each man in his place, and play the game!" See John Springhall, *Youth, Empire and Society: British Youth Movements, 1883–1940* (London, 1977), 58; for the source of Baden-Powell's wishy-washy Romans, see chapter 6.

> Where the old trade's plyin' and the old flag flyin'
> They shall find him ware and wakin', as they found him long
>   ago![59]

Although Newbolt assayed dialect poetry, he merely insulted it. His notion of natural language is to inject an occasional "ye" and to drop a final "g" (but never drop an "haitch"). Next to Kipling, who was writing soldier poems during this period, Newbolt sounds like a eunuch chorister. Yet the Admiralty became attentive to this bard of the couchant lion, and after Newbolt wrote a centenary account of Trafalgar he was rewarded by a week's cruise with the Channel Fleet. He repaid his debt with *Songs of the Fleet*. The Royal Navy had found its laureate. A knighthood followed in 1913. Newbolt had beaten his way into the College of Heralds by grafting a middle-class work ethic onto an ancillary stem of English poetry.

As poet, Newbolt reads like a junior-grade Tennyson trapped in the "Light Brigade" phase but revving up for an audience thirsting for red blood at a time when the British Empire is bleeding. He never sloughed off his infatuation with public school life, which in his mind became fused with the imagined splendors of the English race as these were defined by isolated, and often idiosyncratic, deeds of martial valor. A truncated schoolboy reverie advanced center stage in his poem "He Fell Among Thieves." This memorializes Lieutenant George Hayward, captured by Afghans in 1870 and sentenced to be shot at dawn. The Englishman broods all night, but he does not think of his impending death or of loved ones at home. Of course not—for this is a Newbolt poem. The thoughts of the doomed man focus upon his days at public school.

> He saw the School Close, sunny and green,
> The runner beside him, the stand by the parapet wall,
> The distant tape, and the crowd roaring between
> His name over all.
>
> He saw the dark wainscot and timbered roof,
> The long tables, and the faces merry and keen;
> The College Eight and their trainers dining aloof,
> The Dons on the dais serene.[60]

Fortified by these recollections, he stoically accepts his fate and even praises his English God for having given him a "glorious life." (We wait for a line about "playing the game," but Newbolt spares us.) As in

"Vitai Lampada," the major value of a public school education is that it teaches how to die violently, but properly. In Newbolt's poems of school life there is no room for bullies, weedy lawns, or dank weather: he is haunted by a dreamy landscape filled with green sward, flanneled youths, and gothicized halls.

What of the stay-at-homes, that comfortable majority of middle-class Englishmen who (like Sir Henry himself) were never given the opportunity to serve with Wolfe at Quebec or Gordon at Khartoum? Newbolt had a poem for them, too. "Ionicus" commemorated William Cory, an aging teacher at Eton who would break off lessons whenever soldiers marched past and take his class outdoors to watch them. Despite his "failing feet" and his "shoulders bowed," Cory would storm the Afghan mountain track or watch from *Victory's* deck "the sweep and splendour of England's war," thereby transcending his dull existence by vicarious participation in battle.[61] (There may have been other reasons for Cory's infatuation with soldiers and sailors: Eton eventually sacked him on suspicion of homosexuality.)

For Newbolt the Great War came as a moral crusade against Germany which "broke rules" by invading Belgium and sinking the *Lusitania.* Yet not even reports from the mayhem of Flanders and Picardy dislodged his romantic notions about heroism. Safely ensconced in his job as controller of wireless and cables at the Admiralty (later he joined Beaverbrook's propaganda operation, the Ministry of Information), he amused himself by fantasizing about what the Great-English-Poets would be doing in the war if resurrected: Shelley, a conscientious objector at first, ultimately proves his mettle by joining the Royal Flying Corps; Byron dies in Greece while waiting for an advance against the Turks; and Browning, as motorcycle dispatch rider, brings news to the British Expeditionary Force (B.E.F.) from Ghent.[62] When a fellow poet, Lawrence Binyon, showed him photographs of a French hospital where he had assisted in carrying in wounded from Verdun, Sir Henry confessed himself "mad with envy."[63] But he did not volunteer. Not even the sight and smell of actual wounded and mutilated soldiers ever quite turned into real flesh and blood for Newbolt. Walking in the garden of New College at Oxford, where the wounded of the Somme lay in tents on the lawn, he noted their empty sleeves and compared them with "the Homeric heroes in Elysium, talking of 'the ten years war in Troy.'"[64] One can only guess how these crippled veterans would have characterized Newbolt and company.

Perhaps Sir Henry's crowning achievement in the falsification of history is *The Book of the Happy Warrior* (1917), which attempted to demonstrate that public school boys (provided they were neither slackers nor pacifists) were direct descendants of the knights of yore, while Boy Scouts were the equivalent of their loyal squires.* Embellished with eight colored plates and twenty-five black-and-white illustrations, this book was written for the adolescent trade. According to Newbolt's argument, "Chivalry was a plan of life, a conscious ideal, an ardent attempt to save Europe from barbarism."[65] Far from being defunct, the "school of the Happy Warrior" still lies open to all nations and all classes "so long as there remain in the world wild beasts, savages, maniacs, autocrats, and worshippers of Woden"—a cut at the Kaiser's henchmen, who are the modern equivalent of ancient ogres and dragons.[66]

After chapters on Roland, Richard Coeur de Lion, Robin Hood (promoted by the author to knighthood because he loved sports and "knew how a gentleman should feel"), and other paladins, Newbolt expatiated on his favorite topic, the public school. This English institution combined two forms of education, the monastic and the chivalric. The earliest schools had an "inferior" purpose—training boys' minds for the church without regard for the values of the soldier, country gentleman, or businessman. William of Wykeham established the house system, and the housemaster became the schoolboy's equivalent of knight. It was he who "made men, not sneaks or bookworms" or "sham Latinists and sham saints."[67] The generation of 1793 saved Europe from Caesarism, but after Waterloo soldiering receded until the Boer War when it became apparent that "if our games are to be a thorough training for war, they must include throwing the bomb as well as the cricket ball."[68] In 1914 the enemy mistakenly believed that we could not develop an officer class in time, but they overlooked the men trained by the public school. Today there are only two classes "those who have been in the trenches and those who have not [sic]."[69] If chivalric fellowship prevails it will free the world of both the militarists and the pacifists. Of these two the pacifists are the greater menace because they desire peace through impossible means. They practice their passive virtue under protection of military force and to avoid

*The title is cribbed from Wordsworth's poem "Character of the Happy Warrior," which Newbolt willfully wrenches out of context. Wordsworth had nothing to say of chivalry, public schools, or martial display. His purpose was to define the moral qualities necessary for any man, in whatever station, who deserves the title of greatness.

service they use as justification the argument that Christianity forbids men to hate their neighbors. But the British soldier honors, not hates, his enemy even as he does his best to kill him.* And so on till the final line. "Peace is given only to the Happy Warrior, in life or in death."[70] Whether *The Book of the Happy Warrior* was written out of sheer ignorance or with malice aforethought, it is nonetheless an unconscionably jingoist book designed to wrench history into the service of recruiting fresh fodder for the guns of the Western Front.

Like many other emotional refugees from the Victorian era, Newbolt registered his distress when he read the war poets of the Sassoon-Owen generation with their unvarnished realism and their scorn for "dulce et decorum est . . ." abstractions. He regarded Wilfred Owen's work as the product of a mind somehow unhinged—certainly not that of a good team player, like Sir Douglas Haig:

> When I looked into Douglas Haig I saw what is really great,— perfect acceptance, which means perfect faith. Owen and the rest of the broken men rail at the old men who sent the young to die: they have suffered cruelly, but in the nerves and not the heart. . . . Paternity apart, what Englishman of fifty wouldn't far rather stop the shot himself than see the boys do it for him? I don't think these shell-shocked war poems will move our grand-children greatly— there's nothing fundamental or final about them.[71]

Since Newbolt had turned fifty-two in 1914, he was conveniently exempt from offering himself as a sacrifice.

Presumably more suitable as a war poem for grandchildren was Newbolt's "The Toy Band: A Song of the Great Retreat," a poem published in the *Times* in December 1914 and designed to boost morale at a period when England was doing poorly in the war.[72] (For Newbolt, even an English military disaster had to be warped into a euphemism like "Great Retreat.") This treats a battle-worn dragoon on the long withdrawal from Mons who regrets the absence of his regimental band. Finding a toy store, he distributes whistles and drums to his men, whose spirits soar nearly as high as the author's as they march to the

---

*In a letter written six days before the Armistice, Newbolt revealed a less benign view of how Germany must be treated: "I have come to believe that the best thing we can do is kill the accursed and that isn't a job to rejoice over. To *win a game* makes the pulses leap but not to massacre—that only chokes and disgusts [my italics]." See Patric Dickinson (ed.), *Selected Poems of Henry Newbolt* (London, 1981), 21. If it came to massacre as public policy, probably Sir Henry could have found reasons to justify it.

tunes of their improvised band. Wilfred Owen never wrote about adolescent frolics of toy soldiers in Never-Neverland.

The poetry of Sir Henry Newbolt is long on war and dying but short on blood and corpses. But then, as Ezra Pound wrote in retrospection, Newbolt was one of those literary figures who always looked "twice bathed."[73]

Homo newboltiensis was the demonstration of what Cyril Connolly, an Etonian of the postwar decade, called the Theory of Permanent Adolescence—a condition where the glories and sorrows of school life have become so intense that they dominate the youth's later life and arrest his emotional development. Connolly attributed this to the presence of the tag ends of a degenerate romanticism which emphasized growing up as a fall from grace without the compensation of future redemption. Reworking Wordsworth, he writes, "We enter the world trailing clouds of glory, childhood and boyhood follow and we are damned."[74] This accounted for, in his view, the number of public school men who become "haunted ruins" in middle life as they look back yearningly on their school years as a vanished Eden of grace and security. Memories of school become then a sequence of random events embalmed, like stray flies in amber—the clock striking the hours late at night, the rattle of tea things, the poking of smoldering wood fires—all "recollected in anguish" because they are unrecoverable. (Marcel Proust felt much the same way about evoking his childhood, but *school* life played only a minor part in it.) Other memoirs testify to the powerful impact of the public school on subsequent reconstructions of the experience. Robert Graves, who left Charterhouse on the eve of the Great War convinced that the public school spirit was a "fundamental evil," nevertheless records in *Good-bye to All That* a conversation with a classmate during their last days at the school. Despite their disaffection, they both recognize that in twenty years "we'll send our sons to Charterhouse for sentiment's sake, and they'll go through all we did."[75] This speaks volumes for the potency of the public school ideal in inculcating conformity even among those who are intellectually alienated from it.

Only about one-third of Newbolt's novel *The Twynams: A Tale of Youth* (1911) treats the school years of his hero, Percival Twynam, but as the title suggests that period figures as the most important. After five years at Downton School, Percy (a thinly disguised portrait of the author) acquires its tone—devotion without apparent enthusiasm, stoical Christianity, and self-mastery held in check by "the coolest common sense." Harsher features of public school life are excised completely from this narrative. There is none of the rugged vitality that carried *Tom Brown's School Days* through seventy editions during the author's lifetime and still makes the novel a good read. The raw strength of Tom Brown's "muscular Christianity" has degenerated in Percy Twynam into languid aestheticism and supine gentility. The post-Darwinist justification of the public school as appropriate incubator for "the struggle for life" is replaced by Newbolt with a conception that the school is a club for meeting the right people—and "right people" are defined as those exactly like yourself, except perhaps better connected and with more money.

The lesson contained in *The Twynams* is that playing the game means doing the right thing and awaiting the inevitable reward. Eventually Percy inherits the ancient Wiltshire seat of the Twynams because his principal rival, also a public school product, sends him a missing deed that invalidates his own claim! Impressed by the nobility of this sacrifice, Percy reciprocates by throwing the deed into the fire. All is not lost, however, for he marries his rival's sister and all three presumably live happily ever after. As a novel, *The Twynams* is important only because it reflects the exaggerated idealism of Newbolt, who in turn is only important because he mirrored the public school ethos on the eve of the Great War. For it required but few switches of emotional gears to exchange unquestioning loyalty to one's school for a blind enthusiasm for England's war.

Patriotism is not necessarily a vice (and it might even be argued that habits of blind obedience nurtured by the public school were a positive asset in the war), but hindsight suggests that England might have been better served had the leadership cadre, the majority of whom were public school men, been able to address themselves to the real causes of the war and to oppose the final drift over the brink. Unfortunately the habit of opposition, of going against the current, was not nurtured by the public school creed. It was simply much easier to adapt the idiom and the ritual of the great match at Rugby-Harrow-Eton to the new contest shaping up on the spongy plains of Ypres. For newcomers to battle, war *was* football, as this passage from a British captain's handbook of that epoch shows:

An army, in fact, tries to *work together* in a battle or a large manoeuvre in much the same way as a football team *plays together* in a match; and you need scarcely be told what an important thing that is if you want to win. The army *fights* for the good of its country as the *team plays* for the honour of its school. Regiments *assist* each other as players do when they *shove together* or *pass the ball* from one to another; exceptionally gallant *charges* and heroic *defences* correspond to brilliant *runs* and fine *tackling*. All work with one common impulse, given to the army by its general, to the team by its captain.[76]

The captain fails to discuss the many differences between a football and a grenade or a 5.9 shell.

The Great War resulted in the near-extinction of the species *Homo newboltiensis*. During the 1920s there was a reaction against the "old men" of the Victorian establishment, who were blamed for the extermination of nearly a million English lives—the original "lost generation." Increasingly, one heard from the young a satiric codicil attached to Wellington's reputed line about the playing fields of Eton—"Yes, but the Battle of the Somme was *lost* on the playing fields of Sherborne."[77] (For Sherborne read Eton, Harrow, Wellington, Marlborough. . . .) The gamesmanship taught on the playing field proved to be an inadequate preparation for the pitiless dehumanization of modern warfare encountered on the Western Front. As players in a new game in which one machine gunner—and the keyword here is *machine*—could bowl out the combined elevens of Eton and Harrow, the public school youth found, at first hand, the liabilities of his education. Kicking a football toward the German lines as one went over the top at the Battle of Loos in 1915 made cheerful news copy for folks keeping the home fires burning, but it failed to demoralize the enemy or to mitigate the attendant slaughter.

The pretty version of martial valor promulgated by Sir Henry Newbolt was effectively detonated by the high explosives of the Western Front even though it took the extermination of a new children's crusade to effect it. He retained his old following, yet for those who had been shocked into maturity by the war the poetry of Newbolt was as extinct as the droppings of the dodo bird. When the post of poet laureate was vacated in 1930, he was eliminated from the competition because the values he had espoused had become archaic, if not ridiculous. In Richard Aldington's novel *Death of a Hero* (1929), the protagonist George Winterbourne discovers that the horrors of war include not only killing Germans but enduring fossilized Englishmen at home like his mother's vacuous lover—"an adult Boy Scout, a Public School fag in shining armour, the armour of obtuseness."[78] That might also serve as an appropriate epitaph for the species *Homo newboltiensis*.

6 AT THE WICKET

▼

Then ye returned to your trinkets;
then ye contented your souls
With the flanneled fools at the wicket
or the muddied oafs at the goals.
RUDYARD KIPLING, *"The Islanders"*

Novels treating public schools constitute a large subgenre of English
fiction during the period immediately preceding the Great War, although their quality is uniformly undistinguished. In his preface to *The
Oppidan* Shane Leslie alludes to some forty novels that had attempted
to catch the essence of public school life before his student days at Eton
during the Boer War. While perhaps the majority of these were uncritical glorifications of the old school in the Newbolt vein, others
began to edge warily toward serious critiques of the system. An encroaching disenchantment rather than outright repudiation characterizes the mood of the rebel fringe, which includes three texts deserving extended commentary: Leslie's *The Oppidan* (1922), Arnold Lunn's
The Harrovian (1913), and Alex Waugh's *The Loom of Youth* (1917).

Although *The Oppidan* was written after the Great War, the events
portrayed and the attitudes conveyed in this novel about Eton place it at
century's end—marked in the book both by the Boer War that ended
the imperial dream and the death of the Queen whose departure defined
the end of an epoch of English history. In meticulously recreating
conditions experienced at Eton College by that schoolboy generation
which would be abruptly plunged into the Great War, Shane Leslie
(1885–1971) shows major cracks in the public school veneer which
would be opened by the harsh realities of the twentieth century. So long
as the world seemed the exclusive club of the British Empire, Eton was
no more challenged than the Academy of Noble Ecclesiastics in Rome

which functioned for the Church as a nursery for cardinals and nuncios. But the solid phalanx of Etonians in Parliament and in cabinets would shortly be swept away by the reforms of 1906 with its attendant political and social leveling. Public school men still had a head start in the race, but they no longer wore seven-league boots.

The Oppidan is a tale of failed initiation for a promising youth abruptly thrust into a repressive atmosphere ruled by exotic customs and unwritten laws "which were stronger than the Ten Commandments but, unfortunately, for new boys, not recited on Sundays."[1]* Two new boys, Darley and Socston, attempt to feel their way through this confusing microcosm in which the wrong step—failure to conform—can plummet the neophyte into excruciating self-torment. Peter Darley finds the pathway to acceptance narrow indeed, for he is a budding intellectual—or "sap," to use the Etonian term—in a country of Philistines and Philathletes. His fatal flaw lies in his eagerness to discover at school a place to develop his mind and to satisfy his idealistic spirit. What he finds is that "at Eton books were treated like outlaws and vermin, something outside the Mosaic code."[2] His friend Socston, however, is cut from the proper Eton cloth. Learning that success lies in becoming an ardent "wet-bob" or a "dry-bob"—Eton slang for aquatic and field sports—he opts for the river and in time rows for the College Eight, a major achievement because, among the students, the captain of Eton Boats outranks the admiral of the English fleet. Once he earns his colors as an oarsman, Socston terminates his friendship with Darley, for a "blood" loses face if he dares to fraternize with a despised "sap."

Leslie soft-pedals the overt brutality which characterizes so many memoirs and novels of public school life. Peter Darley, as the sensitive plant in a rank jungle, escapes the kind of torture inflicted on Cyril Connolly, who attended Eton just after the Great War and was made to stand on a mantle while a senior boy brandished a hot poker between his legs and made him dance and state his real name was "Ugly."[3] But Peter is nonetheless intimidated by the predatory atmosphere of the

*Oppidans are nonscholarship boys at Eton College. The scholars, or "Tugs," are separated from the Oppidans by "the same gulf that lay between Professionals and Gentlemen in the world of sport." Earlier the gulf had been wider. According to E. D. Coleridge, an Eton chronicler of the 1840s, no aristocrat would have been a Collegian because "such associates, cheek by jowl with the sons of Windsor tradesmen, would no more have amalgamated than the Rhine with the Rhone." See Shane Leslie, *The Oppidan* (New York, 1922), 48; Edward C. Mack, *British Schools and British Opinion, 1780 to 1860* (London, 1938), 363.

school, reduced by Leslie to ichthyic phyla: "In the Eton pool every fish sports and swims in awe of another minutely bigger or socially distinct."[4] This requires learning quickly a rigid code based upon inscrutable rules: only boys elected to "Pop," the exclusive honor society, are allowed to walk arm in arm; one is branded a "cad" if he is caught wearing a derby hat; sweaters are outlawed except for athletes (until a boy nearly dies of exposure in an unheated house and the rule must be changed).

Wherever Peter turns he faces the mindless idols of athleticism. His housemaster is universally acknowledged as a fool but retains his position because of his fine bowling for Cambridge in a match against the Australians a generation before. (That English loss in 1878 to the Australians—"raw-boned bearded giants"[5]—had produced a deep wound, one which never completely healed, for the Down-Under contingent with their harsh cockneyized language were never regarded as true gentlemen.) Eton had become an *athletocracy*. If there is one collective agony, however, it lies in the fact that within recent years Eton has been repeatedly downed by the "cads" of Harrow at the annual matches at Lord's. As one Old Boy, exploring ideas of how to improve the school, proclaims—"Of one thing I am certain. We all have one object in view, the improvement of cricket at Eton."[6] In such an atmosphere a boy like Peter Darley, useless at sports, learns to keep his mouth shut and to pretend to worship the local deities. If a boy grumbles, he will be told that worse things can happen to him—"You might be a cad and have to go to Harrow."[7] With a shudder, Peter recalls that his grandfather had been a Harrovian, but he has the good sense not to tell anyone.

Alienated by his incapacity for sports, Peter Darley wishes to prove his mettle by excellence in scholarship, defined at Eton by Greek and Latin. Science exists as a strange caddish dominion inhabited by freaks only a step or two removed from alchemists and conjurors. Curious chaps, these scientists—one boy gets an Oxbridge scholarship for his work in chemically analyzing a sixpence, another boy is at work dissecting a frog! A rumor ripples through the school that a science master has been detected taking photographs at the Windsor Fair. Decidedly not the thing to do—"he would want to take pupils next."[8] The assumption by the science teachers that they are equals with the classicists marks the first hint of revolution about to disrupt the equanimity of Eton. It was tarred with the same brush as the outlandish behavior of the women's movement: women who desired equal rights with men "could only be very unusual women"—and "unusual" for an Oppidan

meant odious.[9] For some masters Eton has already been too radi-
calized. For instance, German is now studied in the college, and all
because "the Prince Consort had set prizes for his horrible language."[10]
Not even the church is sacred anymore. A science teacher who had once
been invited to speak in chapel lectured on the probable gases let loose
at the Creation. Geography might prove useful if it described places
that England included in her empire, but it is not formally studied. In
classrooms students continue to use maps marked with places called
Byzantium and Euxine yet have never heard of Constantinople or the
Black Sea. All of them know something about Troy—but have never
heard of Gallipoli.

Driven inward, Peter responds favorably to the awesome majesty of
Eton as place, particularly at night when his predators are asleep in
their lairs and he has the freedom to dream: "The great buttresses,
caught in the freezing enchantment of the moon, seemed to pour like
icy waterfalls from the Chapel roof, thickening in their fall, until they
touched the white lunar lake which filled the School yard."[11] At such
times Eton becomes an extension of his own frozen, isolated sensibility.
Like a bad Georgian poet, Peter has become a diseased romantic, de-
tached from communal reality, inhabiting the cold surface of the moon.
In a telling episode, having heard a master expound the theory that
those whom the gods love die young, Peter wishes that he might die at
Eton and achieve recognition: "Could there be a sweeter fate than to die
in battle under the Wall and be gathered into the bosom of a mourning
Mother?"[12] Pathetically, the "battle under the Wall" refers not even to
combat in some far-flung corner of empire à la Newbolt, but only to
"Fives," a game originating at Eton. Games and gamesmanship seep
into every cranny of school life. As Peter stares at the Watts painting of
Sir Galahad in Upper Chapel, he thinks how remote the gentle pre-
Raphaelite face and clasped hands of the knight are from the present
Eton ideal, and he concludes that if Galahad were to return to earth he
would come not in armor to seek the Holy Grail but in pads to play for
Eton at the Wall.[13]*

*Such associations are legion in literature treating public school life. A St. Paul's graduate
remembered how a schoolboy, a Rowing Blue, read a fragment from the Bible at a
religious meeting and followed it with his exegesis. It meant "we must play hard. . . .
Christ would have played hard for His school, if He was at school today. . . . He said,
Christ might have rowed for the Varsity if there'd been any Varsity to row for." (Or
would Christ have acted as coxswain for the University of Galilee eight, while Simon
Peter and other disciples manned the oars?) Some years later he recorded that at
Cambridge he was rebuked for his agnosticism by another militant Christian who ex-

The Boer War comes and goes, the casualty lists overshadowed by the saturnalia that follows news of the Mafeking relief. "It was maddening to think that Baden-Powell was not an Etonian."[14] Beating on tin trays gummed with B-P's portrait, the boys file up the hill to Windsor Castle, that puissant symbol of imperial glory. Townspeople, when not "howling obscene references to Mr. Kruger's family life," give "three cheers for *Florit Etona*."[15] Only on such patriotic occasions are relationships with town cads acceptable, as Socston learns to his dismay after he is expelled for fraternizing with a lower-class girl at a local dance. All is not lost for him, however. As the school clerk puts it, "All you have to do is to go out to India or South Africa and win a D.S.O. Then they'll forgive you."[16]

In concluding *The Oppidan*, Leslie drew upon a shocking episode that had occurred during the great fire at Eton in 1903. A boy temporarily deranged after being tortured by older students set fire to a dormitory and two Etonians trapped in an upper room by the barred windows (installed to prevent boys from sneaking out at night) perished in the blaze. Edmond Warre, the headmaster, tried in vain to suppress references in the press to the barred windows, but he did not trouble to attend the double funeral.[17] In Leslie's novel one of the dead boys is Peter Darley, who had ironically yearned for death as a means of merging with the heroic ideals fostered by the school. Salvaged from the fire is a scrap of paper on which he had written:

> Stranger to Eton, a *sap* and misanthrope lies here,
> Shunned of all, yet only to the Muses dear.[18]

Fortunately for the headmaster, Darley was an orphan and no outraged and influential parent was at hand to demand an explanation for his death. In the concluding scene of the novel the funeral of an obscure Eton misfit serves as a portent for the generation shortly to be consumed by the flames of the Great War: "Slowly the School poured into the familiar Yard and into the Long Walk as though their generation had been consecrated by the Service they had attended, and as though they were also doomed to pass through some far-off and fiery harvest, of which the first fruits had been mysteriously reaped before their eyes."[19]

---

claimed, "Why don't you believe in Jesus, you bloody bastard? Why don't you fall down on your knees and pray to the bleeding God?" Here was "muscular Christianity," quite literally. See Arthur Calder-Marshall, "More Frank than Buchman," in Graham Greene (ed.), *The Old School* (London, 1934), 64, 68.

The principal value of *The Oppidan* lies in its exploitation of a rich vein of social history rather than its delineation of character. If it survives as a novel, it will be read as an ethnographical document like *Coming of Age in Samoa* rather than as an English version of *Portrait of the Artist as a Young Man*. As the author noted in his preface, the problem of creating a novel from the "Matter of Eton"—or any other public school—lies in creating three-dimensional characters out of an environment in which stereotypes were the ideal as well as the norm. Whatever its limitations, *The Oppidan* forcefully draws attention to the mindlessness and absurdities in a sacrosanct English institution by describing conditions which, in the author's view, were in part responsible for the complacent sacrifice of a generation of young Englishmen.

▼

"On or about December 1910 human character changed."[20] Virginia Woolf's famous remark, in reference to the appearance of iconoclastic books like *The Way of All Flesh* and to the notorious Postimpressionist Exhibition in London, finds its echo elsewhere in the political and economic character of England in this period. The Irish were demanding home rule, women were demanding the vote, the passing of Edward VII marked the end of a brief cosmopolitan outlook on the part of the monarchy. Yet, the most far-reaching changes were being enacted in Parliament. In 1909 Lloyd George had prepared his "People's Budget" aimed to diminish the power of the rich by increasing death duties, imposing an income tax on incomes above 5,000 pounds per annum, and taxing undeveloped land. The House of Lords responded by overwhelmingly rejecting this budget only to be stripped of its veto power by the Parliament Act of 1911, which in effect terminated the political power of the English aristocracy.

As a class, however, the aristocracy continued to play the dominant role in social and cultural affairs, for it set standards which were mimicked and revered by large numbers of English citizens of all ranks. Democracy was not achieved merely by passing an act of legislation. In *The Decline of Aristocracy* (1912) Arthur Ponsonby (1871–1946), a Liberal M.P., addressed this problem of influence for good or for ill. Starting from the premise that "aristocrats, however decadent, cannot be abolished any more than anarchists, however dangerous," he argues that the present aristocracy as a class has no outstanding qualities, being neither elected nor selected.[21]

Their boast of distinguished lineage he exposes as a sham; the peerage contains only thirty-seven members whose ancestors held their titles prior to the seventeenth century, while the greatest number has been recruited from the middle class within the past fifty years. Their values had deteriorated with surprising swiftness. Their appetite for money was as ravenous as it was for the middle classes, which they professed to despise. The root cause of their failure lay with their education—or lack of it. Once a good education had been the mark of a gentleman, but about the time that educational opportunities had filtered down into the commercial classes, the old landed aristocracy began to lose its incentives for intellectual distinction. Ponsonby noted the contrast between the libraries of old country houses, which revealed superb collections of literature and history, and the reading matter of the present aristocracy, who seemed consumed by vulgar weekly magazines and cheap novels. Modern gentlemen had lost their knowledge of the classics and failed to fill the blank with proficiency in anything else. Worse, "they are not only proud they do not understand but also proud that they understand that it is better not to understand."[22]

Ponsonby did not call for elimination of the aristocracy but only a heightened awareness within this class of their moral lassitude so that they might assist the rising middle class in combatting what he feared would become the great evil of the future—a spawning, self-serving plutocracy. The key to opening a great future for England lay in major reforms of the public schools. Not even the best of these pioneered new ideas but lagged behind until outside pressure compelled changes. What was taught, without exception, was class prejudice. Locked within a curriculum designed not for utility but for providing a cachet of gentility, the schoolboy was taught to believe, as though it were a scientific law, that ninety-five percent of the nation existed solely to serve the remaining five. He acquired "no idea of how wealth of a nation is built up, how the business of a nation is carried on, or even how their own needs and requirements are satisfied."[23] A telltale signal that the public school had lost itself in the modern age was the fact that the Royal Navy chose to recruit its future officers from its own schools rather than rely upon gentlemen amateurs, one of whom told Ponsonby that the only *practical* skill he had learned at public school was how to bank a proper fire.

The Decline of Aristocracy is an impressionistic but sensible work which examines social conditions on the eve of the Great War. Ponsonby offered a series of radical measures in education to allow England to catch up with progressive nations on the Continent. Boys should be taught political economy, industrial history, economics, natural science, and *recent* English history. Above all, a strategy had to be found to correct the major flaw in public school education—"an entire absorption in games to the exclusion of practically all other interests."[24]

It was too late for reform. Games by this time were so deeply tentacled in the root of the public school ideal that to wrench them out would have torn the organism to pieces. It had not always been so. Originally only informal diversions for boys at schools, games had been institutionalized in the early 1850s at Marlborough specifically as a means of controlling what the headmaster called "a school of mutineers" who bullied the staff and spread havoc among the local residents by their poaching, fighting, and stealing.[25]* This expedient proved so successful that other schools, most of them beset with similar problems in social control, gratefully followed. Moreover, on grounds—probably mistaken—that intense physical activity served to deplete the sexual libido, some masters took the attitude, "Send the boys to bed tired, and you'll have no trouble."[26] In 1853 Harrow organized its Philathletic Club, consisting of thirty pupils as an elite corps, which promised to utilize recreation leading "to the maintenance of order and discipline through the school."[27] It was truly the beginning of a revolution in the value system of the Victorians. Between 1850 and 1900 the number of acres used exclusively for school games increased from 8 to 146 at Harrow, from 2 to 68 at Marlborough, with comparable increases estimated elsewhere.[28] Matches between houses were succeeded by interscholastic battles like the fiercely contested Eton-Harrow cricket match which had to be fought on neutral ground to prevent physical harassment of the visiting team. During the 1850s there were scarcely enough spectators at this match to form a line around the ground; however, by 1871 more then 27,000 viewers paid their shilling to watch the match at Lord's (an appropriate name for the playing field).[29] Fanatical partisanship gripped the spectators. At the Eton victory of 1910 a distinguished cabinet minister was observed hysterically dancing on the Harrovian flag—perfectly reasonable behavior.[30]

From recreation, games evolved with explosive force into religion.

---

*According to J. R. S. Honey, an historian of English public schools, the remark ascribed to Wellington about Waterloo and Eton's playing fields would have referred mainly to "semi-organised brawls and fisticuffs—on at least one occasion involving a boy's death— at Eton during the early part of the century." See J. R. S. Honey, *Tom Brown's Universe: The Development of the Victorian Public School* (London, 1977), 111. Cricket existed that early but was not compulsory or even highly regarded as an activity for youths.

Between 1880 and 1900 they became compulsory in most public schools. During important matches boys not playing were required to become cheering spectators, and if their cheers were not lusty enough, they might be whipped by prefects afterward or slashed on the legs on the spot. Physical punishment was de rigueur. Sports that inflicted no pain got on slowly. Tennis—called "pat-ball" by bloods—could even be played by girls, while golf was favored by peculiar Scotsmen in skirts. The goal for all boys seemed to be some kind of physical suffering as the primary rite de passage to manhood. It was only fair that if bloods took their punishment on the playing fields, then lesser youths should take it at the end of switch, paddle, or strap. Beatings were a kind of vicarious athletics, recalled an Etonian: "Flogging there, and the endurance of flogging, were as much a form of athletics as compulsory football."[31]

This was the age of gorgeous athletic millinery in which the participants created for themselves honorific trappings as badges of their prowess—caps, badges, ties, belts, blazers, buttons, tassels, and scarves—as complex in nuance as the bones and feathers adorning an African warrior or the regalia of the Grenadier Guard. A major growth industry arose of school fiction which quickly became standard fare in magazines for boys like *Boys' Own Paper* and *Union Jack*. One of the first novels of P. G. Wodehouse, *Mike. A Public School Story*, was first serialized in *The Captain*, a boys' magazine, and typifies the genre. It is a school novel in which the school does not figure at all except as a vehicle for cricket and a brief account of a boy shooting cats in the headmaster's garden with an air pistol. What readers wanted at that time, Wodehouse explained forty years later, was "lots of cricket."[32] They got it. Except for a donnybrook between the Wrykyn boys and a gang of town rowdies which climaxed by throwing a police officer into a horsepond, there is very little else.

The English infatuation with sports during the late Victorian period reflected the desire of a burgeoning, wealthy middle class to acquire the honorary status of instant gentleman for their male offspring by rigid conformity to the mores of the public school. Fox hunting and grouse shooting, which had been the dominant sports of the eighteenth-century aristocrat, were slowly drying up in industrialized England and, except for the very rich, were inaccessible to the new monied class. School games gave this class an opportunity to compete with the landed aristocracy on even terms. The rising middle class of the Victorian era had little access to the shooting, fishing, and riding which had formerly defined "sport" for the gentry, but this disadvantage had largely been neutralized by the ability to hit, throw, bump, or kick a ball. As a means of providing youths with an acceptable caste mark, the public school attracted the new monied class "as filings to a magnet."[33] Insecure about their status and hopelessly in awe of the traditional gentleman, such people were the last to insist upon reforms in an antiquated educational system. What they desired for their male children were certificates of membership into the English elite caste; education was of secondary importance, when it was considered at all. Although it seems incongruous that sons of businessmen and manufacturers, saturated as they were in the work-ethic, would accept the "romantic" frivolity implicit in the public school obsession with games, they acquiesced as the price to pay for climbing the social ladder. They recognized as gospel truth what the headmaster at Rodley School announced in 1872: "The public school can confer an aristocracy on boys who do not inherit it."[34] Perhaps, too, as a scholar of English athleticism has suggested, upper middle-class fathers, acutely aware that they were undistinguished in anything except making money, sought a heroic ideal for their sons.[35] Certainly the connection between athletics and future success as a captain of empire was not lost upon a youth at Shrewsbury School who cleverly sized up the system and charted his personal course to match: "I shall row myself into the Sudan, a country of Blacks ruled by Blues."[36]

A novel which captures public school at the peak of its prestige and prosperity, just before the outbreak of the Great War, is Arnold Lunn's *The Harrovian* (1913), which passed through four editions in its first year. It has been called by a scholar of English public schools "an acid piece of muckraking" for its critique of life at Harrow.[37] Muckraking it surely is not, although Lunn (1888–1974) displays none of the reverence that had marked Newbolt's groveling worship before the public school idols.

Lunn's quarrel is less with Harrow than with the stuffiness of the adult world which imposes Harrow as a goal for impressionable youths. His protagonist, Peter O'Brien, is a tough-minded skeptic who has been adopted, after his parents' death, by an aunt and uncle, a couple that "most resembled Euclidean definition of a surface—that which has breadth without depth."[38] The Hampdens inhabit a middle-class burrow, place their faith in a "vague unmiraculous Christianity," and believe as an article of faith that the unemployed exist because God intended them to be unemployed. The uncle has somehow contracted the "Oxford manner" and cultivates a voice that seems to issue with difficulty from the roof of his mouth—a sound like "a man talking down the nozzle of a water-can." Lunn posits the existence of an unbridgeable generation gap: whatever the liabilities of the young, they are nevertheless distinct and preferable to those of their elders.

At Harrow Peter is subjected to the usual physical harassment both on and off the playing field, but he has luck in falling in with a group of new boys who, while acquiescing in the modus operandi of the school, fortify each other through their trenchant criticism of it. Their absence of illusions would have repelled *Homo newboltiensis*. In discussing "footer," one asks, "Did you ever hear anyone say, 'Play up, you fellow?,'" to which another responds, "They once worked down to 'Play up, you ugly swine!'—that was the mildest they ever go to."[39] From start to finish football is synonymous with verbal and physical abuse. There is nothing gentlemanly about throwing a small boy into a game against those twice his size, and they know it.* They dissect the monitorial system, which provides older boys with an opportunity for beating younger ones, not to improve their character but simply because "the average man likes whopping others."[40] Since no new boy can possibly master all the unwritten rules, the "priv" can lie in wait until he finds his prey ignorant of the prohibition against wearing carpet slippers, or something as trivial, and then decree an "official" punishment. Peter's friend Kendal mockingly refers to "'our grand old monitorial system, the bulwark of our great Public Schools.' Wasn't Arnold the name of the blighter who patented it?"[41] On another occasion the young rebels quote from a newspaper which pushes the weary playing-fields-of-Eton theme: "It is precisely the discipline of the Playing Fields, the suppression of individual display in the interests of the side, that wins not only the mimic warfare of the playing field. . . ." To this Kendal exclaims, "Chuck it away! A man who uses a tag which one's aunts are beginning to understand should be shot."[42] They ceremonially burn the offending article.

Despite their disclaimers, the boys are not exempt from the virus of athleticism. After all, they are only boys susceptible to hero worship,

---

*An American physical culturist touring English public schools during the 1920s, after observing the punishment administered small boys by large ones in football games, suggested that the nearest American equivalent to "blood," the slang term for athlete, was the word "bully"—designating those whose aim was to domineer by sheer brute force. See J. A. Mangan, *Athleticism in the Victorian and Edwardian Public School* (Cambridge, 1977), 177.

and what other models exist for emulation? The "beaks," or masters, are a poor lot. (A chapter titled "Comic Relief" recounts how boys team up to humiliate a weak master.) Religion offers no guide. The chapel exists primarily for pompous celebrations or asylum for boys escaping persecution. Peter imagines how a housemaster might lecture young Jesus on His indiscreet behavior: "Your views, dear boy, are Quixotic. They might go down in a Quaker School, but they won't help you in the rough and tumble of Harrow life."[43] When hunger marchers come from London and gather outside the Bill Yard, the boys laugh at the illiterate speech of the leader, because they have been taught by their fathers that poverty is the direct result of laziness, drunkenness, or worse. The failure to sympathize "was not their fault. It was not the fault of Harrow. Public Schools do not create—they only fail to expel— class insolence."[44] Peter's letter protesting the boys' insensitivity is not published in *The Harrovian*, which had already endorsed the house- master whose solution to the problem is to turn a hose on the marchers.

What system of values remains except that offered by the example of the Harrow cricketeer scoring his century at Lord's? Peter O'Brien admits that "there is something of religion in it," not derived from the Hebraic tradition but "Greek in its frank worship of physical prowess, and catching the note of the Olympic Games, where religion and athlet- ics went hand in hand."[45] Lunn honestly confronts the paradox that had baffled two generations of public school reformers: games are at once rationally ridiculous yet emotionally sublime. A boy may hate his house, yet in the heat of a contest "he will forget everything save that he is a unit in a society represented by eleven good men and true, and that a rival House must be humbled in the dust."[46] Here was xenophobic nationalism on a schoolboy level, which would be readily transmuted into jingoistic ethnocentrism in the war against the Germans, which lay only a year in the future.* Boys are not the only celebrants in the hysterical saturnalia taking place each year at Lord's. Among the heat- ed spectators are "the Cabinet Minister who's much more excited in the match than in the Cabinet crisis; and there's the Bishop, who looks gratified when the bluff old General says 'damn' on the fall of a Harrow wicket; and the ol' Harrovian master who can't bear the strain and retires behind the Pavy [Pavilion] to pray."[47]

*In his autobiography Lunn refers to the bloods as a samurai caste, "trained for England and Empire." The function of the intellectuals at Harrow is to do their academic work for them. He recalls how one cricketeer raffled his homework assignments each Saturday evening, using tickets drawn from a bag. See Arnold Lunn, *Come What May: An Auto- biography* (London, 1940), 29.

Eventually Peter O'Brien becomes head of his house at Harrow and effects a few minor reforms like taking away "whopping privileges" from certain (but not all) senior boys. Like most public school novels, *The Harrovian* ends with the departure of the protagonist to the outer world. While Lunn concludes on a rising note—his belief that the system may be reshaped from within—this seems contrived, for the Harrow he has depicted is oppressively parochial, trivial, and cruel. The best, and worst, that can be said of it as a training ground for young Englishmen had already been stated by Peter earlier in the novel: "Blessed are those that learn to kill the young men of other countries with the greatest possible dispatch."[48] For 1913 this was a prescient observation; opportunities for testing it lay immediately ahead.

By far the most notorious public school novel of this period was *The Loom of Youth*, written by Alec Waugh (1898–1981) about his experiences at Sherborne School during the Great War. Published in July 1917, while Waugh was posted as a subaltern on the Western Front, the book unleashed a heated controversy in the press, which elevated it to best-seller status by Christmas. Anxious parents barraged housemasters throughout England demanding assurances that their sons would not be exposed to attitudes and conditions described in Waugh's novel. An ex-headmaster of Eton penned a ten-page rebuttal, while a critic predicted that the work would become the *Uncle Tom's Cabin* of the public school system.[49] Evelyn Waugh has recorded that his brother's novel destroyed friendships in their father's circle and forced him to Lancing School because he would have been persona non grata at Sherborne.[50]

Adding to the furor aroused by the book, Thomas Seccombe, an instructor at Sandhurst (and therefore a voice presumed to be speaking for the army), wrote a preface which debunked the role of the public school as a preparation for modern war. The problem with such schools, Seccombe declared, was that they created "Little Englanders" with the attitude that "England is top dog, that's enough." It was true that the patriotism inculcated by the public school tradition had "fairly helped to get us out of the mess of August 1914," he conceded. "Yes, but it contributed heavily to get us into it."[51] This was a strong indictment, coming as it did in 1917 when school honor rolls listing the war dead had already reached shocking proportions. (A final tally would show that approximately one-quarter of all public school men who served in the war had been killed.)[52]

The opening scenes of *The Loom of Youth* might have been written by Henry Newbolt. Gordon Caruthers arrives at Fernhurst School and is awed by the antique grandeur of the place. In the dining room a statue of Edward VI looks down on rows of tables and creates a mood that wafts one back to a chivalric age. But once incorporated within this facade, Gordon experiences rapid disenchantment. The primitive physical conditions—ten boys sleeping in one room contemptuously called "The Nursery" and four baths for eighty boys—Gordon gamely accepts.* He is less prepared for the foul language and the nearly exclusive focus of Fernhurst on sports. At his preparatory school athletics existed merely to condition the body; at Fernhurst "they seemed the one thing that mattered."[53] With their blue and gold ribbons the bloods are exempt from laws that govern mere mortal boys. Fortunately, Gordon has a keen appetite for sports and a capacity for taking physical punishment. His first step out of the limbo of new boy status comes when he is given the choice of learning a hundred lines or taking a beating. He opts for the six strokes and afterward is congratulated by a blood—"Damned plucky of you."[54] Gordon tastes his first success at Fernhurst.†

In *The Oppidan* the young protagonist is destroyed because he fails to fit into the iron mail of the public school; in *The Loom of Youth* the youth degenerates because he wears the armor all too well. The loom determines what design must be woven from its raw materials. Gordon arrived at Fernhurst with a desire to excel, and he assumed that the measure of excellence would be intellectual and moral. He discovers that "success lay in a blind worship at the shrine of the god of Athleticism. Honesty, virtue, moral determination—these mattered not at all."[55] Cheating is rampant. Translations of classical texts (officially prohibited in the school) are passed from boy to boy under the nose of a senile master. Lying is a natural first line of defense for a boy accused of violating a rule; he confesses only when proof against him is irrefutable. The masters make a travesty of intellectual pursuit. Imitation is the backbone of their method, which is "mould your Latin on Vergil, your

*By standards of the time these conditions were almost luxurious. At Charterhouse no baths at all existed until 1903. As late as 1912 the head of an Oxford college acidly opposed installing a bathroom, because the young men were in residence for only eight weeks at a time. Let them bathe when they got home. See Honey, *Tom Brown's Universe*, 212.

†English social behavior changed but slowly. Fifty years earlier, the father of Virginia Woolf had written of his public school days, "To be flogged in accordance with traditions handed down from hoar antiquity, and embodied in a special local jargon, is to have gone through a sacred initiating rite." See Edward C. Mack, *Public Schools and British Opinion Since 1860* (New York, 1941), 136.

English on Matthew Arnold but don't think for yourself."⁵⁶ By the time he reaches the fifth form, the standard Fernhurst boy has read all the poetry he will ever know; he appreciates Kipling's rousing lines about empire, some choice bits of *Don Juan* as legitimate pornography, and a few scraps and tags of Shakespeare. Keats—no sportsman and mucky about women—is so much nonsense.

Waugh uses a dialectical method to perform his biopsy of the public school ethos. Caruthers is midrope in an ideological tug-of-war between Buller, the games master seeking to control his body, and Ferrers, a new master seeking to open his mind. Although Gordon succeeds on Buller's turf, he begins to question the value of being able to kick goals from the twenty-five. Ferrers, on the other hand, represents the winds of change beginning to blow through England and gusting even at a traditionalist stronghold like Fernhurst. He denounces the study of classics as merely mimetic exercise, quotes *Sinister Street* as evidence of the shallowness of conventional education, and argues that the best minds, like those of Wells and Bennett, missed public school altogether. He scorns games as nothing more than recreation and school ideals as "a mud-heap that had to be washed clean."⁵⁷ Ferrers altogether represents the spirit of a new iconoclastic generation of intellectuals "heedless of tradition, probing the root of everything."⁵⁸ Through his influence Caruthers rediscovers the life of the mind, attends readings at the Poetry Bookshop in Devonshire Street (a haunt of the Georgian poets prior to the war), and becomes a devotee of Rupert Brooke.

When the war breaks out Ferrers is ecstatic. War will be the crucible in which ossified traditions and ideas will be turned to ashes: "Glorious! Glorious! A war is what we want. It will wake us up from sleeping; stir us into life; inform our literature. There's a real chance now of sweeping away the old outworn traditions. In a great fire they will all be burned. Then we can build afresh."⁵⁹ Ferrers loosely paraphrases Rupert Brooke's hawkish sonnet of 1914, "Peace," with its endorsement of war as means of self-purification and escape from a corrupt environment.⁶⁰ He only regrets that his disability, a weak heart, must bar him from joining the fight—but it is a great opportunity for healthy youths like Gordon! Under the stimulation of this false prophet Gordon envisions "an age rising out of these purging fires that would rival the Elizabethan."⁶¹ The fallacy of this argument, as he soon learns, is that his generation, entrusted with the mission of effecting a spiritual rebirth, must fuel the purging flames with their lives. Ferrers' rules for playing the game prove to be as futile as Buller's—and perhaps more dangerous. Mindless conformity may have led England into the war, but radical individualism provides no pathway out. During Gordon's final year at Fernhurst, an old boy who has seen fighting in France revisits the school and confides that the Rupert Brooke vision of war is a fraud. His outburst to Gordon may well be the first articulation of the "lost generation" theme which would become a commonplace in the fiction of writers like Remarque and Hemingway in the 1920s: "All our generation has been sacrificed. . . . For the time being art and literature are dead. Look at the rotten stuff that's being written to-day. At the beginning we were deceived by the tinsel of war; Romance dies hard. But we know now. We're done with fairy tales. There is nothing glorious in war. No good can come of it. It's bloody, utterly bloody."[62]

Near the end of *The Loom of Youth* Gordon participates in a school debate on the question, "The Value of Athletics." He cites A. C. Benson's argument that for twenty years the public schoolboy, conditioned to play rather than work, has been steadily losing ground in competition against those who study hard subjects unrelated to cricket and football. Buller listens with mounting anger as this apostate—no contemptible milksop, but a star athlete—attacks the central pivot of the English educational system: "Some fool said 'the battle of Waterloo was won on the playing fields of Eton'; and a fool he was, too. Games don't win battles, but brains do, and brains aren't trained on the footer field."[63] For all this icon-smashing zeal, Gordon has become so trapped within games worship that he takes particular relish in the victory of his house over Buller's in the final cricket match, even though he consciously knows that he has wasted his last years at Fernhurst by trying to upset Buller, a man whom personally he admires. He had become an egoist and iconoclast without acquiring anything positive by way of values to substitute for games. Gordon has worked through thesis and antithesis, only to find that synthesis has eluded him. In the final scene of the novel, as the train carries him away from Fernhurst, he feels drained of will and purpose, and he knows he will not return because "the glamour with which he had surrounded the grey studies and green walks of Fernhurst [were] merely a mist of sentiment that would fade away."[64]

When placed against postwar critiques of public school life like Robert Graves' *Good-bye to All That* (1929) or Cyril Connolly's *Enemies of Promise* (1939), Waugh's novel seems tame stuff, hardly deserving the hullabaloo that greeted its publication in 1917. But conservatives promptly drew their broadswords and waded into attack. Criticism of the public school tradition was tantamount to criticism of England herself, and this was all the more unsporting because the country was at war. Martin Browne, an Etonian, replied with a 120-page rebuttal titled *A Dream of Youth* (1918), a sophomoric work which mustered all the hackneyed arguments that had been used for half a century in boosting the sagging system; namely, public schools inculcate a sense of duty, there is great freedom in the system, athletics are necessary for exercise, and yawningly so forth.[65] Of greater weight, Edward Lyttelton, headmaster at Eton whose brother Alfred had been the most gifted athlete in England during the Edwardian period, warned that Waugh's novel should not be read, particularly during wartime, because of its distortions of school life.[66] (This from a former cricketeer who confessed that he never walked up the aisle of a church without bowling an imaginary ball down it and wondering about its spin.)[67] Nearly ten years later public school supporters were still licking wounds inflicted by Waugh, for a writer in *Quarterly Review*, lacking any argument more potent, accused him of "blasphemy and meanness just because his own mind is a naturally unpleasant one."[68] Had Waugh not shown his readiness to "play the game" by frontline service as a machine gun commander in France (he was captured in the big German push of March 1918 and imprisoned in Mainz till the end of the war), attacks on his book and his character would doubtless have been more corrosive.

What the war years required were books like Ian Hay's *The Lighter Side of School Life* (1915), which simply transmogrified the defects of the English system—xenophobia, athleticism, rote learning, and conformity—into virtues which accounted for the superiority of Englishmen.* These frothy sketches, originally circulated in *Blackwood's Magazine*, were designed to dispel whatever doubts arose about the value of the public school product. At school the boy is taught to worship "bodily strength, bodily grace, swiftness of foot, straightness of eye, dashing courage, and ability to handle a bat or a gun."[69] Furthermore, these must be *natural* attainments, acquired without undue practice or pains. The ideal is to jump five feet four inches without training for the event, because only then can one preserve his amateur status. Gentlemen must be amateurs in war and in peace, never professionals. "To an Englishman, a real hero is a man who wins a champion-

*Ian Hay was the pen name of John Hay Beith (1876–1952), whose fictionalized account of a "typical regiment in Kitchener's Army," *The First Hundred Thousand* (1915), was a runaway best-seller which glorified the BEF during the opening phase of the Great War.

ship in the morning, despite the fact that he was dead drunk the night before."[70] True Englishmen deplore the "unsportsmanlike" way in which American oarsmen train for a race; to reveal yourself eager to win is very bad form.

This amateur status must also inform the schoolboy's study pattern. Brilliance in scholarship is acceptable only if the student is not suspected of application, otherwise he is nothing but a "swat." Moreover, he must be careful not to show that he takes pleasure in his work and always to present a "flippant front to the world."[71] Often the academic star is that boy who disappears on Sunday walks to sit behind hedges in a cold east wind and read his Thucydides. "An Englishman dislikes brains almost as much as he worships force of character."[72] Mere cleverness he associates with sharp practices. Even worse is the vice of boasting, which is as epidemic among Prussians as their ludicrous attempts to speak the King's English. Hay lampoons a German master in an English school who regales his class with accounts of how he had been warmly thanked by the Emperor, Moltke, and Bismarck for his service at the Battle of Sedan. "You liddle Engleesh boys," he says, "you think your Army is great. In my gontry it would be noding—noding!"[73] Germans replace Frenchmen as the butt of jokes in English schools—at least for the duration of the war.

Hay assures his readers that public schools are directed by gentlemen of the first rank, for it is well established that "a man who can run a great public school can run an Empire."[74] In answering those reformers who have urged revision of the curriculum to adapt to modern times, Hay cites the reply of a headmaster to a brash parent who complained that his boy was not being prepared for a specific profession: "Unfortunately, sir, the fees of this school and the members of its Staff are calculated upon a *table d'hôte* basis. If you want to have your son educated *à la carte,* you must get a private tutor for him."[75]

The final lines of *The Lighter Side of School Life* epitomize the public school ethos as it existed before the breakup of the empire after the Great War:

> When the daily, hourly business of a nation is to govern hundreds of other nations, perhaps it is well to do so through the medium of men who, by merging their own individuality in a common stock, have evolved a standard of Character and Manners which while never meteoric, seldom brilliant, too often hopelessly dull, is always conscientious, generally efficient, and never, never tyrannical or corrupt. If this be mediocrity, who would soar?[76]

It is revealing that Hay capitalized *Character* and *Manners,* as though these pretty abstractions drawn from ancient codes of chivalry were adequate weaponry in facing dragons of twentieth-century technology and democracy. Faced with these dismal expectations for their youth, it is little wonder that thoughtful Englishmen began to question the goals of public school education. A Conservative like Sir Ian Hamilton might manage a hesitant endorsement—"Through Eton lay the royal road— to something," while a Liberal like George Bernard Shaw could exclaim in exasperation, "Eton, Harrow, Winchester . . . and their cheaper and more pernicious imitators should be razed to the ground and their foundations sown with salt."[77]

There exist documents without number testifying to the value of the public school experience as a training ground for the Great War. After all, it was relatively easy to convert one's inventory of loyalties from school to king-and-country. Playing field simply became battlefield. In peace only a privilege few could play for their school at Lord's, but in war every boy could take his bat and face the Germans at the wicket. Ronald Gurner, a war poet from Marlborough, recalled that at his school boys responded to the outbreak of war as if it were "a glorified football match in which, if peace did not come, they might take their places in the English team."[78] It might be argued that the values inculcated by the public school were a positive asset for those engaged in a war calling primarily for physical endurance rather than mental facility. After all, what good was imagination or intellect to a soldier undergoing the mindless pounding of trench warfare? What counted was one's ability to take punishment, and in that subject the public school boy had received a superb education. The proposition was contained in the words of a late Victorian headmaster preparing a boy for a thrashing, "TAKE DOWN YOUR BREECHES LIKE A MAN!"[79] Having endured this sort of education, the public school boy was probably as ready for the carrion fields of Flanders as the Tynesider or the Lancashire collier who had graduated only from the school of hard knocks.

7 PETER PAN'S ENGLAND

▼

To die will be an awfully big adventure.
J. M. BARRIE, *Peter Pan*

As we have seen, much of the popular literature of England written during the four decades that preceded the Great War contains heavy infusions of patriotic tonic concocted to stiffen the backbone and to thicken the blood of an effete readership on the verge of forgetting that the price to be paid for basking in the late Victorian sunshine must ultimately be an unstinting willingness to sacrifice self for king and country. While the decision to fight or not to fight rested with politicians reacting to the imagined, or actual, weather vanes of Realpolitik, many writers helped to make that decision palatable by fabricating tales which fostered a spirit of bellicose nationalism. Sometimes their work blew trumpets of alarm; at other times their writings functioned like subliminal recruitment posters which deposited messages in the reader's brain to be retrieved and acted on at a future time. It would be absurd to claim that popular literature *caused* the Great War, but its impregnation with xenophobic and paranoid warnings of Armageddon did assist in creating a climate of popular opinion that almost unanimously cheered the decision of Parliament to declare war on imperial Germany in August 1914. War fever has a way of encroaching into literary works which, on first reading, one would suspect were immune to the contagion. A case in point is *Peter Pan* (1904), attended by more English viewers than any other play of the prewar period and probably seen by more English-speaking children than any other play in history. On the surface it is an innocent fantasy, a "safe" spectacle appealing to the young and the young at heart, but imbedded within the fairy drama are behavioral keys which instruct proper children how to go about the urgent business of serving—and dying for—their country.

One problem in discussing *Peter Pan* lies in establishing a definitive text, for the play underwent many textual changes following its first production, and the original manuscript has disappeared. Subsequently the author, James Matthew Barrie (1860–1937), claimed that he had no recollection of writing *Peter Pan*, although he could remember details about the genesis of his other plays. For him it was always a very special work—almost an inspired book, like a gospel—that originated in some unconscious recess of his mind. In his preface to the 1928 edition (usually regarded as "definitive") Barrie dedicated his play to "The Five"—the five sons of Sylvia Llewelyn Davies—who as children had fired his imagination. At the time of this dedication his two favorites were dead: George, killed in the war, and Michael, a presumed suicide at Oxford.

Peter Pan is so inextricably bound up with Barrie's complex attachment to the Davies family that some biographical commentary is called for. The crucial year was 1897 when Barrie met Sylvia Davies, the daughter of the novelist George du Maurier and the wife of Arthur Llewelyn Davies, a barrister of Inner Temple. Unhappy in a marriage—said to have been unconsummated—to a bit actress, Barrie gradually appropriated Sylvia and her sons. She was a beautiful woman (safely married to someone else) who embodied the spirit of motherhood, which Barrie worshipped.* For a long period Barrie met Sylvia and her sons daily in Kensington Gardens and made up fantastic games to amuse the boys. For George (b. 1893) and Jack (b. 1894) he elaborated a complex yarn about baby Peter (b. 1897), which evolved into a fable about Peter Pan, a deathless boy living on an island in the Serpentine with a flock of faeries, who teach him how to fly. Although there was always a morbid and violent strain in his stories, apparently Sylvia was never able to detect this, or flattered by this attention from a famous playwright she chose to ignore it. Among other things, Barrie told the boys that the surveyor's markers in the park were the tombstones of babies who had died and that Peter Pan would dance on their graves and lead these dead children to Never-Neverland. (It was in

*Barrie's pedophilia was keyed to a nostalgic and imagined recreation of his mother as a child. Years later he wrote of his mother fixation: ". . . I grow tired of writing tales unless I can see a little girl, of whom my mother has told me, wandering confidently through the pages. Such a girl as her memory of her girlhood had upon me since I was a boy of six." He seemed unable to please her. Her favorite son died in childhood. Once Barrie dressed in his brother's clothes to console her, but only made her distraught. See Janet Dunbar, *J. M. Barrie: The Man Behind the Image* (Boston, 1970), 16.

response to this that George uttered the famous line, later incorporated into *Peter Pan*, "To die will be an awfully big adventure."[1]) The three oldest children enjoyed the lavish attention and gifts which Barrie showered on them and in the main never wholly confused fantasy with reality. It was different with Michael (b. 1900), who suffered terrible nightmares about strange people and things coming through the windows. Unlike his older brothers, he had been brought up to believe in the existence of Peter Pan, not to relegate him to a dreamworld. A fifth son, Nico (b. 1903), arrived well after Barrie had purged himself of the initial Peter Pan fever.

The Davies boys and their mother were frequent guests at Barrie's suburban estate, "Black Lake." (Arthur Davies must have resented Barrie's strange absorption in his sons' lives but as a struggling barrister he stood in awe of Barrie's affluence and doubtless saw financial advantages in tolerating the relationship.) The dwarfish playwright joined in the boys' games—which excluded Sylvia Davies and his wife Mary— and documented their complicated frolics with photographs. In 1901 he commissioned his publishers to print a special book titled *The Boy Castaways of Black Lake Island*, which displayed thirty-five of these photographs with fanciful captions.[2] The putative author was Peter Llewelyn Davies. The villain of the piece is Captain Swarthy, a black man—the earliest model for Captain Hook. The picture on the cover shows the three boys (George, Jack, and Peter) paddling a raft and, significantly, bears the title "Setting out to be wrecked." Only two copies of this work were printed, one of them a gift to the father (who said he "lost" it on a train.)

At this time Barrie was also writing *The Little White Bird* (1902), a work of fiction which probes more deeply, though inadvertently, his infatuation with young boys. In one chapter, significantly titled "The Interloper," a child named David spends the night with the narrator, a bachelor unaccustomed to the presence of children. After taking off David's boots the narrator exclaims "This was a delightful experience, but I think I remained wonderfully calm."[3] David is fearful of sleeping alone, and when he learns he will be sleeping with his elderly friend he calls it "The Adventure." The narrator describes how in bed "the little white figure rose and flung itself at me" and then clings tightly to his finger all night. The narrator is unable to sleep, "thinking of the boy who had buried his head on his knees while being undressed," and so on.[4] Although few readers of 1902 would have found anything in this scene except a transcript of innocent love on the part of an avuncular narrator, any post-Freudian reading of Barrie's absorption in the details of undressing, sleeping together, and squeezing the finger, brings to mind a sublimated pedophilic seduction. By this time Barrie's immersion in the world of the Davies boys had become nearly total. Another chapter announced the presence of Peter Pan, a boy who was neither old nor young, a preternatural being who had escaped from humanity when only seven days old and who lives on an island in the Serpentine. Barrie was creating for himself the role of Peter Pan, "ever so old, but he is really always the same age,"[5] who would abduct the boys (Davies/David) from their false parents and save them from commercialism and mediocrity.

Rehearsals for *Peter Pan* (1904), produced by Charles Frohman, were conducted in an atmosphere more appropriate for the launching of a dreadnought than a mere play. Few actors were trusted with pages of the script not bearing upon their parts, and the special effects were as closely guarded as state secrets. To capture the school holiday crowd it opened on December 27, 1904, with Gerald du Maurier (Sylvia's brother) in the role of Captain Hook. It was an instant success with grownups as well as children. Although George Bernard Shaw crustily charged that it was "foisted on children by grown-ups,"[6] children themselves were wildly happy with the play, while adults vicariously reverted to childhood. The sinister features of the play were overlooked—the gratuitous violence, the repudiation of adult and bourgeois values, the blatant appeal to do-or-die patriotism, and the necrotic messages.

A major theme of *Peter Pan*, appropriately subtitled *The Boy Who Would Not Grow Up*, is rejection of the traditional Victorian family, which placed the father as the central luminary around which wife and children revolved as dependent satellites. The contemptible Mr. Darling, a clerk who sits atop a stool "as fixed as a postage stamp," regards his children as chattels.[7] He threatens them with visions of starvation if his tie is not tied properly for a dinner party, and when he hears that his wife has trapped the shadow of a mysterious creature (Peter Pan) he remarks, "There is money in this, my love. I shall take it to the British Museum tomorrow and have it priced."[8] With the soul of a Dickensian bookkeeper, he represents for Barrie the nonheroic, middle-class patriarch who measures the world with a stick calibrated in pounds and shillings. In creating Mr. Darling, Barrie was scoring on his chief rival, Arthur Llewelyn Davies, and twisting Sylvia's affectionate term for her husband into an anathema. The values of the workaday world are loathed by Peter Pan, who had fled from home on the day he was born, "Because I heard father and mother talking of what I was to be when I became a man. I want always to be a little boy and to have fun."[9] (This is but a variant of what Cyril Connolly called the Theory of Arrested Development, except that Barrie pushes the ideal age back before the public school years.) Although Peter wages a ferocious war against pirates, his deepest scorn is reserved for clockwork bondsmen like Mr. Darling. Arthur Davies is maliciously destroyed by Barrie for fathering real children which he (Barrie) could only possess by fantasizing.

The Neverland to which the Darling children escape is populated almost entirely by boys, and girls when they appear at all are either faeries or midget matrons. Peter and Wendy Darling become surrogate parents without becoming spouses. When Wendy darns the children's socks she enacts a proper role, but when she probes Peter's feelings about her she violates the faery rules. Peter becomes puzzled by her exploratory sexual language, and he consistently rebuffs her attempts to kiss him. Homophilic protocol is as rigidly enforced in *Peter Pan* as in an English public school. Mermaids, traditionally creatures associated with destructive female sexuality, become the object of jolly hunting expeditions—but they are dangerous game because they pull boys into the water and drown them. *Peter Pan* restructures the ideal world according to a parthenogenetic model of women as mothers but never wives or lovers.

Peter serves as a tutor figure for the boys, showing them how to cast aside the dull, programmed workaday world of their father for a life dedicated to adventure—invariably destructive. As they prepare for their battle against the pirates Peter utters his most famous line, "To die will be an awfully big adventure."[10] In a sense Peter is already dead, for he is permanently self-exiled to a spirit world where he will never grow old. The only way to arrest growth is to die, and it is appropriate that Peter's distinctive costume—cobwebs and autumn leaves—are death symbols more suitable for a corpse than a living boy.

The climax of the play occurs when the boys battle the pirates, led by Captain Hook. Superficially this anarchical brigand seems nothing more than a prototypical villain found in any melodrama—a readily identified personification of evil which must be defeated by the "good" characters. Certainly most viewers have responded to him in just this way. Daphne du Maurier recalled that when her father paced the quarterdeck as Hook, children had to be carried screaming from the theater: "How he was hated, with his flourish, his poses, his dreaded diabolical smile! . . .

There was no peace in those days until the monster was destroyed, and the fight upon the pirate ship was a fight to the death."[11]

But Captain Hook is not your average brigand. Barrie's stage directions carefully set him apart from his crew as a "solitary among uncultured companions." Having heard that he bears a resemblance to the House of Stuarts, Hook "apes the dandiacal associated with Charles II."[12] The House of Hohenzollern might be closer to the mark. The appearance on the stage of an invader from the sea with fierce mustache and mutilated arm must have brought to the mind of many adult viewers the sinister figure of Kaiser Wilhelm with his withered arm. By 1904, as we have seen, the tangled yarns which comprise the invasion stories had been wound into a single thread stretching to the beaches of imperial Germany. And like Hook, the Kaiser fancied he had a claim to the English throne through family connections.

Whether by design or by unconscious process, the conflict between the true Englishman and the dastardly foreign invader splashing ashore with his minions falls within the narrative perimeters worked out by Chesney, Le Queux, and others.* Hook is the consummate bully who violates the "laws" of civilized warfare by attacking the Indians first— and not at dawn. Moreover, he is a poor sportsman. In the grand battle he tries to set fire to a powder magazine. As the children beg for mercy, he shouts, "I'll show you now the road to dusty death. A holocaust of children, there is something grand in the idea!"[13] He is foiled by the *Überkind* Peter Pan who forces Hook over the side into the jaws of a crocodile and thereby saves the day as effectively as the Royal Navy saves England from enemies in countless invasion stories. Ten years after this first production of *Peter Pan* the Great War would introduce a new and horrible dimension to the phrase "a holocaust of children," for which the Kaiser would be held personally responsible by those Englishmen calling for his execution as war criminal.†

In creating Captain Hook, Barrie tapped other springs, among them his growing aversion to the public school type who held the reins of political power and social prestige during this period when he, a Scottish weaver's son, had to struggle upward through crusty layers of class

*Pirates, islands, and invasion had been the primary stuff from which Barrie wove his elaborate games for the Davies boys at Black Lake and which he commemorated in *The Boy Castaways*.

†Productions of *Peter Pan* during the war years deleted lines having ghastly (and tasteless) associations, like "To die will be an awfully big adventure." In view of the weekly casualty lists, "holocaust of children" was also inappropriate. See Andrew Birkin, *J. M. Barrie and the Lost Boys* (London, 1979), 252.

Peter Pan by F. D. Bedford. From James Matthew Barrie's
Peter Pan and Wendy (1911).

prejudice. In a note for the 1920 production of *Peter Pan* he wrote: "Hook. Eton & Magdalen. . . . Studied for Mods. Took to drink in 1881, elected M.P. following year."[14] While ruthless and violent, Hook is portrayed as a decayed gentleman who says "Sorry" as he makes a victim walk the plank, and his last words before plunging into the crocodile's jaws are "Floreat Etona"—the Eton College motto.[15] It appears that Barrie was simultaneously drawn to and repelled by the public school type. After the death of Arthur Davies from facial cancer in 1906, Barrie contributed substantially to the support of George, Peter, and Michael at Eton, and he behaved like a proud father when George distinguished himself in the Harrow match at Lord's by knocking up the second highest score and by making a spectacular left-handed catch that was photographed and featured in the newspapers. At the same time he jealously resented the insidious power of public schools which "draw from their sons a devotion that is deeper, more lasting than almost any other love."[16] Embittered that his cherished "sons" were growing up and leaving him alone in Neverland, Barrie began to excoriate the public school stereotype. After watching a gentlemanly game of tennis in 1920, he summarized the protocol in an acidulous letter to a friend: "The chief word in it seems to be 'sorry' and admiration of each other's play crosses the net as frequently as the ball. I fancy this is all part of the 'something' you get at public schools and can't get anywhere else. I feel sure that when my English public school boy shot a Boche he called out 'Sorry.' If he was hit himself he cried, 'Oh, well shot.' "[17] The remark was deeply personal, for George Llewelyn Davies, his favorite boy, had been killed by a "Boche" sniper near Voormezeele in 1915. In a private moment Barrie had shifted the responsibility for his senseless death from the Kaiser's "holocaust of children" to the sporting codes of the English public school.

Toward the end of *Peter Pan* Captain Hook holds the children captive on his pirate ship but offers to set them free if they will submit to ignominious conditions; they must enlist in his band and proclaim, as oath of allegiance, "Down with King Edward!" Like Flashman, the public school bully in *Tom Brown's School Days*, Hook intends to acquire an obedient troop of fags. However, Wendy rallies the boys with her rousing call to arms, "I have a message to you from your real mothers, and it is this, 'We hope that our sons will die like English gentlemen.' "[18] At this, the boys "go on fire." Led by Peter Pan, who appears like a visitation of St. George, and singing "God Save the

King," they join in a murderous free-for-all.* Michael reports exultantly that he has killed a pirate. Horrified, Wendy cries, "It's awful, awful," only to be contradicted by Michael, "No, it isn't, I like it, I like it."[19] Sanctioned by patriotic fervor, the act concludes in an orgy of delighted slaughter. The point could hardly be missed by any viewer over four years old; when properly instructed by faery avengers, English boys can vanquish enemies of king and country. Lord Roberts and Baden-Powell, if they witnessed the play, must have approved, for every production of *Peter Pan* was the lollipop counterpart of a patriotic rally.

Peter Pan ends where it began—in the nursery. Humiliated by his failure as a father, but enjoying his status as the parent of children who have flown away. Mr. Darling now lives in a dog house (a malicious gibe at Arthur Davies as breadwinner). The boys have come into an awareness of life as adventure and derring-do, in contrast with their father's stodgy dullness. They have broken free of middle-class stultification. Significantly, Michael observes, after peering into the dog house, that his father is not as big as the pirate he killed. Parricide is unnecessary, for the Victorian father has shriveled up to a nonentity. In the final scene the real world dissolves into nothingness. In a treetop Peter plays on his pipes. His adventure with the Darling children is fading from his memory, for he is a creature without nostalgia, sentiment, or affection. Having indoctrinated the children into the manly art of warfare, the solitary piper abdicates from his tutorial role. What the children do with their new knowledge is not his affair—or the author's. Beyond the surface layers of fun and fancy looms a wholly different sort of message—death, not life, is the "awfully big adventure."

Testimonials to the impact of *Peter Pan* on young boys of the prewar generation abound. For Anthony Powell, visits to Kensington Gardens as a toddler were indelibly associated with the fear of disappearing.[20] Graham Greene saw the play once each year in London. His favorite scene was when Peter fought the pirates and he thrilled at the line "To die will be an awfully big adventure," which echoed through his adolescence—at least until the time during the war "when death became for all of us a common every day risk."[21] George Orwell came to feel the

*In American versions "Down with the stars and stripes!" and "Yankee Doodle" replaced their English equivalents. One can imagine what substitutions were supplied in German productions of the play. See Roger L. Green, *Fifty Years of Peter Pan* (London, 1954), 107.

excessive morbidity of the play, and wrote of it, "Personally I would sooner give a child a copy of Petronius Arbiter than *Peter Pan*."[22]

▼

On January 27, 1909, Viscount Esher, a member of the Committee of Imperial Defence, attended the theater and jotted in his diary: "A play of 'Invasion' most excitingly acted."[23] It had opened at Wyndham's Theatre and proved such a sensation that it was shortly being produced at three London theaters simultaneously. Directed by Gerald du Maurier, *An Englishman's Home* treated the invasion of England by foreigners known as Nearlanders but whose behavior and names conjured up Germans. (Niderland in the Middle High German epic *Das Nibelungenlied* is the birthplace of Siegfried, victor over the Saxons.) The author was known only by his pseudonym, "A Patriot," and a rumor got about that Matthew Barrie had written the play. It was a good guess, in view of his intimacy with Gerald du Maurier and his sister Sylvia Davies, but it happened to be wrong. The play, a crude, scaremongering melodrama, had been written by Guy du Maurier, Gerald's older brother, who was then second in command of the Royal Fusiliers in South Africa. Convinced by army talk about the German preparation for war against England, Guy had scratched it out and sent it to Gerald for an opinion. Without Guy's knowledge or permission, Gerald collected a cast, apparently obtained Barrie's help in smoothing off the more protuberant knots and lumps, and began production.[24] Finding no German uniforms in London prop inventories, he clothed the invaders in Balkan outfits—possibly the same ones used by the cast of Shaw's *Arms and the Man* back in the 1890s. The result was electrifying—as well as disturbing for an audience already conditioned to fear invasion like an epidemic. For three chilling acts they watched in horror as brutalizing foreigners desecrated a conventional middleclass Essex household. Until the truth leaked out, the public attributed authorship to Barrie.

An Englishman's home is his castle, and the lord of this one is Mr. Brown, a middle-aged commuter with muttonchop whiskers, four spoiled children, and a statue of Britannia on the mantle. Fogbound on a dreary Boxing Day, the children devour the sporting page and sing snatches of cheap music hall ditties while the father, an empty blowhard, blames everything, including the fog, on incompetents in the government. Paul Robinson, a guest wearing the ill-fitting uniform of the Territorial Army, arouses Mr. Brown's ire because of wasted money on the military, while the young people ridicule Paul's patriotism by performing parodies of military drills and speeches. The first act concludes with the arrival of Prince Yoland, a thick-jowled Nearlander, who announces to the shocked Britons that he is in the vanguard of invasion.*

On the following morning Mr. Brown seethes with indignation when he discovers Nearlander dragoons (many of them ex-waiters in English hotels, a staple of invasion stories of the period) camping without permission in his yard. Maggie, a spunky daughter, protests at this violation of personal property rights. In rebuking the Nearlanders, she speaks for an audience conditioned to believe that war should be a matter for soldiers only. It is not cricket to involve civilians: "War is made by soldiers—on soldiers. We are all helpless here."[25] After the battle develops and the invaders move elsewhere, Paul reappears, muddy and exhausted. He had joined his Territorial unit only to find that they had no weapons, no ammunition, no orders, and no discipline. When the others joke about the whole situation, Paul renders the author's impacted warning: "The whole damned country is coming down like a house of cards, and you, and thousands like you, are saying it's not your business, as long as it doesn't interfere with you."[26] The Browns' complacency abruptly ends when a squad of Nearlanders approaches, spots one of the boys at a window, and shoots him through the heart. Down curtain on act two.

For a brief period the Browns' house becomes a stronghold for the English defensive lines, but when the roof catches fire, the Territorials retreat. Now committed by his anger to the fight, Mr. Brown picks up an abandoned rifle and opens fire on the Nearlanders. The stage direction is blunt: "He becomes from instinct a fighting man. The lust of battle comes over him."[27] Guttural shouts outside come closer. Finally enemy soldiers break down the door. A Nearlander rushes at Mr. Brown with fixed bayonet, misses his thrust, and is felled by the valiant freeholder. Prince Yoland enters and orders Mr. Brown to be shot as a bushwhacker. On her knees Maggie pleads with the Prince for her father's life, but the cruel martinet refuses to countermand the order. A volley of rifle fire is heard. Maggie exits screaming as the final curtain drops.

*This act of du Maurier's play provided P. G. Wodehouse with the launching platform for *The Swoop!*, his lampoon of invasion stories, which appeared the same year.

It is as difficult to find literary merit in this play as it is to exaggerate its impact upon that prewar generation of viewers. Sylvia Davies wrote glowingly to her brother of its London reception: "My beloved Guy, the world is writing and talking of nothing else but your play. . . . Mummy tells people the author's name is a profound secret, but in my heart I know she tells everyone she meets."[28] Guy had asked for anonymity because as an officer of the British army he doubted the propriety of stirring up the already muddy waters of Anglo-German relations. He need not have worried. After his authorship was leaked to the public he received congratulatory letters from both Lord Roberts and Richard Haldane (who had implemented the Territorial Army scheme) for alerting the nation to the invasion danger. Formerly one had to be able to *read* in order to be spooked by invasion fears; now a blind illiterate had access to scaremongering literature. Photographs featuring scenes from the play and scraps of its dialogue circulated in newspapers throughout Britain; a gramophone company turned out records excerpting exciting parts of the play.[29] At precisely the time when Baden-Powell was drawing youths into his Boy Scout movement (while serving as a regional commander of the Territorial Army), du Maurier's melodrama was bombarding adults with the same message—Be Prepared. Haldane wrote that the play had "created an extraordinary agitation in favour of the Territorials."[30] The Territorials even set up a recruiting booth at one of the London theaters to accommodate the press of volunteers eager to sign on to defend their country. The government moved quickly to protect the play from satirists; a director planning a spoof of du Maurier's play was informed by the Lord Chamberlain's office that no such skit would be allowed.[31]

The staging of *An Englishman's Home* was complicated by the fact that there were two endings available. Guy's version ended with the execution of Mr. Brown and a temporary Nearlander victory. However, at some point in his stage version Gerald du Maurier and Barrie tagged on a last-minute victory. Presumably directors could take their pick of versions on the basis of what the local traffic would bear. George Llewelyn Davies assessed his uncle's play in a note to his mother, "Of course the ending does rather spoil the lesson—it makes one think that even if the Germans [*sic*] did have a high old time for a bit, England would win in the end all right. I suppose it had to be put in to please the average audience."[32] At the time he wrote this, George was preparing for the Officers' Training Corps (OTC) Field Day exercises at Eton, which he called "a topping rag." It never crossed his mind that he would be fighting "Nearlanders" on the Western Front just five years in the future.

With or without the happy ending, An Englishman's Home had a six-month run, "gaining its effects by shock tactics on an audience's nerves," as Barrie's biographer termed it.[33] To see on a stage the violation of an Englishman's home, castle, and sanctuary by a brutal gang of offshore pirates was the next thing to watching the real thing. Like the Darling children of Peter Pan, Mr. Brown had found himself transported into a violent world not of his own making; once in, he had achieved a kind of transcendence by behaving like a proper Englishman. As anti-German propagandist, du Maurier probably had a greater impact on the English public than that master of scaremongery, William Le Queux.

Although An Englishman's Home was not produced in Germany, reports of its bias were widely circulated in their newspapers. Katherine Mansfield amusingly recounts German reactions to the play in her story "Germans at Meat" (1911). Guests in her pension gloat over the panic in England caused by the play. A German says, "I suppose you are frightened of an invasion, too, eh? Oh, that's good. I've been reading all about your English play in a newspaper. You ought to be. You have got no army at all—a few little boys with their veins full of nicotine poisoning." Another guest chimes in, offering oily reassurance, "Don't be afraid. We don't want England. If we did we would have had her long ago. We really do not want you." To this the narrator, having listened to these well-fed Germans describe the effects of sauerkraut and beer on their digestive organs, replies ironically, "We certainly do not want Germany."[34]

Hate campaigns worked both ways. In 1909 Stanley Casson was studying German with a Bonn family and found that discussion of a future war with England was constant table talk. When a zeppelin passed over the city, he asked what it was for, and his host replied jovially, "To drop bombs on your British navy."[35] Later, on returning to England, Casson attended a performance of An Englishman's Home and thought it very effective propaganda. In 1916, as zeppelins bombed the Liverpool Street Station, he had occasion to make connections between German airships and an English play.[36]

Having warned his countrymen of the German menace, Guy du Maurier did not capitalize on his extraordinary debut by writing another play. He genuinely hated war. He had seen hard fighting during the Boer War where it was said that his hair turned completely white after a friend next to him had been killed. On his return from South Africa shortly before the outbreak of the Great War he became a model of emulation for the Davies boys at a time when Barrie was losing his hold over their affection. After Sylvia's death in 1910 Barrie had offended some of her sons by claiming that she had promised to marry him. Peter Davies found it incongruous that Barrie believed Sylvia would have taken seriously "the strange little creature who adored her and dreamed . . . of stepping into Arthur's shoes."[37] Moreover, one can imagine the tortures inflicted upon him by fellow Etonians jeeringly dubbing him "Peter Pan."

Because of the impact of *Peter Pan* on the prewar generation of young English children, it is instructive to follow the models for Barrie's famous character as they underwent the transition from Neverland to No Man's Land. Two days after the declaration of war, George and Peter Davies volunteered for service in the King's Royal Rifles. The colonel commanding remembered George's spectacular cricket plays at Lord's and booked him without question. Peter was accepted because the colonel assumed that as George's brother he surely knew how "to play the game."[38] Nor was the importance of cricket as a reasonable preparation for war lost upon their godfather. Somewhat later Barrie wrote George that getting ready to go into the trenches must be "uncommonly like 'putting on your pads.' "[39]

Meanwhile, Barrie put on his own pads. On behalf of the patriotic muse he wrote a one-act morality play, *"Der Tag" or the Tragic Man*, which was staged at the Coliseum in December 1914. The subject is the Kaiser's unleashing of world war and his dream of invading England. The Emperor is a Faustian figure who feels that his power is irresistible. "Red Blood boils in my veins," he exclaims to his chancellor and a German officer; "I would eat all the elephants in Hindustan and pick my teeth with the spire of Strassburg Cathedral."[40] He anticipates the fall of France in three weeks, Russia in six, then "The Day! We sweep the English Channel. . . . Dover to London is a week of leisured marching, and London itself, unfortified and panic-stricken, falls in a day!"[41] (Since the play was designed as propaganda and was published simultaneously in New York, invasion of the United States figures on the Kaiser's agenda). His megalomaniacal musings are interrupted by the Spirit of Culture, appropriately a "noble woman in white robes." She congratulates him on German progress—filled granaries, busy mills, teeming commerce, and seats of learning—but she is not taken in by his argument that he wishes to control the world only to bring culture and order to it. "I am not of German make," she says. "My banner is already in every land on which you would place your heel." She disappears and a chastened Kaiser tears up his proclamation of war. But what has transpired in the play is only a dream of the Kaiser. The war has actually begun. Culture now appears before him in the flesh, so to speak, and explains that his destruction is assured by the violation of Belgium and arousing of England's sense of justice. England had grown degenerate through idleness but has been rejuvenated by the war. Pointing her finger at the Kaiser, she exclaims, "you, *you,* have made her great." As she leaves him she places his pistol in his hand—"It is all she can do for her old friend."[42] The curtain falls as a single candle burns low, leaving the Emperor alone in shadows. Poor as it is, this play, unabashedly designed to give viewers a patriotic boost, differs from similar effusions of the London stage during that period by its comparatively gentle treatment of the Kaiser, who is depicted as a troubled and mistaken man rather than a bloodthirsty fiend.

The departure of George's unit for the front late in 1914 provided Barrie with the raw material for his one-act play, "The New Word" (1915), which explores the deep affection between father and son which lies deeply buried beneath their mutual veneer of insouciance. Roger Torrance, a newly commissioned second lieutenant, prepares to leave for the front. While his sister and mother ogle him, his father cracks jokes and deflates the importance of the occasion; two men are not supposed to show affection for one another. When the womenfolk are out of the room, Mr. Torrance says, "We have, as it were, signed a compact, Roger, never to let on that we care for each other. As gentlemen, we must stick to it."[43] Then he painfully adds, "I am fond of you, my boy," while Roger cringes, fearful that someone might hear this mortifying confession. When Mrs. Torrance interrupts, both sputter that they have been discussing military affairs: "I have been helping Roger to take his first trench," says the father.[44] Both males comprehend that the war has broken down the icy barriers of reserve hitherto inhibiting father-son relationships among the English.

In the letters that George wrote to Barrie from the front he carefully censored details which might have conveyed the horrors of trench warfare. Instead he emphasized such Peter Pan effects as the spectral appearance of a shrapnel-flecked chateau in bright moonlight, as though evoking the habitation of gnomes and faeries. Only two miles farther down the line his uncle, Lieutenant Colonel Guy du Maurier of the

Royal Fusiliers, was graphically describing in letters to his wife what modern war was really like:

> The trenches are full of dead Frenchmen. When one is killed they let him lie in the squelching mud and water at the bottom; and when you try and drain or dig you unearth them in an advanced state of decomposition. . . . All the filth of an Army lies around rotting. . . . The stink is awful. There are many dead Highlanders just in front—killed in December I think—and they aren't pleasant. . . . I'll try and go over and see George who I think is only two miles off. I haven't seen anyone I know lately. I fancy most of the Army I know are killed or wounded.[45]

Early in March, 1915, Barrie heard that Guy had been killed. On the eleventh he wrote a letter of consolation to George—his last one—which indirectly spoke to his own frustrations; Uncle Guy had reached a time of life "when the best things have come to one if they are to come at all, and he had no children, which is the best reason for caring to live on after the sun has set."[46] As the realization dawned on him that his Peter Pans had truly grown up and were not exempt from mortal coil by flights to Neverland, Barrie grew apprehensive. In his letter he went on to say: "I don't have any little iota of desire for you to get military glory. I do not care a farthing for anything of the kind, but I have the one passionate desire that we may all be together again once at least. You would not mean a featherweight more to me tho' you came back a General. I just want yourself." In conclusion he wrote, "I have lost all sense I ever had of war being glorious. It is just unspeakably monstrous to me now."

Four days later, during the English advance on St. Eloi, George was "shot through the head, and died almost immediately, so that he can have felt nothing"—or so went the report of Lord Tennyson's son Aubrey, a fellow officer.[47] (Nearly all such accounts of deaths in the Great War assured loved ones that the victim had "felt nothing"—what else could they say?) The news reached Barrie that evening at the Davies house. What ensued was a scene that was duplicated in thousands of British households during the Great War. Eleven-year-old Nico was awakened by a banging at the front door. Mary Hodgson, the family nurse, got out of bed and went downstairs, while Nico sat up with his ears pricked. "Then I heard Uncle Jim's voice, an eerie

Banshee wail—'Sh-h-h! They'll all go, Mary—Jack, Peter, Michael—
even little Nico—This dreadful war will get them all in the end!' "[48]

On the following day, among telegrams and letters of condolence,
Barrie received, as though from the world of the dead, George's last
letter, urging him not to lose faith: "Keep your heart up, Uncle Jim,
and remember how good an experience like this is for a chap who's been
very idle before. Lord, I shall be proud when I'm home again, and
talking to you about all this. That old dinner at the Savoy will be pretty
grand."[49]

A week later came news of the sinking of the *Lusitania*. Among the
deaths was Charles Frohman, the producer of *Peter Pan*, whose last
words were publicized by an actress who survived: "Why fear death? It
is the greatest adventure in life." Barrie believed Frohman was mis-
quoted, and made the correction in a letter to a friend: "His last
words . . . were really, I feel sure, 'Death will be an awfully big
adventure.' "[50]

George had been the linchpin holding together the flagging relationships between Barrie and his five godsons. His death brought a
tragic dimension into the three playlets that Barrie wrote in direct
reaction to the war, each of which treats the effect of death at the front
upon the inner life of real or surrogate parent at home.* "A Well-
Remembered Voice" explores the possibility of spiritualism as a means
of regaining communication with a son killed in France and serves as a
kind of sequel to "A New Word," which dealt with communication
problems with a living son. Mr. Don, a colorless man of fifty, sits aloof
from a séance at center stage, where his wife, with the help of a spiritualist, tries to draw her son Dick from the spirit world. After a
rapping singles out FATHER, the message fades, and Mrs. Don blames
her husband for breaking the spell. Mothers are more important than
fathers, she says, and Mr. Don abjectly agrees. But after she leaves,
Dick's ghost appears and explains that ghosts are allowed to appear
only to one chosen person: "Mother's a darling, but she doesn't need
me as much as you do."[51] He describes his own experience of painless
death in battle and touches upon his peaceful existence in death's kingdom—an updated version of Peter Pan's bland Neverland. Dick van-
ishes after promising to reappear so long as his father remains "bright"
and gets to work again. This playlet turns the familial themes of *Peter*

*With "A New Word," these playlets—"The Old Lady Shows Her Medals" (1917), "A
Well-Remembered Voice" (1918), and "Barbara's Wedding" (1918)—were published in
his collection, *Echoes of the War* (1918).

Pan inside out. Here the adventurous boy repudiates the mother—the "darling" (perhaps an unconscious allusion to Mrs. Darling of *Peter Pan*)—and vindicates the self-effacing father. While it capitalizes on the hysteria of loss which characterized English families during the final years of the war, Barrie leaves open the question of whether contact with the spirit world can be achieved.* What is conveyed is an imagination stripped of the playful attitudes that orbited his famous line, "To die will be an awfully big adventure."

Despite the reassuring account of George's painless death, there persisted always terrifying doubts about how soldiers in the war really died. That Barrie brooded on such possibilities for George is suggested by Gerrie Llewelyn Davis, Jack's wife, who stayed with him for a short period during the war while her husband was at sea. Quite out of context Barrie asked her if she knew how Guy du Maurier had been killed. When she replied that she had heard that he had been shot, he said bitterly, "Yes. He was shot. And he wandered about the battlefield for half-an-hour with his stomach hanging out, begging somebody to finish him off."[52] Since her husband was on active duty in the navy, the remark horrified her as being "so queer, so cruel." "He just told it to me point-blank, then went on with whatever he was doing." Added to his worries, Peter Davies was shipped out to France in time for the Somme carnage. After two months he was invalided home safely with nothing more dangerous than eczema and shell shock, but Barrie's relief was short lived. Peter became involved with a married woman twice his age, a relationship which deeply shocked his guardian, whose own divorce brought about by Mary Barrie's affair with the novelist Gilbert Cannan had been a major scandal a few years back. Barrie probably understood why Peter was attracted to a mother figure—it was evidently the only male-female relationship he did understand—but Peter's presumed carnal liaison bordered on incest for Barrie, because it turned mother into mistress.

With the original Peter Pan trio lost to him—George dead, Peter corrupted, and Jack married—Barrie turned to Michael and Nico, then students at Eton and dependent on him financially. He wrote them each

---

*This hysteria of loss proved to be a bonanza for charlatans promising to raise the ghosts of dead soldiers. A popular handbook during the war was J. Hewat McKenzie's *Spirit Intercourse* (1916), which discussed such phenomena as the "psychic umbilical cord" and published "photographs" of deceased relatives. Converts to spiritualism included A. Conan Doyle and his wife, who had lost a son in the war and who traveled 50,000 miles searching for psychic evidence of communion with the dead. See chapter 9.

day and agonized over their possible incorporation into the war. The Armistice ended that fear, but just three years later he was devastated when Michael and a companion were drowned near Oxford in what was rumored to be a suicide pact. Presumably the two were lovers, for Nico later confessed that Michael was "going through something of a homosexual phase."[53] Newspapers made sensational copy out of the tragedy, the Peter Pan connection proving irresistible: "Now both boys who are most closely associated with the fashioning of *Peter Pan* are dead. One recalls the words of Peter himself: 'To die would be an awfully big adventure.' "[54] So went the account in the *Evening Standard* under the headline THE TRAGEDY OF PETER PAN.* It seemed impossible for the public to divest itself of that terrible line.

Two years after Michael's death Barrie recorded in a notebook a dream about Michael:

> I dreamt that he came back to me, not knowing that he was drowned and that I kept this knowledge from him, and we went on for another year in old way till the fatal 19th approached & he became very sad not knowing why and I feared what was to happen but never let on—and as the day drew nearer he understood more & thought I didn't—and gradually each knew the other knew but still we didn't speak of it—and when the day came I had devised schemes to make it impossible for him to leave me yet doubted they could help—and he rose in the night and put on the old clothes and came to look at me as he thought asleep. I tried to prevent him going but he had to go and I knew it and he said he thought it would be harder if I didn't let him go alone, but I went with him, holding his hand and he liked it and when we came to the place—that pool—he said goodbye to me and went into it and sank just as before. At this point I woke but feeling that he had walked cheerily into my room as if another year had again begun for us.[55]

Dreams about young men who returned from the dead proliferated in the 1920s, and whether the youth drowned in the mud of Passchendaele or in an Oxford pool was immaterial to a grieving parent. In this

*In 1960 Peter Llewelyn Davies, at that time a leading London publisher, threw himself under an underground train. At Eton he had loathed being called Peter Pan; in later years he alluded to the play as "that terrible masterpiece." He would have foreseen the headlines which announced his death: PETER PAN'S DEATH LEAP and THE BOY WHO NEVER GREW UP IS DEAD. See Birkin, *J. M. Barrie*, 1.

succession of images the dreamer turned the clock backwards, like reversing a motion picture, till it coincided with a time in which the dead youth came alive again, and then let time resume. There were two possible endings to such a dream; either the young man would be resurrected permanently, or he would revert to death. Barrie's unconscious chose the destructive outcome. Black Lake, where Barrie had played pirate games with the Davies boys, had evolved into the lake where Peter Pan and his boys fought Captain Hook. This lake, in turn, had become for Michael (who was always afraid of water) a dark tarn that swallowed up real boys. With some justification Barrie could in part blame himself for Michael's death through imposing on this most impressionable of the Davies boys the strange clutter of the Peter Pan imagery. The unhealthy nature of Barrie's relationship with Michael had been analyzed by one of Michael's friends: "It was morbid, and it went beyond the bonds of ordinary affection. . . . Michael was very prone to melancholy and when Barrie was in a dark mood, he tended to *pull Michael down* with him [my italics]."[56]

The possibility of returning to a moment of the past and of having a second chance for happiness by making a different choice haunted Barrie during these years. It is the theme of his play *Dear Brutus* (1917), in which characters enter an enchanted forest controlled by Lob, an ancient gnomish creature who resembles a grown-up Peter Pan. They momentarily cast aside what they are for what they might have been, only to discover that their second chance brings greater unhappiness. Only Mr. Dearth, an artist crippled by a cruel wife, finds temporary joy in the forest through the discovery of a dream daughter, Margaret (not surprisingly the Christian name of Barrie's mother). In shifting his attention from dream sons to dream daughter it was as though Barrie had recognized that, in time of war, fathers with girls had far greater immunity.

▼

Probably above all others Baden-Powell and Barrie had the greatest impact upon the thinking of young men growing up during the decade immediately preceding the Great War—B-P by instilling in them the imperatives of duty and sacrifice, and Barrie by foisting on them the particularly malignant messages that their youth alone mattered, that death was preferable to growing old, and that death was itself a great adventure. While B-P wanted boys to grow up fast so that they could assume the responsibility of running the empire, Barrie did not want them to grow up at all. The postwar generation showed little tolerance for either ideology. Recognizing this, Barrie in his notebooks of the early 1920s tried to sort out his views of "Age & Youth the two great enemies" separated by a gulf of misunderstanding. The occasion was his installation as rector of St. Andrews University (an honorary post) in his native Scotland, for which he chose "Courage" as the theme of his speech. While his speech was a great success—he was cheered and borne out of the hall on the shoulders of the students—the notebooks come closer to revealing Barrie's innermost feelings about the Great War, his personal anguish, and the lost generation. After much bitter reflection on recent history, he had begun to agree with the rebels, who charged that the Great War had been an old man's war and a young man's fight.

> Age (wisdom) failed—Now let us see what youth
> (audacity) can do. The 2 great Partners in state shdn't
> be Tory, Liberal or Labour—but Age & Youth. . . .
> Youth already knows nearly as much as Old & feel far
> more. Old advising young with advice rather a mockery
> just after War which young men died for. . . .
> They shd put statesmen who make war in front line. They
> shd be convicting me in dock (instead of my addressing)
> & condemning. . . .
> It may be a mood (but it is perhaps something better),
> but they [youth] are out for dissection, exposure, they
> have lost simple faith—probably the War is main cause
> of it—they query everything. Perhaps they accept too
> little & we accepted too much. . . .
> We can't be sure that they are wrong & we right—*we
> who seem to have made the greatest mess of things that
> has ever been made in the history of the world.*[57]

8 MISSIONARY OF EMPIRE

▼

*We happen to be the best people in the world, with
the highest ideals of decency and justice and liberty
and peace, and the more of the world we inhabit,
the better it is for humanity.*
CECIL RHODES

Whether the British Empire created Rudyard Kipling or whether
Rudyard Kipling created the British Empire might be a question worth
debating. In that queasy epoch marking century's end, a period when
self-satisfaction with a century of material progress conflicted with a
want of confidence about the future, it was perhaps inevitable that a
stormy prophet would arise from somewhere east of Suez and attempt
to pump red blood back into the blue veins of the English nation. Using
his formidable literary energy, he tried to hammer into apathetic skulls
his basic message: the nation had become effete, self-absorbed, and
costive with petty domestic affairs, and it would not survive unless it
took stock of its moral laxness and reverted to a more "primitive"
ethos. His literature spoke with unfamiliar tones and accents; the voice
was gruff and aggressive like that of a barbarian only recently over the
wall. It was wholly at odds with the drowsy equivocation of English
psychological fiction and with the weary falsettos of the art-for-art's-
sake crowd. Without question, the literary marvel of the age was the
meteoric rise of Rudyard Kipling, the "man from nowhere" (Matthew
Barrie's phrase), who arrived in London almost unknown in 1889 and
who became in less than ten years the universally accepted laureate of
Pax Britannica—the thesis that holding England together required, as
inevitable corollary, holding on to empire.

Prior to Kipling, English literature had been largely preoccupied
with the activities of men and women during their leisure rather than

The Age of Kipling. Kitchener and Kipling as guardians
of the British Empire.

their working hours. Kipling staked his claim for the dominion of work. For him a man—and there were few women in his work—was defined not by who he was but by what he did. To deserve his bread he had to be *useful*, and utility would be defined by his relation to empire rather than to Little England. A reviewer in *Blackwood's* summarized it well: "It was he and no other who first brought home to the average Englishman something like an adequate conception of what our Indian Empire means."[1] Max Beerbohm, who admired Kipling's genius as much as he loathed his ideas, caught what he thought was the quintessential Kipling in his famous cartoon of 1904 featuring a horn-tooting dwarfish bounder in a Roman helmet being dragged along by an Amazonian female in derby hat, the caption reading, "Mr. Rudyard Kipling takes a bloomin' day aht, on the blasted 'eath, along with Britannia, 'is gurl."

Traditionalists in morality and taste could not decide what they disliked more—Kipling's affectionate use of slang (particularly his version of the despised cockney dialect) or his characters, many of them roughnecks engaged in raising "the flag of Hooligan Imperialism."[2] While, of course, these same readers enjoyed the luxuries provided by colonialism, they preferred not to think about the brutal force and raw energy required for placing tea and chutney on their tables. Victorian England regarded the army as a barely necessary evil, a caste shunted out of sight at the ends of the earth and without the glamour of the navy—which was associated with bread-and-butter issues attending commerce and trade. Kipling tapped this ignored arm. His soldiers were a spanking new phenomenon in military fiction. Gone were the inanities of the officer's mess where monosyllabic dragoons gurgled through their mustaches as they waited for their chance to charge with the Light Brigade. Populating his poems and stories was pugnacious and thievish Tommy Atkins, officered by renegade gentlemen whose Sandhurst manners had been scaled away by the dust and sun of the outer fringes of empire. The secret of Kipling's popularity, as some contemporary reviewers perceived, was that he created characters who were doing things and not simply whining at existence. Intellect and untried virtue were of little importance to Kipling; character—always in the context of activity—was paramount.

Like other London litterateurs Henry James watched Kipling's conquest of the English-speaking world in mild surprise. At first he inclined toward heavily qualified admiration—"an infant master" and "the most complete man of genius (as distinct from fine intelligence) that I have ever known." In his introduction to Kipling's *Mine Own People* (1891), James highlighted those things which the young writer did exceedingly well: "his smoking room manner . . . , his delight in battle; his 'cheek' about women . . . , his 'imperial' fibre . . . ; the private soldier and the primitive man."[3] When Kipling married Carrie Balestier of Vermont in 1892, James gave the bride away, but increasingly he was becoming annoyed by the absence, in the younger man's work, of complex human relationships, particularly those involving what he called "the female form." Next he registered distress when Kipling's love of sheer power led him to write pieces about machinery which thought, felt, and even copulated. Once he had hoped that Kipling's incredible gift for probing character might allow him to become the English Balzac, but, distressed by the mechanical stories which appeared in the late nineties, James registered his despair: "he has come down steadily from the simple in subject to the more simple— from the Anglo-Indians to the natives, from the natives to the Tommies, from the Tommies to the quadrupeds, from the quadrupeds to the fish, and from the fish to the engines and screws."[4] Kipling's gifts, according to James, belonged in the domain of public address and propaganda rather than literature. Other writers shared James' doubts. Reading Kipling, asserted Virginia Woolf, was like being "caught eavesdropping at some purely masculine orgy."[5] Max Beerbohm objected to "the smell of blood, beer, and 'baccy" exhaled from his works.[6] Oscar Wilde put it more bluntly: "He is a reporter who knows vulgarity better than anyone has ever known it. Dickens knew its clothes. Mr. Kipling knows its essence. He is our best authority on the second-rate."[7] Rejection by literary coteries mattered not a whit to Kipling, however, for he had no use for "long-haired things" who seemed to have no other function in life except to "moo and coo with womenfolk about their blessed souls."[8]

While purists in aesthetics and liberals in politics generally agreed with James and Wilde, their appraisal was not shared by the English public at large, which responded enthusiastically to Kipling's thumping rhymes, to his unconventional characters, and to his conservative ideology. His art was the music hall and the yellow press come to life and disguised as literature, while his message called for service and sacrifice without stint or apology. A fair specimen is "The English Flag" (1891), a poem published shortly after his arrival in London from India, which unashamedly celebrated conquest and commerce at the ends of the earth as the foundation of English prosperity. What the "poor little street-bred people"—his contemptuous label for Londoners—forget is that their luxurious standard of living exists solely because of the hardship and hard knocks endured by generations of soldiers, sailors, and other empire builders:

Never the lotus closes, never the wild-fowl wake,
But a soul goes out on the East Wind that died for England's
sake—

Man or woman or suckling, mother or bride or maid—
Because on the bones of the English the English Flag is stayed.[9]

At first glance this message, calling as it does for individual sacrifice to a collective idea, bears a superficial similarity to Henry Newbolt's vision of English destiny abroad, and, in fact, a reviewer once characterized Newbolt's poetry as "Kipling without the brutality."[10] Both writers did believe that the twentieth century belonged to the Anglo-Saxon, and both were belligerent patriots infatuated with military and naval lore. The likenesses ended there. The difference was that while Newbolt looked backward to a patrician version of schoolboy athleticism and neverland chivalry, Kipling—ever the plebeian—conceived empire in terms of steam and sweat and slang. Newbolt resembled a hothouse plant—Kipling a rank jungle weed. The one fancied the soldier as a chivalrous gentleman playing with fixed rules; the other focused on the roustabout "other ranks" making or breaking rules as they went along. The showdown, when it came, would depend upon rifle shots at the Khyber Pass, not upon cricket bats at Lord's. These two patriot-poets never met, but it is likely that Kipling had "Vitai Lampada" in mind when he alluded in his poem "The Islanders" to "the flanneled fools at the wicket or the muddied oafs at the goals."

The impact of this and other Kipling works on the prewar generation cannot be overemphasized, because his work today is not well known, even among academics. Yet in *The New Machiavelli* (1911) H. G. Wells noted that the Edwardian age was dominated by Kiplingism, with its "wild shouts of boyish enthusiasm for effective force . . . its wondrous discovery of machinery and cotton waste."[11] This view is supported by the memoir of Major General Sir George Younghusband, a professional soldier, who recorded that early in his career no soldiers talked like Kipling's martial characters but that just prior to the Great War all of them did. The General's verdict—"Rudyard Kipling made the modern soldier."[12] It was a clear case of life imitating art, of Kipling's altering the psyche of the modern soldier by providing him with a vocabulary and a recognizable personality. During the Boer War Kipling and Cecil Rhodes, on departing from the headquarters of the Third Imperial Yeomanry, were greeted by cheers by the soldiers. Rhodes said, "Take off your cap, they are cheering you," to which Kipling replied, "They are cheering you." An adjutant explained. "I think they are cheering you both," at which both shyly took off their caps.[13] For these soldiers Rhodes and Kipling personified the empire. Moreover, for that generation of schoolboys who would shortly be transmogrified into subalterns and dispatched to Flanders, Kipling's work provided a kind of manual for proper army behavior with its depiction of that brotherhood among frontline soldiers, their distrust of politicians, and their pride in enduring hardship. Robert Graves, who entered the Royal Welch Fusiliers direct from Charterhouse School, found himself at once on familiar turf because the soldiers of his unit spoke and acted like Kipling "characters."[14]

Barrack-Room Ballads (1892), Kipling's most influential collection of soldier verse, passed through fifty printings in thirty years. His Tommy Atkins conforms to no parade ground or fashion plate stereotype. He joins in a brawl with a rival regiment using belt and buckle weapons ("Belts"); he gets stinking drunk and leaves his mark on the face of the corporal of the guard ("Cells"); he steals whatever he can from civilians ("Loot"); and he turns out to witness the hanging of a fellow soldier executed for the dastardly crime of shooting a sleeping comrade ("Danny Deever"). His code for living and dying is summarized in "The Young British Soldier," which wastes no words on love of mankind— or womankind:

> If the wife should go wrong with a comrade, be loth
> To shoot when you catch 'em—you'll swing, on my oath!—
> Make 'im take 'er: that's Hell for them both,
> An' you're shut o' the curse of a soldier.[15]

Kipling exults in defying Victorian taboos, whether these bear upon female virtue or upon the sanctity of human life. His soldier can expect neither rewards nor gratitude from an indifferent public for upholding the empire. He cannot be assured of even a clean death:

> When you're wounded and left on Afghanistan's plains,
> And the women come out to cut up what remains,
> Jest roll to your rifle and blow out your brains
> An' go to your Gawd like a soldier.

Men had no monopoly on cruelty and aggressiveness in Kipling's vision. Beneath their corsets and coverings women were as ferocious as men, because they were equally human. He dared, during an era when it was fashionable to be protective of women, to write a poem like "The Female of the Species," which listed shocking examples of female malignity, the lesson drubbed home with his refrain, "The female of the species is more deadly than the male." War came as no surprise to Kipling because ferocity was a normal instinct—the surprise for him would have been peace, the abnormal state of human affairs.

Kipling's infatuation with soldiers impregnated his life and his work. They belonged to the "legion of the lost ones," who were, like his Gentlemen-Rankers, "damned from here to eternity." He admired them not just because they were licensed outlaws who gratified a submerged appetite for destructiveness, but also because they were paradoxically essential instruments for the survival of the British Empire. He was aware of the irony in the conditions of this survival: that the men buttressing the front line of defense gave no thought to the political structure or the ideology which they gave their lives for. Moreover, he had no doubts about their superiority as human beings to the stay-at-homes who believed that human nature could be changed by sliding a slip of paper in a ballot box. A major Kipling theme is the gulf that separates the soldier from the civilian; the former give, and the latter only take. In "The Last of the Light Brigade" (1891) his subject is the niggardly ingratitude of the English nation which subscribes only twenty-four pounds for the relief of twenty destitute survivors of the famous Crimean charge. Their spokesman, the old Troop Sergeant, appeals to the Master-singer (Tennyson) who once made them immortals (of poetry):

> We think that someone has blundered, an' couldn't you tell 'em
>   how?
> You wrote we were heroes once, sir. Please write we are starving
>   now.

The poem concludes with an excoriating indictment of English selfishness and hypocrisy—which remained consistent targets for Kipling in the years ahead:

> O thirty million English that babble of England's might,
> Behold there are twenty heroes who lack their food to-night;
> Our children's children are lisping to "honour the charge they
>   made—"

And we leave to the streets and the workhouse the charge of the
Light Brigade![16]

▼

Kipling delivered a frontal assault on that supreme incubator of upper
class values, the public school, in his episodic novel, *Stalky & Co.*
(1899), a work that turned on its head the easy morality which had been
fossilized in the popular mind by *Tom Brown's Schooldays.* Loosely
based on his experiences at the United Services College at Westward
Ho! in Devonshire, which he had attended in the late 1870s, the novel
featured no Arnoldian uplift or muscular Christianity, but rather a dog-
eat-dog environment where only the fit survived. The college was no
Harrow or Eton, rimed with ancient rites and arcane traditions. Founded only four years before Kipling arrived there, it occupied a grim line
of nondescript buildings and was designed as a forcing house to get
boys, the majority of whom were sons of imperial officers, into Woolwich or Sandhurst.* Its motto was "Fear God, Honour the King," and
its graduates went off to colonial posts as servants of the empire. "India," Kipling wrote exultantly, "was only Westward Ho! spread
thin."[17] Success was measured by making a mark somewhere, not by
learning complex nuances of snobbery or a few lines of Greek. In *Stalky*
the boys have no illusions about their school; as one of them says,
"We're a limited liability company payin' four per cent. My father's a
stockholder, too."[18] To Etonians or Harrovians, youths from the
United Services colleges would be cads—or at least "bounders."

   The novel treats the school activities of Stalky, McTurk, and Beetle
("three fiends in human likeness" wrote one outraged reviewer),[19] who
flagrantly avoid cricket, football, and other character-building games in
order to lounge about, smoke, and swear. The trio wander about with a
pistol, pawn watches for treats, and make up scathing nicknames for
fellow collegians. Revenge is sweet—and swift. They bully the brute
who had bullied a frightened little boy, trussing and beating the of-
fender beyond the level of punishment and well over the threshold of
torture. When an officious housemaster accuses them of being dirty,
they push a putrescent cat under the floorboards of his apartment and
gleefully enjoy the aftermath. While their pranks are cruel, even sadis-
tic, they operate with an elemental sense of rough justice, punishing

---

*In the school magazine Kipling published his first poem, "Ave Imperatrix," inspired by
the foiling of a lunatic's attempt to assassinate Queen Victoria.

only those who deserve it yet cannot be reached by ordinary channels. The key here is punishment for evil, not reward for good; the Code of Hammurabi, not the Golden Rule, motivates these vigilantes.*

Kipling's departure from the norms of public school fiction is best seen in his chapter, "The Flag of Their Country," where an M.P. arrives at the school to deliver a booster patriotic speech in support of a cadet corps. He mouths a belief that boys hold private and sacrosanct— love of country. "He cried aloud little matters, like the hope of Honour and the dream of Glory that boys do not discuss even with their most intimate equals."[20] Among English boyhood, patriotism, like sex, is better acted upon than talked about. Finally the M.P. hauls out a large Union Jack, shakes it, and waits for a thunderous applause. The boys look on in silence. They had seen the flag at the coastguard station, above the roof at the golf club, or as wrapper on a sweetmeat; but they never alluded to it. "It was a matter shut up, sacred and apart." Their verdict on the jingoist M.P.—"a Flopshus Cad, an Outrageous Stinker, a Jelly-bellied Flag-Flapper."[21] They are unanimous in rejecting the proposed cadet corps because for youths bound for army careers it is only "playing at soldier."

The boys are not anarchs, lacking respect for flag and law. As sons of imperial officers they do not need to be instructed in patriotism by a jingoist charlatan. They reserve their admiration for men of deeds, not words—for heroes like their headmaster, who saved the life of a boy with diphtheria by sucking poison out of his throat through a tube.

For Kipling the college serves as a training ground for the officer caste which will command the Tommies which he had deified ten years earlier. This is made clear in the final chapter of *Stalky & Co.*, which shifts to the future and to an outpost on the Indian frontier attacked by two bands of natives. Stalky's army exploits have made him the "great man of his Century." In a seemingly hopeless fight he arranges to cross through the enemies' lines and kill a warrior, leaving the mark of a rival tribe on his chest. As a result the bands turn against one another and the English garrison is saved by the sort of prank that Stalky excelled in at school. Kipling's point is that the best hope for the empire lies in maverick officers like Stalky, "chaps that we don't know anything

---

*Major General L. C. Dunsterville (the model for Stalky) in later years recalled his schooldays at Westward Ho!—"Like a hunted animal I had to keep all my senses on the alert to escape from the toils of the hunter—good training in a way, but likely to injure permanently a not very robust temperament." See Edmund Wilson, "The Kipling that Nobody Read," *The Wound and the Bow* (Oxford, 1947), 112.

"John Bull in Trouble": "Can I stand this for long?"
From *Gott Strafe England!*

about, and the surprises will begin when there is really a big row on."[22] Minor lawbreaking at school proves to be excellent preparation for the man's work of beating the barbarians back from the gates. Kipling's performance in *Stalky & Co.*, wrote an angry but discerning critic, was in effect "a crowning achievement as the supreme Recruiting Sergeant."[23]

▼

The years of the Boer War (1899–1902) brought Kipling into the mainstream of political activism and into the fraternity of imperial leadership as he began to move in the circle of men like Cecil Rhodes and Lord Roberts. In February 1900 he journeyed to Capetown, received a pass from Lord Roberts allowing him to go wherever he wished—an astonishing testimonial of trust in view of the skittishness with which authorities viewed journalists during their well-botched African war—and helped edit a newspaper for the troops. For years he had belabored the English for their softness and insularity. Who could forget the Cassandra mood of his poem, "The Recessional" (1897), which had appeared during the year of Victoria's Jubilee and reminded the En-

Cecil Rhodes as the personification of the British Empire, bestriding Africa from Cairo to the Cape. From *Punch*, 1892.

glish race that it might be as transient on God's earth as the populace of Nineveh and Tyre or "lesser breeds without the Law"? Now he saw at first hand the humiliation of a major power struggling to subdue a ragtag army of Dutch guerrillas.

Paradoxically, Kipling rejoiced in the English embarrassment because he believed that the setback was only temporary and that England would be forced to wake up to the threats to her hegemony that lay ahead in the twentieth century. Once he toasted the health of the man who "has taught the British Empire its responsibilities" and "has turned the loafer of the London streets into a man," and to the great surprise of his auditors uttered the name *Stephanus Paulus Kruger*—the Boer leader.[24] Kipling was even prepared to rationalize the English defeat into a victory. In his short story, "The Captive" (1903), when a captured Boer officer accuses the English general of not wanting the war to end, the general agrees: "It's a first-class dress-parade for Armageddon. With luck, we ought to run half a million men through the mill. Why, we might even be able to give our Native Army a look in. . . . The native troops are splendid men." This is one of many allusions to "Armageddon" in Kipling's work. It would appear that his personal contacts with empire builders like Rhodes (who gave the Kipling family the use of a house for their lifetime) and Lord Roberts (with whom Kipling later collaborated in schemes for national defense) gave Kipling a vivid sense of how fragile the empire truly was, and these experiences turned him from a theoretical critic of English decadence into an activist whose mission was to employ his literature both to warn of lurking dangers from outside powers and to support movements or schemes which attempted to reinvigorate the effete body or languid will of the nation. He was by this time a doctrinaire apologist for the English position on the war. While the civilized world shuddered at reports of atrocities and mass deaths in concentration camps set up by British authorities to contain displaced Boer families, Kipling referred to these pens in his writing as places for "nursing and doctoring" and complained about the cost of providing "maintenance of all Boerdom."[25] In view of his involvement with South Africa it is not surprising that he became a friend of Lord Baden-Powell, wrote the "Patrol Song" for his fledgling Boy Scout organization, and directly influenced the Wolf Cub offshoot of B-P's operation through his Mowgli stories in *The Jungle Book* (1894). Both men knew how precarious were the balances that held an empire together, just as both were haunted by the specter of Great Britain's decline. The need to save England from a similar fate is a major Kipling theme in the years following the Boer War, and undoubtedly his invasion-saturated works, like *Puck of Pook's Hill,* influenced Baden-Powell's 1908 edition of *Scouting for Boys,* which alluded to the fall of Rome and to the need of saving Britain from a similar fate.

After his return to England from South Africa, Kipling became obsessed with invasion fears. In his Sussex village he started a rifle club which was drilled by coastguard officers and armed with Lee-Enfield rifles. (Later, troubled about their slow rate of fire, he presented the club with a working machine gun used in the Boer War.) At the same time he wrote to an American friend that England had to turn against the old "soft rubber-tyred" life: "Now we are slowly coming back to the primitives, and realising that a lot of what we call civilisation was another name for shirking."[26] Moreover, what had originally been only an indefinite sense that England was effete—an attitude common among young colonials newly arrived in the mother country—now hardened into a conviction that Germany was the villain of the piece. As he explained the situation in a letter to Charles Norton: "We are girded and goaded by Germany, and there is an uneasy feeling that the continent is getting ready for the big squeeze. . . . When Armageddon comes, remember . . . England is still engaged in saving the peace of the world."[27] His imagination was filled with visions of war. The noise of hunters in the woods near his Sussex manor evoked thoughts of "how it would be if all the wounded birds now lying in the woods were wounded men."[28]

He was now seething with hostilities—toward England for being weak, toward Germany for being strong. His poem "The Islanders" (1902) was both a rebuke for the shoddy English performance in the Boer War and a veiled warning of imminent catastrophe for a nation too supine and spoiled to engage in the struggle for existence. Published in the *Times* it reached a vast audience, and with its gibes at "the flanneled fools at the wicket or the muddied oafs at the goals" it lashed out at those public school devotees who still believed that wars were won on the playing fields of Eton. Its theme paralleled "The Recessional" in warning that the good fortune of England might become reversible, but its tone was heavier and more biting. This poem was a jeremiad designed to lash the public into an awareness of Realpolitik.

> Ye stopped your ears to the warning—ye would
> neither look nor heed—
> Ye set your leisure before their toil and your
> lusts above their need.

„So, Kinder, durch Belgien wären wir jetzt durch. Da drüben liegt England!"

"At the finish": "All right, boys. We have finally made it through
Belgium. England lies over there!" From *Gott Strafe England!*

> Because of your witless learning and your beasts
> of warren and chase,
> Ye grudged your sons to their service and your
> fields for their camping-place.[29]

The result was a foregone conclusion: "Sons of the sheltered city" were no match for a "little people, few but apt in the field."

England survived that test, but more dangerous ones lay ahead. Only through a willingness to prepare to meet new enemies and to sacrifice for the common good could the nation prevail. The first step, according to the argument of this poem, is a year of national service for all young men in order to make them

> Cleansed of servile panic, slow to dread or
> despise,
> Humble because of knowledge, mighty by
> sacrifice.

Kipling knew that this cure, for most Englishmen, was worse than the impending epidemic, no matter how toxic, but he had lost all patience with the national habit of relying upon God's personal intervention in snatching a last-minute victory. He did not doubt that major wars for survival lay ahead for England, and the conclusion of his poem, in the cadences of an Old Testament prophet, drove home the age-old invasion fears that had spooked the English for centuries.

> When ye are ringed as with iron, when ye are
> scourged as with whips,
> When the meat is yet in your belly and the
> boast is yet on your lips;
> When ye go forth at morning and the noon beholds
> you broke,
> Ere ye lie down at even, your remnant, under
> the yoke?

From this point onward the specter of invasion stalks Kipling's work. In *Puck of Pook's Hill* (1906), Robin Goodfellow of Shakespeare's dominion embodies the spirit of England, kept alive through all the centuries and all the racial displacements which have occurred since the Roman occupation. He has watched the approach of Philip's armada, witnessed the death of the last Saxon king, seen Caesar's legions disembark, and observed the Flint Men building their fortifications. The history of England is an evolving narrative of "Old Wars, old Peace, old Arts that cease, / And so was England born!"[30] Puck conveys this cyclical theory of history to two Sussex children, Una and Dan (modeled on Kipling's son and daughter), as he introduces them to figures from the heroic past who have once inhabited their neighborhood. As in *Peter Pan*—which appeared two years earlier—the visionary figures and actions are visible only to young people. For both Barrie and Kipling, grownups, because of their corruption by the gross materialism of the modern age, cannot be recruited in a spiritual cause calling for a revitalized England prepared to sacrifice in order to survive. The similarities end there; Barrie's vision is ahistorical and narcissistic, while Kipling's rigidly conforms to patterns of *Sturm und Drang* as these relate to national destiny.

The three chapters treating Parnesius, a Brito-Roman centurion of the Thirtieth Legion entrusted with the defense of Hadrian's Wall from attacks by both the Painted People (Picts) and the Winged Hats (Danes), form the core of the book. As in his earliest stories, which treated the British armies holding the "wall"—the northwest frontier in India—so two decades later we find Kipling still mulling over the prospect of barbarians vaulting the wall, which now has an explicit English context. One imperial system has been exchanged for another, but the issue is the same—the necessity of a strong people to endure sacrifice in order to prevent the invader from encroaching upon a corner of their empire. Moreover, as in most invasion narratives, there is an explicit causal link between spiritual malaise and national collapse that provides the didactic underpinning of the work. The father of Parnesius tells his son of the necessary work to be done at the Wall: "Rome has forsaken her Gods, and must be punished. The great war with the Painted People broke out in the very year the temples of our Gods were destroyed. We beat the Painted People in the very year our temples were rebuilt. . . . If your heart is set on service, your place is among men on the Wall—and not with women among the cities."[31] The Roman paterfamilias speaks, like Kipling himself, in behalf of preparedness and national service. Parnesius and Pertinax, his Gallic comrade at arms, successfully hold the wall, despite the constant erosion of legionnaires by emperors on the Continent desperately patching holes in the defensive Roman perimeter. When promised reinforcements finally arrive, the defenders are old and gray-haired—but the enemies are still north of the wall.

Charles Carrington, Kipling's most sympathetic biographer, calls these stories "a panegyric of duty and service" and claims that no other works of the prewar epoch were more effective in molding the thought of a generation and strengthening the nerve of a young soldier in the dark days of 1915.[32] Since Carrington was a combat veteran of the Somme and later a distinguished military historian, his viewpoint carries considerable authority. Clearly, many other young Englishmen found in *Puck of Pook's Hill* a well-researched and vividly written series of historical fables that opened up possibilities for heroism. Invasion, Kipling warned, was the normal, not the aberrant, pattern of English history. Hadrian's Wall is a strange choice for his cautionary tale, since as barrier it ultimately failed to check the advance of the barbarians. Yet by making Parnesius a Briton, the effect is to make a contemporary Briton feel more Roman. Rome's imperial mission is used to justify England's own defensive policies, at the Khyber Pass, in the North Sea, or wherever. Moreover, every schoolboy had heard his mentors pontificate on the reasons for the decline and fall of the Roman Empire; Kipling took this inquiry from its italic contexts and anglicized it. The implication was clear: unless young men like Parnesius came forward, England could again be faced with repelling an invasion, this time not from barbarians in winged hats, but in spiked helmets. It behooved the patriot to see that the collapse of the Roman Empire was not to be reenacted in the present.

For Kipling the Liberal sweep of Parliament in 1906 was like a plague, for they were as great a menace to the British Empire as the Germans. In 1907 he wrote that the "only serious enemy to the Empire, within or without, is that very Democracy which depends on the Empire for its proper comforts."[33] Five years later his distrust had deepened into bitter hatred of what he thought was cowardice and duplicity in Liberal policies: "I don't suppose you could prevent a Liberal from lying any more than you could stop a little dog from lifting up his leg against a lamp post."[34]

Kipling's attitude is a classic example of social Darwinism in its aggravated literary phase. This hypothesized that organisms, whether individual or social, were either improving or they were degenerating. The Boers had been sustained by their conviction that the British were decadent, and many officers like Baden-Powell and Lord Roberts agreed with them—thus their campaigns in support of Boy Scouts and National Service as corrective anodynes. In the aftermath of the Boer War, there developed a desperate attempt among Englishmen to convince themselves and the developing world powers—Russia, Germany, and the United States—that they were not witnessing an end to something.

In 1911 Kipling published a children's history of Great Britain and her empire with C. F. L. Fletcher. Although presented as a legitimate historical work by the Clarendon Press at Oxford, it stands as a blood-drenched chronicle serving as blatant propaganda for the National Service League. No child could miss the point: England's prosperity was directly proportionate to its military power and preparedness. In the succession of events from the arrival of the Celts to the Franco-Prussian War the lesson was always the same—"He who has the best weapons will beat his fellow men in battle." History, for the authors, is only a tool for political indoctrination. The Romans, admired because they created a great empire, collapsed because of "too much power, too much prosperity, too much luxury." Lest the young reader miss the parallel, the authors supply an aside, "What a lesson for us all to-day." The Danes overthrow King Alfred's kingdom because the "wise men" of Ethelred's court "were as useless as the House of Commons would be to-day if there were a big invasion. They talked, but did nothing." In a crisis a *man* is required, not "six hundred members of Parliament, with a sprinkling of traitors among them, to discuss how to make peace." The Civil War brings a mixed reaction. While it is true that Cromwell's crack cavalry units were the "direct forerunners of the cavalry regiments of our present gallant little army," the authors deplored the rebellion because it "prevented men from seeing that to serve the King and country in the Army is the second best profession of Englishmen of all classes; to serve the Navy, I suppose we all admit, is the best." The book is generously garnished with illustrations calculated to glorify leaders at the expense of human fodder: at Hastings William stands on top of a great mound of writhing bodies; at Waterloo Wellington stands amid the carnage while his officers wave their hats in victory. In concluding their volume, the authors allude to the speed and efficiency of Germany in overwhelming France in 1870 and warn their readers that all "civilized nations" except the Americans and British have armed their citizenry "so as to fit themselves for war on a gigantic scale at any moment." The surest way to avert disaster is to form a federation of the whole empire with a central parliament, but this is impossible because England has no great statesmen any more. In lieu of this, the only recourse "for all of us who love our country is to learn soldiering at once, and to be prepared."[35]

In this book Kipling inserted narrative songs treating wars with each
of the invading hosts who had threatened England during her history—
the Romans, the Saxons, the Danes, the Normans, the Dutch in the
Medway, and Napoleon. The mood varies from defiant to anxious. In
"The Pirates in England" he describes how "The pestilent Picts leaped
over the wall / To harry the English land," only to forget that on their
heels were the Saxons, the next wave of conquerors, who take the
beaches "with a grind and a roar" and rush inland.[36] In "Norman and
Saxon" a Norman baron gives some useful deathbed advice to his heir
about how to get along with the Saxons, who are a breed apart from the
usual conquered race:

> The Saxon is not like us Normans. His manners are not so polite.
> But he never means anything serious till he talks about justice and
>   right.
> When he stands like an ox in the furrow with his sullen set eyes
>   on your own,
> And grumbles, "This isn't fair dealing," my son, leave the Saxon
>   alone.[37]

Although the Saxon was a "drunkard and a gambler, and very stupid,"
when aroused he had a kind of dangerous integrity which present enemies would be advised to take notice of. His song, "The Dutch in the
Medway," treats the aborted invasion of 1664 but also reads like an
appeal for greater military funding to resist the Kaiser's Germany:

> If wars were won by feasting,
>   Or victory by song,
> Or safety found in sleeping sound,
>   How England would be strong!
> But honour and dominion
>   Are not maintained so.
> They're only got by sword and shot,
>   *And this the Dutchmen know!*[38]

What the present "Dutchmen" ruled by Kaiser Wilhelm knew was
the science of war and the means by which a nation could be mobilized
for it, for in these crafty arts Germany was light years ahead of the
English. But Kipling believed that the Englishman, like the Saxon of
his poem, needed only to be aroused by a noble cause for his power to

be exerted in the world. In a letter of this same year, he outlined the prospects ahead:

> Meanwhile the Teuton has his large cold eye on us and prepares to give us toko when he feels good and ready. Our chances are not so slim as they look for the reason that the Teuton knows all about war as it should be waged scientifically, and my experience has been that when a man knows exactly how everything ought to be done under every conceivable contingency he is apt to be tied up by his own knowledge. But we ought to see in a few years now.[39]

The inevitable war of the future would pit the Teutonic man of science against the Anglo-Saxon man of character, the latter motivated (like his oxlike Saxon ancestor) by a deep sense of moral purpose. It would be English grit against German brain, with Stalky to the rescue. In the contest between head and heart, Kipling stood solidly with the heart-of-oak school. In an account of Westward Ho! written for a boys' magazine about this time, he showed his contempt for purely intellectual achievements: "A scholar may, as the Latin masters said, get more pleasure out of his life than an Army officer, but only little children believe that a man's life is given him to decorate pretty little things."[40] In his admiration of men of action Kipling seems to have quite overlooked the fact that he was not a Lord Roberts or a Cecil Rhodes but only a writer—a decorator of pretty little things.

By this time Kipling's most creative period lay behind him. While his reputation among men of letters, with few exceptions, was in shambles and his work was anathema to most Liberals, he held on to his position as the most influential living poet in the English-speaking world. In his autobiography Kipling characterized himself as a "political Calvinist." His prose is packed with biblical allusions, many of them obscure, and he often intones his poetry like a harshly judgmental Old Testament prophet. Lacking traditional religious faith, he adopted simple but very rigorous political ideas which were pandemic among conservatives of the period. These involved the conviction that people were unable to govern themselves effectively; they needed a superior class to show them the way. Further, war was a natural condition of man, and to attempt to avert it was not only fruitless, it might also be harmful to the hidden processes of national growth and social evolution. The nub of Kipling's political philosophy is his notion of "The Law," which envisions a nondemocratic system ruled by a benign body dedicated to implementing the ideas of Peace, Order, Justice, and Public Works.

The essence is found in a single stanza of "A Song of the English" (1893):

Keep ye the Law—be swift in all obedience—
Clear the land of evil, drive the road and bridge the ford.
Make ye sure to each his own
That he reap where he hath sown;
By the peace among Our peoples let men know we serve the
Lord![41]

The job of the imperialist is to bring the benefits of Western civilization—benefits in the form of roads and sewers, not useless stuff like romantic poetry—to less developed races. (Kipling deplored the Portuguese version of imperialism because its sovereignty extended only one musket shot into the interior and it failed to build roads.) This is a far cry from imperialism as a purely commercial and exploitative concept, for it involved a sort of messianic zeal for industrial progress in "backward" places that was reminiscent of the original spirit behind Christian missions. As George Orwell noted, the empire affirmed by Kipling was of overworked officials and frontier skirmishes, not of Lord Beaverbrook and Australian butter. At that time "It was still possible to be an imperialist and a gentleman, and of Kipling's *personal* decency there can be no doubt."[42]

Kipling's "law" derived from current notions concerning "the survival of the fittest" but differed from them by entailing a responsibility of the fit to ameliorate conditions among those less endowed with the intelligence or strength to survive unassisted in the sociobiological struggle for life. He never doubted that Nature had made quite unequal rankings among its animal creations or that the process of evolution would cause future displacements in these rankings—thus his growing fear of Germany displacing England in the twentieth century. *The Jungle Book* (1894) had presented this idea in fable form through the character of Mowgli, who asserted his natural superiority to control the animals. "The law of the jungle," a favorite catchphrase of that generation, was given popular currency by Kipling. As he told Brander Matthews in 1926, "When I had once found the Law of the Jungle, then the rest followed as a matter of course."[43] The key word here is *law*, not *jungle*, for Kipling recognized that the foundation of a modern state required order, duty, and discipline, all of which could be implemented only by complex agencies of civilization. (Personally, Kipling would not have lasted long in a real jungle: without eyeglasses he was nearly blind; he was afraid of horses; and a Vermont neighbor claimed that he was physically incapable of lifting a fieldstone.) Much of his celebration of primitive characters, whether renegades like the Man Who Would Be King or native tribes like the Fuzzy-Wuzzy, was a way of showing, through an implied contrast, the deficiencies of their opposite numbers in England, those males whose manhood had been ravaged by creature comforts gained without hard work. G. K. Chesterton remarked of Kipling, "He admires England because she is strong, not because she is English."[44] This would suggest that Kipling's personal version of imperialism owed more to biological theories than to nationalism.

As a series of international incidents brought Germany and England closer to the brink of war, Kipling prepared his son John for a military career. In 1910 he visited Wellington School, which specialized in preparing boys for the army, and wrote to his thirteen-year-old glowingly about its motto FILII HEROUM (Sons of Heroes), its military museum which featured as chief relic the cloak worn by Wellington at Waterloo, and—conveniently forgetting his barbed allusions to "flanneled fools" and "muddy oafs"—its cricket and football fields which were "a dream of delight."[45]

He tried his hand at an invasion story, "The Edge of the Evening" (1913), in which two German spies in an airplane equipped with engine silencer land in the garden of a country house leased by an American industrialist who has left his country because it has become "a government of the alien, by the alien, for the alien." When the spies flourish guns, the American lays one of them out cold while a guest, an ex-footballer at Harrow, smashes the other. Both spies are dead—poor physical condition is endemic among Germans—and the friends are faced with a dilemma: "It's our necks or Armageddon." Even though there is proof that the spies have been photographing English fortifications, they know that if they report the deaths the wishy-washy Liberal government will convict them as murderers in order to avoid an ugly incident with Germany. They solve the problem by placing the bodies back in the airplane, locking the controls, and sending it off toward the sea. "Poor chaps! We'd have had 'em to dinner if they hadn't lost their heads."[46] English coolheaded ingenuity easily foils the Germans, who are more pitiable than formidable when met man-for-man.*

*Max Beerbohm had shown remarkable prescience in anticipating Kipling's story of the German airmen with his parody, "P.C., X, 36" by R*D***RD K*PL*NG in *A Christmas Garland* (1912). The narrator and Police Constable x 36 mistake Santa Claus emerging from a chimney pot for a German spy carrying a suspicious-looking sack. When their

August 4, 1914. On the day when England declared war against Germany, Kipling jotted in his wife's diary the line, "Incidentally Armageddon begins," as though the event had been ordained years before—as indeed it had.[47] The war brought him a swift sense of relief; at one stroke many of the social and economic problems that had dogged England fell away—the industrial strikes, the Irish troubles, the suffragette violence. Within days he dashed off a poem for the *Times*, "For All We Have and Are," which explained that through wantonness England had lost the old comfortable world, and again raised the invasion specter with its lines

> For all we have and are,
> For all our children's fate,
> Stand up and take the war.
> The Hun is at the gate![48]

(Kipling was not the sort to mince words or to muffle his cudgel— Germans were Huns, and that was that.) His object was not to intimidate the English, but to prod them to accept their heritage, the ancient law of force. What was required was ". . . iron sacrifice / Of body, will, and soul." It concluded with the rousing Anglocentric lines

> What stands if Freedom fall?
> Who dies if England live?

This widely reprinted poem set the tone for the home front yellow press during the next four years.

Too old to fight, Kipling like thousands of venerable Abrahams offered his son for whatever sacrifice was required. On John's seventeenth birthday Kipling personally conveyed him to a recruiter only to suffer a bitter disappointment when the boy was rejected because of defective eyesight. Undaunted, Kipling obtained an audience with Lord Roberts and arranged for his son's commission in the Irish Guards. After John completed his basic training, Kipling praised him: "You have stood it like a white man and a son to be proud of."[49] Through his son, Kipling had become what he most admired, a soldier of the King.

---

captive snivels something about peace on earth, goodwill toward men, the constable replies: "The Noo Testament contains some uncommon nice readin' for old gents an' young ladies. But it ain't included in the librery o' the Force. We confine ourselves to the Old Testament—o.t., 'ot. An' 'ot you'll get it. Hup with that sack, an' quick march!"

Meanwhile, Kipling employed his pen on behalf of the English nation in what he conceived was nothing less than a holy war. Always he had been a good hater, but the war years brought out a ferocity and vindictiveness that has often embarrassed his admirers. "Mary Postgate," once characterized as "the wickedest story ever written,"[50] treats the supreme moment of a pathetic and lonely paid companion who lives vicariously through the nephew of her employer. She idolizes young Fowler, whom she helped to rear, although he treats her shabbily. When he is killed in a training flight, she is unable to cry and feels only anger at the Germans. Mrs. Fowler instructs her to burn his toys and books, which she collects and carries to the garden incinerator. While fetching paraffin from the village she encounters the body of a nine-year-old girl just killed in an air raid. Then, as she lights her fire, she hears groans behind the hedge and finds a badly wounded German pilot. He begs her for a doctor, but she refuses, vowing to stay till "the thing" is dead. This, she thinks, is proper women's work, for men would be required to be "sportsmen" and save the creature. She reflects in her matter-of-fact way: "Tea would be at five. If It did not die before that time, she would be soaked and would have to change."[51] Patiently she stokes her incinerator, and commands him to stop groaning. After hearing the German's dying gasps she rises contentedly, takes a hot bath before tea to ward off the chill, and comes down looking "quite handsome," in the words of her employer.*

If pity is not an appropriate emotion for an enemy, neither is it suitable for that more verminous creature in Kipling's nest of hatreds—the neutral. In "The Sea Constables," one Maddington, a middle-aged businessman serving as a naval reserve officer, tells a band of similar officers how he had stalked a neutral vessel which was carrying diesel fuel destined for a German submarine. Unable to blow "Uncle Newt" from the water because it might provoke a diplomatic rupture, he nonetheless sticks so close that the refueling has to be abandoned. Frustrated, the neutral skipper puts in at an out-of-the-way Irish port and sells his fuel to the locals. Maddington boards the neutral vessel and finds the skipper desperately ill. When he tells Maddington that unless he is carried at

---

*The source of "Mary Postgate" was an anti-German poster, based on a report from the front, which featured a smirking German nurse pouring water onto the ground as a wounded English soldier reached for it. Part of the caption reads: "There is no woman in Britain who would do it / There is no woman in Britain who will forget it." Kipling apparently wished to show his approval of an English woman's unexpected capacity for revenge.

A wartime recruiting poster, said to be the inspiration for Kipling's story, "Mary Postgate."

once to the mainland for medical aid he will die, Maddington replies, "That's *your* business. Good afternoon." The reserve officers drink a toast—"Damnation to all neutrals."[52] For Kipling no middle ground existed. He never forgave the United States for its delay in entering the war, and after meeting Woodrow Wilson at Buckingham Palace following the war he dismissed him as an "arid Schoolmaster."[53] As might be expected, he admired Theodore Roosevelt.

When the Huns failed to capitulate before the English and the mounting casualty lists brought a horrible new genre of reading matter before the English public, Kipling betrayed uneasiness about the progress of the war. Writing to his friend H. Rider Haggard about the Battle of Neuve Chapelle, acclaimed as a victory by the press, Kipling expressed concern about the 724 officer casualties and exclaimed, "Heaven save us from more such 'victories.'"[54] Haggard wrote in his diary that the Kiplings were "terrified lest he [John] should be sent to the front and killed, as has happened to nearly all the young men they know."[55] In August 1915 the Second Irish Guards were ordered across the Channel, and in the same month Kipling went to France as guest of the French. He visited Clemenceau, talked with General Nivelle, and toured a quiet sector of the front. He marveled at a surrealist landscape poisoned by German gas, enjoyed a fifteen-course lunch which included crayfish and fillet of beef, and peeped through a loophole at a German trench only "the length of a cricket-pitch" distant. The general told him that all his soldiers knew Kipling's books—"Yes, yes, especially the Jungle Books." Kipling found the trenches "beautifully clean and kept like a museum . . . There was no smell save the smell of cookery." With the air of a seasoned campaigner he wrote his son, who was moving up into trenches less savory, that he should be sure to put boric acid in his socks and rabbit netting overhead as a protection against hand grenades. (He thought tennis netting might also work, but did not suggest where this might be found at the front.) From his Paris hotel he added, "It's a grand life though and does not give you a dull moment."[56]

One month later John Kipling became one of the estimated 20,000 British dead in the failed attempt to break the German line at Loos. He was last seen falling to the rear while trying to tie a field dressing around his mouth shattered by a shell fragment. He was crying with pain. Another shell dropped nearby and, when the smoke cleared away, John Kipling, who had just turned eighteen, had vanished forever.[57]

In November Kipling wrote about John's death to his old schoolmate, General L. C. Dunsterville (the original of Stalky): "I'm sorry that all the years' work ended in that one afternoon but—lots of people are in our position—and it's something to have bred a man."[58] Despite the bold front, he was deeply embittered against those whom he regarded as responsible for John's death—the Germans, the labor unions, the Radical Party, the Irish. Never gentle with an enemy, he now wrote with pen dipped in black bile, registering most of his hatred upon the Germans, who were seen as a species of humanity apart from Homo sapiens. For the *Daily Express* he contributed this denunciation:

> One thing we must get into our thick heads is that whenever the German man or woman gets a suitable culture to thrive in he or she means death and loss to civilized people, precisely as the germs of any disease mean death or loss to mankind. There is no question of hate or anger or excitement in the matter, any more than there is flushing out sinks. . . . The German is typhoid or plague—*Pestio teutonicus* if you like.[59]

After hearing that certain English officers had condoned the execution of German prisoners of war, he expressed his satisfaction to Dunsterville, "I almost begin to hope that when we have done with him there will be very little Hun left."[60] Annihilation of the German race became a motif of his writing, as in his book for the navy written to encourage the auxiliary services: "We shall finish the German eagle as the merciful lady killed the chicken. It took her the whole afternoon, and then, you will remember, the carcass had to be thrown away."[61] In 1917 when the rumor mills ground out the story that Germans had constructed a corpse factory in which their war dead were being processed into pig food, Kipling gleefully wrote his supreme denunciation of Hunnery:

> Charlotte, when she saw what Herman
> Yielded after he was dead,
> Like a well-conducted German,
> Spread him lightly on her bread.[62]

The war provided Kipling with a concentrated target for his anger. His carping attacks on English decadence had given way, under the press of personal agony, to attacks upon the Germans that were as far beyond good taste as they were beyond reasonable cause. He had always had a genius for echoing the vox populi, and now, in a war which demanded for its continuance the support of the entire empire, the British had found their minnesinger of hatred.

▼

After the war Kipling became England's paramount custodian of the War Dead. As a member of the Imperial War Graves Commission he authored the inscription used in the military cemeteries throughout France and Belgium: "Their Name Liveth For Evermore." On one visitation he did find the chewed stumps of Chalk-Pit Wood, where John had disappeared, but his son's body was never located. In 1922 he joined the King's pilgrimage to the devastated war zone, their party including Field Marshal Sir Douglas Haig, whose strategy had contributed mightily to the ubiquitous cemeteries. Kipling wrote *The Irish Guards in the Great War* (1923), a two-volume history of John's regiment, an eerie work in which battlefield maps are drawn like charts for children's folk stories and adorned with winsome skulls and hourglasses. Its deepest defects, in the opinion of Edmund Blunden, a poet who fought in Flanders, were a frivolous tone and a failure to comprehend the suffering and agony of a real battlefield.[63] This is understandable, for by this time most memories of John Kipling had relapsed into nursery and boyhood years. It was far better to erect a mental shield and to convert the nightmarish realities of wartime France into an adventure story that might have been written by Henty or Stevenson.

T. S. Eliot has expressed his admiration for two categories of Kipling's verse—his hymns, like "The Recessional" and his epigrams, notably his *Epitaphs of the War* (1919), a series of terse, often ironic poems commemorating those killed in the war.[64] Curbing his tendency toward overkill, Kipling removed all the detritus from his portraits, which are sharp and clear as if etched in stone. They range in subject from native water carriers to nurses' aides and as in his early work, his sympathy lay with the naive and the obscure:

THE BEGINNER
On my first hour of my first day
In the front trench I fell.
(Children in boxes at a play
Stand up to watch it well.)[65]

For the slack or manipulator Kipling fetched his fluoride stylus:

BOMBED IN LONDON
On land and sea I strove with anxious care
To escape conscription. It was in the air![66]

A DEAD STATESMAN

I could not dig: I dared not rob:
Therefore I lied to please the mob.
Now all my lies are proved untrue
And I must face the men I slew.
What tale shall serve me here among
Mine angry and defrauded young?[67]

The hatreds of the war years burned out slowly. For a time Kipling and Rider Haggard sponsored the Liberty League, a publicity campaign to warn the nation of bolshevism, but both writers came to feel that they had fallen out of touch with the times. They agreed that contemporary England was going to hell but disagreed about the cause—Kipling blaming the Jews and Haggard the labor unions.[68] With the old verities destroyed by the war, he sought comfort in synthetic mythic structures like the Masons (which figure in *Debits and Credits* (1926), a postwar collection of stories) as a substitute for Christian brotherhood. By this time he had lost caste with most English intellectuals, but King George admired him. After his death in 1936 he was buried in the Poet's Corner of Westminster Abbey. Conspicuous by their absence from the ceremony were English men of letters. Kipling would not have expected their attendance; he had taken their measure, to his own satisfaction, during the war years in a letter to H. Rider Haggard:

> The fine, superior folk, who for years set me down and proclaimed me a barbarian because I wrote of fighting . . . when only the sweet-smelling problems of high civilisation were worthy of treatment, are glad enough today of the virile fighting spirit which I believe I helped to evoke in many of the young men who are all that stand between us and dishonour, the yoke of slavery, and ultimate destruction.[69]

For progressives, Kipling was a disturbing reminder of the war and the war's waste, and worse than that, of the possibility that civilization in this twentieth century of the Christian era was little more than chipped rosewood veneer with rough lumber underneath.

▼

Wonderful is the atmosphere of war. When the millenium comes the world will gain much but it will lose its greatest thrill.
SIR ARTHUR CONAN DOYLE,
Memories and Adventures

"You have been in Afghanistan, I perceive."[1] With these famous words, Sherlock Holmes launched his longstanding but patronizing friendship with Dr. Watson, who, having just come to London to recuperate from a wound received in the recent Afghan War, got his first surprise at the astonishing capacity of Holmes for deduction from simple observation. The occasion was an introduction by a mutual friend, for Watson was seeking some congenial soul with whom he could share lodgings. The meeting occurred in a laboratory, where Watson was perplexed by Holmes' scientific tinkering with hemoglobin. Clearly he was not a medical student, nor was he pursuing a formal course of science. Although he found Holmes' powers of deduction extraordinary, Watson quickly learned that his friend was abysmally ignorant of quite commonplace subjects on which any cultivated gentleman might be expected to have a few ideas. About contemporary literature, philosophy, and politics, for instance, Holmes "knew next to almost nothing." He had never heard of the Copernican system, and on Watson's explaining to him that the Earth went round the Sun, he said that now that he knew it he would do his best to forget it. The capacity of the brain, Holmes explained, was finite, and only a fool would attempt to store mere "useless facts," which could squeeze out important ones. Against these limitations, Watson tallied up the compensating strengths: knowledge of botany ("well up in belladonna, opium, and poisons generally"); geology ("practical but limited"); chemistry ("profound"); and sensational literature ("immense. He appears to know every detail of every horror perpetrated in the century").[2]

As criminologist Sherlock Holmes is the incarnation of the amateur spirit: he is less concerned with bringing a criminal to justice (in many cases he allows the villain to go scot-free) than with savoring the nuances of the crime itself. In his contempt for the banal and the bourgeois values of the middle way, Holmes is as much a dilettante of the decadent nineties as Aubrey Beardsley or Oscar Wilde.* Congratulated by Watson for his easy solution to the Red Headed League conundrum, Holmes replies yawning, "It saved me from ennui. . . . My life is spent in one long effort to escape from the commonplaces of existence."[3] Totally unpredictable, he can swing in one moment from coolheaded grand inquisitor to mawkish sentimentalist rhapsodizing upon the beauty of a rose, and yet remain wholly oblivious, or indifferent, to the effect of this eccentricity upon lesser mortals wholly absorbed in locating a stolen naval treaty. His scientific research is as bizarre and as alien to the average citizen as the laboratory experiments of a Mr. Hyde or the depraved seminars of a Dorian Gray. As the foremost expert on 140 specimens of cigar ash and the author of such works as *Chaldean Roots in the Ancient Cornish Language* and *Practical Handbook of Bee Culture, with some Observations upon the Segregation of the Queen,* Holmes is a connoisseur of exotica wholly beyond the ken of professional bumblers from Scotland Yard like Lestrade and Gregson, who are incapable of solving an unusual crime but not above taking credit for it.[4] Alluding to these boorish professionals, Holmes tells Watson, "If a man is caught, it will be *on account* of their exertions; if he escapes it will be *in spite of* their exertions. It's heads I win, tails you lose."[5] Not that he cares, for recognition by the masses or advancement in some crass professional sense is distasteful to him. What could be more middle class? As Watson says, "His cold and proud nature was always averse to anything in the shape of public applause."[6] On one occasion, when mistaken for an inspector, he grumbles to his loyal Boswell, "Fancy his having the insolence to confound me with the official detective force!"[7]

The social contamination which the late Victorians associated with those engaged in "trade" carried over to the distinction they made

---

*In London during the 1880s, well before Wilde's homosexuality became public knowledge, Doyle had met Wilde and admired him. In discussing wars of the future, Wilde told him, "A chemist on each side will approach the frontier with a bottle." See Sir Arthur Conan Doyle, *Memories and Adventures* (Boston, 1924), 156.

between gentlemen and players, between amateurs and professionals. These nuances are instinctively felt by all characters in the Holmes saga. Holmes, for example, calls Lestrade "the best of the professionals," which makes the "little professional" somehow tolerable (but decidedly *not* a gentleman).[8] Conversely, when a provincial policeman assigned to assist Holmes on a case "looked doubtfully at the amateur," he is reassured by a Scotland Yard official, "I have worked with Mr. Holmes before. He plays the game."[9] Although hacks at Scotland Yard and among the provincial police forces may regard Holmes as nothing more than an "amateur," Doyle uses that term as the highest praise because the amateur labors for the love of adventure, not lucre. After foiling the robbers in "The Red Headed League," Holmes tells the bank manager, "I have been at some small expense over this matter, which I shall expect the bank to refund, but beyond that I am amply repaid by having had an experience which is in many ways unique." Most of the expenses which Holmes incurs in solving other people's problems appear to come from his own pocket. Although money (not passion) constitutes the pith and sinew of a typical Sherlock Holmes story, the author withholds specific information about the financial status of his hero so that we never learn what it is he lives on. Gentlemen are not supposed to inquire about such mundane matters, but by definition they are solvent.

Although we learn little about Holmes' antecedents, his political and social attitudes conform to those of a squirearchical public school man like Tom Brown of Rugby. He admires athletic prowess, and despite his frail appearance he somehow has kept himself fit and has been known to exhibit tremendous strength—sufficient to straighten, with his bare hands, a steel poker bent by the bully in "The Adventure of the Speckled Band." He is a skillful boxer and enjoys a man-to-man contest, especially when it entails the use of his "straight left against a slogging ruffian."[10] In another story he goes to great lengths to locate a missing athlete because "amateur sport is the best and soundest thing in England."[11] A host of public school men would have agreed. (It is characteristic of Doyle that in his autobiography he remarks, "Like most boys, I would rather have been knocked down by a first-class cricketer than picked up by a second-rater.")[12]

Without Sherlock Holmes, Arthur Conan Doyle would figure as little more than an obscure footnote in literary history. The neurasthenic figure of Holmes, with Watson, his tagalong in ubiquitous bowler hat, are fictional characters like Don Quixote and Sancho Panza who have achieved worldwide status. So it is ironical that Doyle came to regard them as a kind of monstrous aberration of his imagination. In his memoirs he writes disparagingly of his creation, whose existence "has tended to obscure my higher work," and peevishly concludes that if Holmes had not existed his position "would at the present moment be a more commanding one."[13] At one point Doyle resolved to free himself from the Baker Street connection by killing off his nemesis. After twenty-two of his Sherlock Holmes tales had appeared in *Strand Magazine* between July 1891 and November 1893, Doyle threw Holmes, locked in the arms of the fiendish Professor Moriarty, into the Reichenbach gorge, but the outcry from disappointed fans was so great—along with loss of income—that the author felt compelled to resurrect him ten years later.*

The Sherlock Holmes tales are relatively free of the jingoist scaremongering associated with the 1890s, a decade when Le Queux, Kipling, and Wells burst into public favor with their analyses of racial decay and warnings of national disaster. Even passing allusions to international events are rare in the first wave of Holmes stories (1891–93). An exception is "The Adventure of the Naval Treaty" in which Holmes is called on to restore a secret treaty between Italy and England, the publication of which would result in great embarrassment, or perhaps a war with France and Russia. (In the early 1890s, as we have seen, the xenophobia of the Foreign Office was directed toward France, not Germany.) Le Queux would not have missed an opportunity to wrench a spy thriller from this situation, but in Doyle's story the thief is revealed as only a brother-in-law-to-be, motivated solely by a sudden itch for money, who stole the treaty after stumbling upon it.

Nor is Professor Moriarty an international villain. Although Holmes calls him "A Napoleon of crime . . . the organizer of half that is evil and of nearly all that is undetected in this great city,"[14] the exact nature of the professor's evil deeds is never made clear. Apparently Doyle wished to increase the odds against Holmes (whom he was coming to resent as a roadblock in his literary career) by giving him a formidable opponent, but his conception of criminal behavior rarely strayed beyond simple theft or an occasional tepid murder.† He was, of course,

---

*He was persuaded to return to Sherlock Holmes by *Collier's Weekly Magazine*, which offered $45,000 for thirteen stories. His agreement was unenthusiastic: on a postcard he wrote, "Very well. A. C. D." See Richard L. Green and John M. Gibson, *A Bibliography of A. Conan Doyle* (Oxford, 1983), 140.

†The remoteness of the writer from criminality is seen in Holmes' statement to Watson

too much a gentleman to inflict upon his readers scenes of rape, bestiality, or perversion. Indeed, Conan Doyle's attitudes toward good and evil have a childlike naïveté. As he conceived it, evil had existence wholly within a rational framework bounded on all sides by the illegal acquisition of money. Crimes committed with irrational purpose or stemming from psychological aberration have small place in the Sherlock Holmes canon. The Marxist critic Georg Lukács makes a telling point when he alludes to the detective genre of Conan Doyle as representative of that species of popular literature firmly grounded in a "philosophy of security," with Sherlock Holmes as the personification of an omniscient overseer "who watched over the stability of bourgeois life."[15] For a reader of these tales, the fear of antisocial behavior (almost always restricted to violations of pound-and-shilling morality) is immediately purged by the timely arrival of Holmes with his eagle eye. Good invariably triumphs; might and right have enlisted in the same legions. These stories reinforced sturdy middle-class values against the floodtides of anarchy at a time when protective dikes appeared to be leaking.

▼

Arthur Conan Doyle (1859–1930) had none of that instinctive distrust of foreigners—especially of Germans—that had characterized Kipling. After attending Stonyhurst, where he approved of beatings as "one of the best trainings for a hard life,"[16] he went on to a Jesuit school in the Vorarlberg and afterward confessed that in Austria he sloughed off a habit of rebelliousness and become a "pillar of law and order." After completing medical school in Edinburgh at age twenty he spent seven months in the Arctic as surgeon aboard a whaling vessel, followed by another term on a merchant ship plying between ports in West Africa. With time on his hands, he began writing stories to supplement his meager income, but at this time had no thought of becoming a professional author. Like Henry Newbolt and others of the period, Doyle was infatuated with the grandeur of the (imagined) English chivalric past. His early novel *The White Company* (1891), set in the Hundred Years' War, abounds in jousts, tavern brawls, distressed maidens, besieged castles, and culminates in a massive battle in which the English com-

---

(vide "The Adventure of the Empty House") that during attempts on his life Moriarty was nowhere near but was "working out problems on a blackboard ten miles away." Why does the professor need a blackboard to dispatch his assassins?

pany acquires honor through its valorous struggle against overwhelming odds. This is "high" literature of a derivative sort, which was intended, as he said, to "illuminate our national traditions,"[17] but it was soon abandoned for the more lucrative Sherlock Holmes tales, which he always regarded as an inferior genre.

It was the Boer War which ignited Doyle's strain of militant—as opposed to romantic—patriotism. Leaving wife and bairn in England, he traveled to South Africa in 1898 to join the crusade against those stubborn Dutch farmers who had defied the empire. His major service as physician came at Bloemfontein where an epidemic of dysentery proved more lethal than Boer guns. Apart from this, Doyle undertook a work of extraordinary ambition—a one-man history of the war based upon observations and interviews, including one with a war correspondent named Winston Churchill. Published in 1901 as *The Great Boer War*, this massive tome went through sixteen editions in three years and upstaged the "official history" of the war prepared by a stable of researchers and writers at a cost of 27,000 pounds. Doyle explained that his title did not denote scale of the war but merely differentiated it from the smaller Boer War of 1881 (in which England was resoundingly defeated at Majuba Hill). Despite his disclaimer, it nonetheless echoes the "great war" theme that was beginning to encroach into the consciousness of so many European intellectuals at century's end. "Great" Britain, Columb's and Le Queux's "great" war fictions, the "Great" Boer War, the "Great" War of 1914–18—size and magnitude, even in visions of destruction, characterized this materialistic era.

The Great Boer War is a partisan work in the sense that it pleads the case for England's initiating and prosecuting the war, but it nevertheless records some situations unflattering to the home team, such as bickering among army commanders, and it characterizes the Boers as a worthy opponent. The book opens with a tribute to "one of the most rugged, virile, unconquerable races ever seen upon earth," a race of "hard-bitten farmers with their ancient theology and their inconveniently modern rifles."[18] While repeatedly granting the Dutch manly physical vigor, Doyle criticizes their ethical standards, their resistance to English demands that slavery be abolished, their extraction of huge taxes from Uitlanders (outsiders) in Transvaal without granting them matching representation in the government, their backward views on education, their intractable attitude toward British commissioners. Having briefly established the causes of the conflict, Doyle moves along rapidly with a comprehensive account of the military campaigns of the war, a work so readable and exhaustive that it is still cited as a primary source by historians of the Boer War. Yet Doyle is more convincing when showing process than when arriving at conclusions. What he wanted the reader to carry away from the final chapter was not that the imperial army in its last campaign opposed a paltry force of no more than twenty thousand Boers—hardly cause for a "victory" parade— but rather that "two sturdy and unemotional races clasped hands the instant that the fight was done." The final paragraphs of the book consist of a paean to imperial unity: England had gone into the war, but the Empire had come out, its fragmented particles—English, Irish, Indian, Canadian, Australian—welded together at last in "the blood brotherhood of the Empire." The British flag in South Africa means "clean government, honest laws, liberty and equality for all [sic] men."[19] Imbedded in this unification rhetoric there lies an apprehension that the historic relationship between mother country and colony has shifted: originally the colony had relied for protection on Britain; now it was the other way round.

That Doyle was profoundly disturbed by his country's poor performance in the Boer War is shown by his essay "Some Military Lessons of the War" in *Cornhill Magazine*. Intended as a final chapter for his history, it caused an outcry from certain quarters of the British army largely because it exposed their limitations in the science of war. Doyle had been astonished that the amateur armies of the Boers had so often outclassed the British professionals and he proposed changes in theory and in tactics. "Our professional soldiers have not shown that they were endowed with clear vision," he wrote. "In the face of their manifest blunders and miscalculations a civilian need not hesitate to express his opinion."[20] Implicit here is Doyle's faith in the superior wisdom of the enlightened amateur in devising means to insure survival of individual and society—a basic Tory premise. Some of his recommendations were as shocking as they were astute. He suggested scrapping the cavalry altogether except as a force of mounted rifles,* relegating swords and revolvers to museums, masking artillery with camouflage and scattering batteries in action, and altering tactics to conform to the idiosyncrasies of terrain. A final lesson transformed outcry into outrage; Doyle argued for mobilization of all civilians capable of bearing arms into a national

---

*Erskine Childers had also concluded that the *arme blanche* ("cold steel") was obsolete and wrote a book on the subject, *War and the Arme Blanche* (1910). On one occasion he and Doyle mounted a platform together to plead the case. Cavalry officers in the audience were incensed by these heretical opinions. See Doyle, *Memories*, 208.

militia responsible for home defense. This flew in the face of an ancient English aversion toward conscription, which was regarded as incompatible with individual liberty and suitable only for lockstep continental nations like Germany and France. Doyle's observation of the Boer's mobilization, in which every man was a potential soldier, reinforced his faith in the untapped resources of the amateur and the patriot as opposed to the professional. Returning to his native heath, Doyle promptly organized a private rifle company in his village of Hindhead and paid the cost of rifles and targets from his own pocket. Thus began his own campaign to arouse England to preparedness.

Within army circles a vanguard of reformists, which included Baden-Powell, Ian Hamilton (Kitchener's chief of staff and later commander of the Gallipoli expedition), and Lord Roberts, endorsed Doyle's criticisms of obsolete army policies and found in him a tireless and able propagandist for their progressive ideas. An immediate problem was the fact that Great Britain had emerged from the Boer War with a bad press. Germany's excoriation of English brutality in South Africa was predictable, but some liberal journalists like W. T. Stead had charged that British troops had committed rape, extortion, and wanton acts of plunder. Moreover, the world press had expressed angry alarm about the concentration camps ringed by barbed wire in which an estimated hundred thousand Boer women, children, and other noncombatants were penned up without adequate food, water, or medical supplies. The result had been epidemics, with measles as the principal killer. It fell to A. Conan Doyle to answer these charges. His pamphlet, *The War in South Africa: Its Cause and Conduct* (1902), written in only eight days, is a masterpiece of special pleading which was widely disseminated throughout the world. (Three hundred thousand copies were sold in the English edition; translations promptly appeared in French, German, Norwegian, and even Tamil and Welsh.) As the internationally famous author of the Sherlock Holmes stories, Doyle spoke from an elevated platform of respectability and cool rationality.

The quarrel with the Boers, according to Doyle, was rooted in England's "philanthropic view of the rights of the native."[21] The abolition of slavery in English territory was resented by the Boers, even though slave owners were compensated for their loss. It was true, of course, that rates of compensation averaged only sixty to seventy pounds per slave—well below the market rates—and that London middlemen took a large percentage as commission, but the Boers in this and in other matters remained less "highly educated and progressive" than the En-

glish settlers in the back country.[22] Doyle referred to the Boers as a
throwback to the seventeenth century—except for their knowledge of
twentieth century firepower. When they withdrew from Cape Colony to
establish their independent state of Transvaal, it was good riddance to
bad rubbish. But the discovery of gold in the Dutch state tipped the
uneasy balance between the two races. The Boer War resulted from the
failure of the Transvaal Volksraad to respect the rights of English
nationals who swarmed into the country during the gold rush. In time
the Uitlanders achieved numerical superiority over the Boers, but they
were not given equal representation in the Raad. (Doyle converted the
Dutch parliament into a comic travesty of democratic process à la
Punch by inserting highlights of proceedings such as the debate over
whether the Raad should define the size and shape of neckties and
characterizations of ignorant delegates who inquired whether an aerial
tramway was a balloon or a machine that could fly in the air.) After
21,000 Uitlanders (which he called "British helots") petitioned the
Queen for redress, Great Britain had no alternative except to intervene
on moral grounds—and the fact that Transvaal possessed the richest
gold fields in the world had not an iota to do with the decision.

Doyle then proceeded to "demolish" certain ill-informed criticisms
of English policy which had circulated widely in the West. The Boer
War had not been a war on behalf of promoters or capitalists ("It is
difficult to imagine how a state of unrest and insecurity can ever be to
the advantage of capital"), while the charge that Britain wanted Transvaal for herself was "ridiculous."[23] He dismissed out of hand the argument that the war had pitted a monarchy against a republic, for Transvaal, not Britain, stood for "tyranny, race ascendancy, corruption,
taxation without representation."[24] To those who objected on grounds
that a strong nation had bullied a weaker one, he responded that the
British were actually outnumbered—at least in the opening rounds of
the war!

Perhaps more nettlesome were specific charges against the British
army which had been documented by neutral journalists countless
times and which violated traditional rules of civilized warfare: the wanton burning of Boer farms and homesteads, along with the execution of
civilians; use of hollow-pointed bullets; putting hostages on trains to
deter derailments; and establishing those terrible concentration camps
for civilians. To vindicate England, Doyle plunged in with all the
confidence of a Sherlock Holmes solving a single-pipe problem. Farms
had been burned but only when they harbored bushwhackers, and

Doyle reminded his readers that the Hague conventions required that authorized combatants wear proper uniforms. (The logic here goes this way: Bushwhackers do not wear uniforms / Most Boers do not wear uniforms / Therefore, most Boers are bushwhackers.) On the explosive bullet scandal Doyle conceded that a quantity of hollow nose had been sent to South Africa before the war "for target-practice only."[25] When the war broke out they had been recalled because this type of ammunition was "not for use in a war with *white* races [my italics]" but a few were unfortunately used against Boers, wholly by accident. As to hostages on trains, this was an acceptable deterrent because the Germans had originated it during the Franco-Prussian War. And finally, in the matter of concentration camps Doyle averred that the sites were well chosen, the captives had a "spare" but not a starvation diet which would have been adequate if the Boer armies had not cut supply lines, and while the water supply was inadequate, this was a general condition throughout South Africa. Doyle admitted that there was a shortage of tents, but there was absolutely no overcrowding for the simple reason that "to overcrowd a tent is hygienically almost impossible, for the atmosphere of a tent, however crowded, will never become tainted in the same sense as a room."[26] While the mortality rate in the camps was "deplorable," Doyle, a licensed physician, argued that death by measles did not result from filth, as with typhus. Moreover, the real culprits were not the English but the Boer mothers, who refused to allow sick children to be separated and insisted upon quack remedies like painting the eruptions with green paint. Finally, a major reason for deaths in the camps was "the dirty habits of the parents themselves."[27] (How to keep clean without providing adequate water the doctor did not trouble to explain.) In sum, Doyle was satisfied with the conduct of the British soldiery in the South African War. After all, Lord Roberts himself had said that his men had "behaved like gentlemen," so it must be true.[28]

For Conan Doyle the most enduring legacy of the Boer War was a bitter dose of Germanophobia. He had been at first troubled, then angered, by the acrimonious denunciations of English policy in the German press. He felt no bitterness toward the French or the Russians, whose public attacks had been equally hostile, because, as he said, the French press was merely spiteful because of English criticism during the Dreyfus case, while nobody took seriously Russian criticism because freedom of the press in that country did not exist. But Doyle bitterly announced that the alliance between Britain and Germany which had existed since the days of Marlborough and Napoleon had been severed by German calumnies, which he attributed to governmental intervention in the press. As such, this was black ingratitude, because throughout history the British navy had saved the Germans from crushing defeats. Five years ago the prospect of Germany's defeat in a European war would have caused Britain to intervene on her behalf. "Now it is certain that in our lifetime no British guinea and no soldier's life would under any circumstances be spent for such an end."[29] In concluding his pamphlet Doyle wrote of this volte-face in Anglo-German relations: "That is one strange result of the Boer War, and in the long run it is possible that it may prove not the least important." Henceforth, the voice of Arthur Conan Doyle would join that of other influential litterateurs in pointing to the German danger. Just three months after the publication of his Boer War apologia, he was offered, and accepted, a knighthood for services rendered. The navy already had its literary mascot in Sir Henry Newbolt; now Sir Arthur Conan Doyle would serve as bristling watchdog for the English army.

▼

The Boer War brought Doyle into the public arena. Although the authorities regarded his service as invaluable, the common folk were less impressed. Twice he ran for Parliament as a Conservative, and was twice defeated. Although far to the right of center on the Irish question and women's suffrage (suffragettes several times poured vitriol into his letter box), his fervent belief in free enterprise led him in 1909 to write *The Crime of the Congo* (1909), an exposé of the rule of Leopold II on grounds that the Belgian monarch had created a family monopoly under the legal fiction of a free state. Doyle gave nine lectures on this subject—one of them at Albert Hall—and eventually Rudyard Kipling had to intervene to call him off. Kipling feared that further criticism of the Congo problem might bring Germany and Belgium into closer diplomatic affinity. Like Doyle, Kipling was wound up tight on the German menace, but he was less confident of a successful outcome in the event of war. "We are in no shape to stand up to Germany on the sea," he warned Doyle. "On land, of course, we haven't an earthly."[30]

Throughout this period Doyle remained an avid amateur sportsman. Hamlin Garland, a visiting American writer who plumed himself on his baseball prowess, was amazed to find that a cricket veteran like Sir Arthur could catch his fast pitch with bare hands. Perhaps seeking the universal nostrum that William James called a "moral equivalent of war," Doyle became intrigued by the Olympic games idea, although as he watched the blatant nationalism of gentlemen amateurs at the 1908 Olympiad—the Americans' lack of modesty he especially deplored—he theorized that the Grecian wars might have had their origin in the ancient games. (Doyle became a member of the committee arranging for the 1916 games—cancelled, of course, when the Great Powers became engrossed in real war.) The same competitive rage marred other international events. He participated in the Prince Henry motor race of 1912, which covered a route in both England and Germany. The fact that the Agadir crisis occurred on the second day convinced Doyle, along with countless Englishmen who read the *Daily Mail*, that Prince Henry, who was also head of the German navy, had engineered the race as a cover for his move in Morocco. If the race was designed to bring the two countries together, it failed miserably. A typical assessment of the Germans was voiced by one of Doyle's fellow drivers, an officer of British intelligence, who snapped, "The only thing I want to do with these people is to fight them."[31] The officer went on to predict that war would break out as soon as Germany finished widening the Kiel Canal—a remarkably accurate guess, since the project was accomplished in June 1914. Ill will seemed to be universal as the first decade of the new century came to an end. One of Doyle's American fans, Theodore Roosevelt, wrote him a letter expounding his theory that the Kaiser had been jealous of King Edward's dog, which had followed the procession at the King's funeral in 1910, because the faithful pet had attracted more attention than the Emperor himself.[32] In such an environment of mistrust and anxiety, abusing the Kaiser and reviling the German character had turned into a slugfest with gentlemanly rules suspended for the duration.

The anger of English officialdom turned into alarm with the publication in 1912 of Count Friedrich von Bernhardi's treatise on war, translated in England as *Germany and the Next War*. World war, according to the author, was not only inevitable, it was desirable. Spinning off from Nietzsche and Spencer and reading like an *ur-Mein Kampf*, the book argued that "war is not merely a necessary element in the life of nations but an indispensable factor of culture, in which a true civilized nation finds the highest expression of strength and vitality."[33] The trouble with modern Germany, according to the count's diagnosis, was not its belligerence but its degeneration into a nation of peacemakers preoccupied with making and spending money. Germany's industrial muscle, coupled with its genius for business—English "shopkeepers" would not have appreciated his boast that "the Germans are born business men, more than any others in the world"[34]—had created a surplus in goods and population which could only be absorbed beyond her borders, but unlike the other Great Powers she had few colonies to accommodate the overflow. Her historical mission lay in guarding her present territory (von Bernhardi made it sound like invasions from France and Russia were imminent) and, after construction of a superior fleet, in pressing outward for sufficient lebensraum. German military policy must exploit weaknesses in the Portuguese empire, invalidate Belgian claims in Africa, assist Austria's position in the Balkans, and leave France "so completely crushed that she can never again come across our path."[35] The next war would be fought against the combined forces of Russia, France, and Britain, but Germany would overcome her numerical inferiority by tactical superiority, intelligent generalship, and "prompt use of opportunity"—which to non-German ears had a particularly ominous sound. Especially disturbing to Whitehall was von Bernhardi's proposal for cutting the British Empire in two by supporting a Turkish invasion of Egypt. Filled with bellicose quotations ransacked from authorities as diverse as Christ, Luther, and Wagner, *Germany and the Next War* seemed to speak for an entire German nation turned rabid with war fever. In view of the epidemic of xenophobia sweeping across Western Europe at this time, the book came at the worst possible time.

Doyle was delegated, or he chose, to answer von Bernhardi in an article titled "Great Britain and the Next War," which first appeared in *Fortnightly Review* (1913) and later as a pamphlet widely circulated in Britain and in America as cement for a dreamed of permanent Anglo-American bond. By coolly summarizing the count's principal arguments, Doyle succeeded in presenting a masterly case for English equanimity when juxtaposed against Prussian fanaticism of the von Bernhardi stripe. While he denied that England could be invaded, he admitted that if France were attacked, England would be obliged to assist her. In that event what he most feared was an unknown factor in naval warfare, the submarine, which "like the fox in the poultry yard" could pick off ships carrying troops and supplies to France.[36] The solution lay in pushing forward with a Channel tunnel to provide a link with British allies on the continent. In conclusion he warned that von Bernhardi spoke for a large segment of Germany and that England would be mad not to take his book seriously.

Now convinced that a war with Germany lay in the offing, Doyle actively campaigned for the Channel tunnel as a way to foil the submarine menace. After being politely ignored by leading naval men, he turned to the medium of popular fiction to sound his personal alarm. "Danger! A Story of England's Peril," which appeared in *Strand Magazine* (which earlier had carried his Sherlock Holmes stories) just a few weeks before the outbreak of war, is narrated by Captain John Sirius, a submariner of Norland, a small country threatened by England because of an insignificant boundary dispute in a far-flung colony. Although the Norland authorities wish to capitulate after receiving an ultimatum, Sirius gains reluctant permission to lead eight submarines into the fray. He has no intention of committing suicide by taking on the British navy; instead, he plans to systematically destroy food ships and thereby starve England into submission. His submarines, lurking outside English ports and linked by wireless, sink freighters with impunity. From captured newspapers he watches as wheat prices in England climb from thirty-five to eighty-four shillings and as bread riots force the authorities to post armed guards outside Parliament to protect the lawmakers from angry mobs.

The English are outraged by these unsportsmanlike attacks on unarmed merchantmen and by the refusal of the Norland submarines to engage "legitimate" warships. Foreigners respect nothing—not even the rules of civilized warfare. But Sirius recognizes that "playing the game" is irrelevant in modern war: "It is like the Arabs who think that a flank attack is a mean, unmanly device. War is not a big game, my English friends. It is a desperate business to gain the upper hand, and one must use one's brains to find the weak spot of the enemy."[37] In an episode that foreshadows the sinking of the *Lusitania* in 1915, Sirius catches the largest liner in the world steaming up the Channel at twenty-three knots and with one torpedo sends her to the bottom "like a broken eggshell." Here is warfare as von Bernhardi taught it. The Admiralty aches to retaliate by invading Norland but dares not move because it is suicidal to send transports loaded with soldiers into a sea infested with invisible submarines. In the end, England has no recourse except to swallow her pride and arrange a peace on Norland's terms. The humiliation suffered by the powerful British navy is even greater than that endured by the army during the Boer War. A *Times* leader proclaims that England had been fortunate in fighting a minor power like Norland: "Had we endured this humiliation at the hands of any of the first-class powers it would certainly have entailed the loss of all our crown colonies . . . besides the payment of a huge indemnity."[38] The veiled allusion to Germany was unmistakable.

On this potential danger from submarines Sir Arthur's was a voice coming straight from the future, but few heeded his warning. *Strand Magazine* published twelve responses to "Danger!" (seven of them from admirals), but only two agreed with him, and one dissenter merely compared him to Jules Verne.[39] The tunnel scheme would be debated without resolution for another seventy years, but the German submarine campaign lay only two years away. Rejected as a prophet in his own country, Doyle, always an ardent patriot, was warmly praised by the German secretary of navy in 1917 for his brilliant insights into submarine warfare!*

Doyle proved less convincing as an augur with his novel *The Poison Belt* (1913), an incursion into the field of apocalyptic fiction staked out by H. G. Wells. The inspiration for his plot apparently came from the panic of 1910, created by quasi-scientists who theorized that when the Earth passed through the tail of Halley's Comet it would enter a "poison belt" fatal to human life. To flesh out his plot he reworked his successful Holmes-Watson relationship—creating an eccentric but brilliant scientist named Professor George Challenger and his awed Boswell, the reporter Malone; Moriarty appears, radically changed from evil mastermind to ineffectual fussbudget, as Professor Summerlee, who invariably guesses wrong and is insanely jealous of Challenger.†

After news arrives in England of strange illnesses sweeping out of control in Sumatra, Challenger warns that the solar system is presently floating through a belt of poisonous ether that may eliminate all life on planet Earth. He summons Malone and Summerlee to his country house so that they may face the catastrophe together. Already symptoms of erratic behavior are apparent in Britain: Summerlee occasionally abandons coherent speech for bird and animal cries; Challenger bites his housekeeper in the leg and must fight an urge to hide behind a door and startle his wife by a wild cry. Reports arrive of decimations

---

*Doyle's submarines were of 800 tons, had 1600 h.p., and attained 18 knots speed on the surface versus the early German U-boats' 900 tons, 2000 h.p., and 16 knots. Obviously these were not the fanciful guesses of an amateur. Presumably Doyle was given this information by someone of major influence in the Admiralty who had access to reports by British spies. See Charles Higham, *The Adventures of Conan Doyle* (New York, 1976), 231; for the Reichstag allusion, see Green and Gibson, *Bibliography*, 189.

†These characters had already appeared in his novel *The Lost World* (1912), an H. Rider Haggard spin-off in which they penetrate the South American hinterland and confront a variety of prehistoric creatures such as "missing links" and pterodactyls. This was about the time that Doyle claimed, quite seriously, that he had found a four-foot ichthyosaurus in the Aegean.

among "the less developed races."[40] (The northern races have greater resistance, for in Austria the Slavs succumb quickly while the Teutons hold on longer).

To prolong their lives, Challenger has prepared a room which has been taped and sealed, fitted with oxygen tanks, and supplied with a large shrub (to absorb some of the carbon dioxide). In a scene worthy of Wodehouse, Challenger informs his faithful chauffeur:

> "I'm expecting the end of the world today, Austin."
> "Yes, sir. What time, sir?"
> "I can't say, Austin. Before evening."
> "Very good, sir."[41]

From time to time Challenger opens a transom to allow the poison ether to escape. (Inexplicably no poison seeps in during this ventilation.) From the window they see distant fires as cities burn. But Challenger is unfazed; like Sherlock Holmes, he believes that the human mind should be able to think out a point of abstract knowledge in the interval between falling from a balloon and smashing into the earth. He has time to outline his philosophical belief that the world was created to produce and sustain human life, and Summerlee has time to counter that this is only a monstrous humanoid conceit.

Quite without warning they discover they have survived: the earth has passed through the fatal poison belt. But the vast horror at inhabiting a dead world robs them of their initial joy. Austin drives them into London through scenes of congested, frozen traffic, relieved only by an asthmatic old woman, spared by her oxygen tank, who has one all-important question: "What effect will these events have upon London and North-Western Railway shares?"[42] After they have returned home the world becomes alive once more. Challenger explains: the world had passed through a twenty-eight hour catalepsy, and now everyone will resume his life where he left it—everyone, that is, except those mistakenly buried during the period of the trance or those killed in the temporary apocalypse.

The Poison Belt is a slipshod, silly work in which Sir Arthur ventured into the dominion of science fiction pioneered by Verne and Wells and quickly found himself well beyond his depth in scientific preparation and ordinary plausibility. Fed up with the failure of mankind to be rational, Doyle toys with the destruction of the world, changes his mind, and emerges with grave doubts about the value and validity of material existence. This novel marks the beginning of the end of his hyperratiocination phase that had begun with the Sherlock Holmes tales and would terminate ignominiously in his twelve-year preoccupation with spiritualism and psychic research after the war. Despite its demerits as a novel, *The Poison Belt* stands with Wells' *The World Set Free*, published during the following year, as a work reflecting the sense of imminent catastrophe which dogged English writers on the eve of the Great War. Both works betray a want of confidence, a sense that the long period of Victorian peace had been an anomalous interlude, an awareness of twilight falling fast. Poison gas, atomic bombs, submarines, invasion fleets, Martian monsters—popular fiction of this epoch offered Everyman a rich array of apocalyptic alternatives dire and dreadful, all of them calculated to move Hell out of the pulpit and into the parlor.

▼

On the day when England finally went to war, Doyle called a meeting in his village of Crowborough, Sussex, and launched the Civilian Reserve, a paramilitary force consisting of those too old, or too feeble, to fight, which would protect the coast from German invaders. Doyle gave himself credit for founding this volunteer legion, which eventually enlisted 200,000 men, although by choice he served only as a private. He volunteered for active service, adducing as support his great booming voice "audible at great distances, which is useful at drill,"[43] but was turned down because of his fifty-five years. Throughout the war he was an ardent *Times* letter writer. Fearing that German submarines would sink British transports crossing the Channel he led a campaign which succeeded in providing each Tommy with an inflatable rubber collar.[44] (As it happened no transports were sunk by the Germans during the war.) He was less successful in persuading the War Office to issue a steel cuirass as part of every soldier's battle kit—an idea undoubtedly stemming from his infatuation with tournaments and chivalry. (Military outfitters supplied such breastplates as optional equipment by private order, but veteran soldiers spurned them as unwieldy, ineffective, and a trifle ridiculous.)

The war inspired what he always believed would become his magnum opus, *The British Campaign in France and Flanders* (1916–20), all six volumes researched and written by Doyle alone. He devoured newspapers, corresponded with the leaders, and interviewed eyewitnesses until his mind had become such a well-stocked encyclopedia of information that he could correctly name the place and regiment of any man wounded in France at a particular date.[45] When the War Office threw barriers in his way, he bypassed officialdom by establishing correspondence with generals at the front—Haig, Gough, Birdswood, Plumer, Allenby, and Robertson—all of whom trusted his patriotism and admired his one-man history of the Boer War. Because of his fame as a writer he had access to both Asquith and Lloyd George, prime ministers during the war years. As he said, "I have wonderfully good inside knowledge."[46] Lloyd George unloaded on him his excoriating assessment of Lord Kitchener—"arrogant . . . usually stupid . . . against tanks . . . ruined the Dardanelles—" which Doyle jotted in his diary but properly withheld from publication.[47] Both of them enjoyed Miss Asquith's quip about Kitchener, "If he is not a great man he is a great poster."*

Twice Doyle was invited to make tours of the front lines, where, he reported, "occasionally there were patches of untidiness."[48] The prejudices and preferences of an English squire were abundantly revealed. Impressed by the keen, clear-cut faces of the Australians, he contrasted them with some captured Germans—"Heavy-jawed, beetle-browed, uncouth louts with ox-like stolidity and dullness."[49] But he was most at home with gentlemen-amateurs like the Twentieth Royal Fusiliers, a public school battalion (later annihilated on the Somme), which radiated "the fresh human faces of boy cricketers" or with the aviators of the RFC, who had retained the chivalric character of their crusader forebears.[50] At the headquarters of the BEF he had coffee with General Haig in the map room, compared him favorably with Lord Wellington, and noted admiringly that he had "a truly British distrust of foreigners."[51] It was certainly true that no one would ever mistake Sir Arthur for a foreigner.

Although Doyle regarded *The British Campaigns in France and Flanders* as his most ambitious work and the one which he expected to be remembered by, it was largely admired by "official" circles and ignored by the public at large. In truth, it is a compilation of battles succeeding one another with grinding monotony. He seemed baffled by the complex and nonheroic aspects of the Western Front, which owed nothing to the idea of warfare which he had described in his historical romances.

*An allusion to the most famous recruiting poster of the Great War (or perhaps any war). Designed by Alfred Leete as a cover of the September 6, 1914 number of *London Opinion*, a weekly magazine, the illustration showed massively mustachioed Kitchener pointing to the viewer with the caption, "Your Country Needs You." In America James Montgomery Flagg based his "I Want You" poster on it, replacing Kitchener with a stern-visaged Uncle Sam.

He insisted upon converting slaughter into heroism, noting of the British troops sweeping across No Man's Land on the first day of the Battle of the Somme, "the men fell in lines, but the survivors with backs bent, heads bowed, and rifles at the port neither quickened nor slackened their advance, but went forward as though it was rain and not lead which lashed them."[52] There were sixty thousand British casualties on this single day, yet Doyle wrote that it "should be for ever marked in British military annals as the glorious First of July."[53] As Kipling had shown, it was the sort of war in which portrayal of German fiendishness came easier than creating British heroes out of French or Belgian clay. A case in point is Doyle's account of the first use of chemical warfare by the Germans at the battle of Langemarck:

> It is with a feeling of loathing that the chronicler turns from such knightly deeds to narrate the next episode of the war, in which the Germans, foiled in fair fighting, stole away a few miles of ground in the arts of the murderer. . . . The poisoning of Langemarck will be recorded as an incident by which warfare was degraded, and a great army, which had long been honored as the finest fighting force in the world, became in a single day an object of horror and contempt.[54]

Words like "chronicler," "knightly deeds," "fair fighting," and "long been honored" come from lexicons of chivalry handed down from Froissart or Malory. As such they had no relevance to the activities of combatants on the Western Front, whether German or English. Doyle resembles Newbolt in his conviction that mass slaughter must somehow conform to genteel rules, fabricated by gentlemen amateurs, of "playing the game." (To his credit, however, he did climb about briefly in trenches, whereas Newbolt in his duties as bard of the Royal Navy never had to soil his white flannels.)

While his book on the Boer War had opened with a lucid account of the causes of the war—however rationalized from the British point of view—and had concluded with a valuable critique of military strategy, his six-volume treatise on the Great War consists primarily as a perfunctory chronicle of operations. It is as if the issues were so tangled in webs of ambiguity and mystery that the creator of Sherlock Holmes was as unable to unravel them as millions of others who reflected on the war.

One result of these excursions to the front was a decision to resuscitate Sherlock Holmes for a third go. On a tour of the French sector during the Verdun campaign, after a French general had asked him what Holmes had done in the war, Doyle replied that he was "trop vieux pour service."[55] Later, presumably as a contribution to the war effort, he determined to bring Holmes back and to show his invaluable service to the government. The result was published in *Strand Magazine* (September 1917) as "His Last Bow: An Epilogue of Sherlock Holmes," a spy story in the worn groove of William Le Queux.

The setting is Dover, two days before the outbreak of the Great War, a time when "one might have thought that God's curse hung heavy over a degenerate world." Two Germans pace the cliffs, the glowing ends of their cigars resembling "the smouldering eyes of some malignant fiend looking down in the darkness." Von Bork, a devoted agent of the Kaiser, plans to turn over to the secretary of the German legation his treasure trove of military secrets so that these may be carried out of country in the diplomatic pouch. For four years Von Bork has played the sportsman with the English upper classes, indulging in polo, yachting, hunting, and boxing in order to win their friendship—so that he can betray them for the Kaiser. The gem of his collection (organized with German thoroughness into neat pigeonholes—"Harbour-defences, aeroplanes, Ireland") is the Admiralty code, which an Irish-American spy will deliver later that night. The secretary departs and Altamont the spy arrives. He resembles a caricature of Uncle Sam, and his speech is awash in American idioms as "the real goods," "stool pigeon," and "mug." Von Bork turns over a check for five hundred pounds, and Altamont hands him not the naval secrets but a copy of *Practical Handbook of Bee Culture*. Before the German can recover from his surprise, Altamont seizes him by the neck and holds a chloroform sponge in front of his "writhing face."

Only then do we learn that Altamont is none other than Sherlock Holmes, who had been pulled from retirement on the Downs (where he had divided his time between bee culture and philosophy) by special request of the prime minister. For the past two years he had been in America, developing his Irish-American disguise in order to infiltrate the German spy network, and he had consistently fed the Germans spurious information such as understating the speed of cruisers or the size of new naval guns. The story concludes with Holmes remarking pregnantly to Watson (also rescued from oblivion): "There's an east wind coming, such a wind as never blew on England yet. It will be cold and bitter, Watson, and a good many of us may wither before the blast.

But it's God's own wind none the less, and a cleaner, better, stronger land will lie in the sunshine when the storm has cleared."[56]

Here we have Sherlock Holmes, especially packaged for wartime consumption. Germans are recognizably German, treacherous and cerebral, while Holmes as pseudo-American counterspy commemorates the United States' late entry into the war. The blatant propaganda intent is obvious. From an Englishman deeply influenced by the discipline which he had admired in an Austrian school, followed by his growing respect for German energy, Doyle had devolved in just three decades to a conventional Germanophobe. The government had always put his influence with the public, particularly the Americans, to good use, and in 1917 he was sounded about accepting the directorship of an official propaganda department which would be supplied with information by the War Office. This he declined. Why should he accept? He was already a one-man department.

Throughout his literary career Doyle conveyed in his work a conservative ethic which had covertly but consistently supported the status quo with Victorian England as its lodestone. Readers could not have missed that Sherlock Holmes was always a gentleman, never a bore, and usually a snob (probably those were reasons why they, particularly Americans, admired him). "My good man . . ." sounds as natural coming from his lips when speaking to an inferior as "My dear sir . . ." when engaged with one of equal or superior rank. Doyle regarded as dangerous whirlpools those social or political eddies which drifted from the prevailing currents of his day. In his novel *The Valley of Fear* (1915), for example, the Molly Maguires, a militant working-class order of the Pennsylvania coal fields, are conceived as a kind of international Irish Mafia which in their bloody thirst for revenge will pursue an informer all the way to the Pacific Slope, then across the Atlantic to England, and finally to St. Helena, where he is thrown overboard. It seems never to have occurred to Doyle that underlying the Mollies' terrorist activities were shocking conditions in the mines for which the managers and capitalists were directly responsible. In his first novel, *A Study in Scarlet* (1888), he attributes a similar international malignancy to Mormonism for no apparent reason except perhaps for their unconventional sexual practices. The gospel according to Sir Arthur is ever the same: whatever has been is right. The masses must stay where they belong, and where they belong is where they are. Change, should it become necessary, will be bestowed by the educated classes—none of whom drop their haitches. Suspicion of change swung abruptly to hor-

ror when he assessed the Russian Revolution, perhaps the most enduring legacy of the Great War: "The phenomenon of that great fermenting, putrefying country was more like some huge cataclysm of nature,
some monstrous convulsion of the elements, than any ordinary political
movement. . . . It was as though a robust man had suddenly softened
into liquid putrescence before one's eyes."[57] Germans, Moriarty, Mor-
mons, Molly Maguires, Bolsheviks—these things were evil because
they were essentially non-English. They were manifestations of a sub-
species of invasion anxiety, one shared by many conservative Englishmen confident that the enemy would not land openly on the beaches but fearful that the Victorian verities could be undermined by
subterfuge. Little wonder that he was approached about filling the
directorship of a propaganda department.

The war had ravaged his family. Among the dead were his son King-
sley (a victim of the flu epidemic), his brother Innes (a brigadier general), and his wife's brother (killed at the Somme). For Sir Arthur and his
wife the solution to sorrow and all other human problems lay in psychic
research, and he plunged into this terra incognita with his usual exuberant energy. Convinced that he had been placed by God in a special
mission for conveying psychic truths to the world, he and his wife
traveled fifty thousand miles in their quest for evidence, and he
preached the gospel of spiritualism to a quarter million people, by his
own reckoning. At Carnegie Hall women in black dresses and with gold
stars fainted when strange faces glowed on the screen, accompanied by
eerie sounds from a Victrola. Others cried out, begging for news of sons
killed in the war. To any who would listen Doyle explained that he had
clasped materialized hands, had smelt the "peculiar ozone-like smell of
ectoplasm," and had seen the "dead" glimmer upon photographic
plates which no hand but his had touched.[58] In front of six witnesses he
had brought his son back; at one rap session his brother returned and
recommended that his wife visit an unknown masseur in Copenhagen
whose existence was later confirmed. Hopelessly naive about the sim-
plest principles of photography, he wrote a book, *The Coming of the
Fairies* (1922), which announced that fairies truly existed and validated
his claim by referring to photographs which two Yorkshire sisters had
taken of their fairy playmates.* London had a field day with this, the
Star publishing a photo of Sir Arthur with fairies dancing round his

*In 1983 one of the Yorkshire girls confessed that they had cut out pictures of fairies from
newspaper advertisements, attached them to bushes, and photographed them. See Dan
Richard Cox, *Arthur Conan Doyle* (New York, 1985), 225.

head, and the joke going around that when Peter Pan asked those in the audience who believed in fairies to clap their hands, Doyle led the applause.[59] Moreover, he accepted as authentic Miss Estelle Stead's famous photograph taken at the Cenotaph during the Armistice ceremony of 1922 which captured faces of several dozen soldiers known to have been killed in the war. The spiritualist movement, he claimed, was the most important event in history since the coming of Christ. Among his many efforts to broadcast the new revelations, he urged that England repeal its witchcraft laws and sought inspiration from dead authors like Oscar Wilde, whose ghost was reported to have remarked: "Being dead is the most boring experience in life. That is, if one excepts being married, or dining with a schoolmaster."[60]

The fruit of these final years was *The History of Spiritualism* (1926) in two volumes, which he hoped would become the definitive work on extraterrestrial phenomena but which became, for Sherlock Holmes admirers, merely an embarrassment. It seemed incongruous that the author who had dramatized for the world Holmes' methods of logical analysis and close observation could now become such a pitiful stooge of mediums and necromancers. In support of other world evidence he cites prophecies that came true—conveniently ignoring those that did not. He tells of a German attack beaten off during the war when a "white, spiritual figure of a soldier rose from a shell-hole . . . and slowly walked along our front for a distance of about one thousand yards." Bullets passed through it, and when it made a dash for the German trenches, the enemy scattered back in confusion. (Some said it looked like Lord Kitchener; others swore it was Lord Roberts). He interrogated spirits about the daily, or rather eternal, activities on the "other side" and recorded that evolution of the species continued through the aeons and that schools existed there to teach spirit children—curriculum not described. In the final chapter he soothed the living by explaining that questions asked of spirits "in the main justify the values held by most religions, and show that the path of virtue is also the road to ultimate happiness."[61] He had formed a friendship with Houdini, who repeatedly exposed to him the quacks, rappers, and charlatans milking the spiritualist racket, but Doyle remained a devout believer in the cozy security of the spirit world. His motivation was not economic—he actually lost money on his spiritualist enterprises. It was rather that he hoped to confirm, by "scientific" demonstration, that the human soul existed and was immortal, ideas that had been badly battered by events of the twentieth century.

How Sherlock Holmes would have enjoyed exposing all this chicanery! But Holmes was now thoroughly dead, and only Dr. Watson lived on.

▼

Holmes' literary alter ego is A. J. Raffles, the creation of E. W. Hornung (1866–1921), who married Constance Doyle in 1895 and followed his famous brother-in-law into the byways of vicarious crime with *The Amateur Cracksman* (1899). Raffles is no ordinary thief, for he is a gentleman, a public school man, and he once played cricket on the English team. Unlike traditional gentlemen, he robs from the rich, not the poor; no Robin Hood, he robs not for the poor but for the exclusive use of his expensive tastes. He is a superbly cool individualist, the sort who at school was rumored to have sneaked out at night and roamed the streets disguised in a check suit and beard; he is likely to quote Keats while engaged in his latest felony. What is most important, he is an *amateur*, not a *professional*, cracksman. He comes from the same layer of fine clay as Sherlock Holmes, but he is the obverse figure; while Holmes passionately pursues the criminal, Raffles assiduously eludes the law. Both have faithful confederates whose chuckleheadedness amplifies the exploits of the master; like Watson, Bunny lives to the full only when following his leader. (On one occasion he serves a prison term for Raffles, but does so without question or complaint.) Doyle was unhappy with his brother-in-law for creating Raffles. After reading the manuscript, he feared that the conception was so clever that it might lead some young men into attempting a life of crime. It distressed his sense of order, and he told Hornung, "You must not make the criminal a hero."[62] Years later Hornung came to agree, calling Raffles a "villain"—no doubt as tired of the character's notoriety as Doyle was of Holmes'.[63]

In a brilliant analysis of the Raffles formula, George Orwell argued that combining a cricketer and a burglar in the same character was "the sharpest moral contrast [Hornung] was able to imagine."[64] Since cricket takes an enormous amount of time to play—compared with football—it is a game more often associated with the leisured upper classes. If Orwell is right, cricket, with its emphasis on "good form," its ill-defined rules subject to a kind of ethical interpretation, and its fusion with Newbolt's "playing the game" syndrome, is a game indelibly associated with amateur athletics. Morever, it is a quintessentially *English* game, with no great following in what one cultural historian calls "the celtic fringe" of the British Isles.[65] (For one who is "outside" the English mind-set, "It's not cricket" is a meaningless expression.) Cricket is particularly suitable as an acceptable activity for a protagonist who moves easily from Mayfair dinners to country weekends. Raffles is neither wealthy nor aristocratic. Yet this society will tolerate him because of his public school background and will honor him because of his fame as a cricketer. He receives attention because of his fame as a cricket player; he is in society but not really of it.

Many of Raffles' most spectacular escapades directly result from his passionate patriotism. When he hears that the Kaiser is sending a fine pearl to the King of the Cannibal Islands for making faces at Queen Victoria, he resolves to steal it. With Bunny in tow, he boards the outward bound *Uhlan*, courts a German schoolgirl as a dodge (she has an unpleasant nasal laugh), chloroforms Herr Captain Wilhelm von Heumann, and takes the jewel. For Hornung Germans are ipso facto ridiculous. Unfortunately Raffles' nemesis, Inspector MacKenzie of Scotland Yard, comes aboard at Genoa and forces Raffles to escape by diving overboard ("his lithe, spare body cut the sunset as cleanly and precisely as though he had played at his leisure from a diver's board!").[66] While the mafiosa track Raffles through Italy, the all-suffering Bunny takes the rap and goes to prison. In another episode Raffles steals a gold vessel from the British Museum, but mails it back to Queen Victoria as a Jubilee gift. As he explains to Bunny: "Taking it was an offense against the laws of the land. That is Nothing. But destroying it would be a crime against God and Art."[67] Appropriately, the venture concludes with Raffles' toast—"The Queen. God Bless Her."

The ultimate test for character comes when one's country goes to war. At first the Boer War is an annoyance to Raffles—it makes for skimpier cricket reports in the newspapers. But as Old Boys fall in battle, he recognizes that the battlefield is the way of moral rehabilitation and renounces his life of crime. After applying dye to mustache and hair, to conceal their age, Raffles and Bunny join the army as gentlemen rankers and sail to South Africa. In an advance Bunny is wounded and, being a thorough realist, is unhappy about it. Raffles rescues him despite murderous fire and gives him his last Sullivan (a cigarette that has become his trademark). Pinned down by a Boer sniper, Raffles wonders whether the enemy is enough of a "sportsman" to show his face if he shows his. He exposes himself and is killed. The Boer was no gentleman, but Raffles dies a hero. As in Newbolt's "Vitai Lampada," the values inculcated by public school cricket, once learned, are never forgotten; they allow one to perform bravely and to die well in serving the empire.*

Like Raffles, Hornung understood the seductive allure of war to all classes. His poem about the outbreak of the Great War (written after the war) shows only jubilation:

> We tumbled out of tradesmen's carts, we fell off office stools—
> Fathers forsook their families, boys ran away from schools;
> Mothers untied their apron-strings, lovers unloosed their arms—
> All Europe was a wedding and the bells were war's alarms![68]

No irony is intended here, for he firmly believed that true sufferers were those "youngish men as have managed to stand out of it to the end . . . who have left it to other men to die and bleed for them."[69] This stiff-upper-lip stoicism taught by the sportsman's code, and perhaps strengthened by a literalist view of the example of Christ, sustained Hornung through the devastating loss of his son in Flanders during the early months of the Great War. Disqualified from service because of his age, he enlisted in the YMCA field service and was posted to the Western Front, where in spare moments he engaged in an agonized search for his son's grave—a futile task as it proved, for the area had been shelled for two years and the ground was no longer recognizable to survivors. If one judges from his verses and his memoir, *Notes of a Camp-Follower on the Western Front* (1919), he never doubted that the game was worth the sacrifice. For Hornung heroism was an absolute "like the beauty of Venus or the goodness of God."[70]

Battle was a nearly exact replica of sporting contests in prewar England. The poem "Last Post" recounts how, in letters to his father, a young soldier easily adapted to the front because it was only an extension of his schooldays.

> Still finding War of games the cream,
> And his platoon a priceless team—

---

*Hornung's public school novel, *Fathers of Men* (1912), like others in this genre of boys' novels written by and for men, opens with the youth's arrival at the school and concludes with his departure. Though of humble origins and further disadvantaged by a "bad accent," young Rutter is fully accepted at the end. His conclusion, "It's what you can do and how you take things that matters here," is assisted by the fact that along the way he has become a cricket star. In the final scene he joins the singing of psalms in the chapel, and admires the great east windows and the tablets commemorating old boys "who lived great lives or died *gallant deaths* [my italics]." See E. W. Hornung, *Fathers of Men* (New York, 1912), 356.

CHAPTER NINE

> Still running it by sportsman's rule,
> Just as he ran his house at school.
> Still wild about the "bombing stunt"
> He makes his hobby at the front.
> Still trustful of his wondrous luck—
> "Prepared to take on old man Kluck!"[71]

The imagery of games permeates Hornung's characterizations and descriptions. An artillery duel is "like the muddle of a tennis-court during a hard rally"; during a German offensive an English gunner is "as cheery as if he had been making another century in the Old Boy's Match instead of having just gone on with his heavies on a new pitch altogether."[72] His poem "Lord's Leave" laments that many Old Boys will not cheer on the Eton-Harrow match but takes consolation in their playing a bigger game against the Germans:

> Bigger the cricket here; yet some who tried
>   In vain to earn a Colour while at Eton,
> Have found a place upon an England side
>   That can't be beaten!

But instead of bowling properly, the boorish Germans hurl "shells from Krupp's Foundry" at English batsmen. It is impossible to convey a sense of fair play to a German:

> Playing a game's beyond him and his hordes;
>   Theirs but to play the snake or wolf or vulture!
> Better one sporting lesson learnt at Lord's
>   Than all their Kultur . . .[73]

For Hornung there is a law of compensation which justifies whatever losses must be endured in the war. While he agrees that it is heartbreaking that half the frontline soldiers will never see their homes again, there is the consolation that "the half who survived would be twice the men they ever would or could have been without the war."[74] For Hornung this was no statistical fallacy. Survivors emerge from the fire with the dross burned away, while those who die in battle win the highest decoration of all—a wooden cross ("You cannot DIE a Failure if you win a Cross in France!").[75]

Presumably, readers who had lost sons or lovers in the war were supposed to find consolation in *Notes of a Campfollower*. It retained a vision of the heroic tradition in the face of modernist writers, like

Hemingway, who would compare the battlefield dead with the stock-yards at Chicago, "if nothing was done with the meat except to bury it."[76]

Like Orwell, Graham Greene saw in the Raffles saga a brilliant period piece that set off clearly the gap between the Edwardians and ourselves. In his play *The Return of A. J. Raffles* (1975), set just before death of the "Old Queen," he corrects Bunny's account of Raffles' death in South Africa. Bunny did not observe this for he was at the time in Reading Gaol with Oscar Wilde. Raffles foils an attempt by a Prussian captain (disguised as a waiter) to steal incriminating letters from the Prince of Wales to his current mistress. The amateur triumphs over the professional as he tells the discomfited spy, "Here in England the Gentlemen quite often beat the Players."[77] Yet stormy weather lies ahead for the English amateur spirit. The Prince, shortly to become King Edward VII, shares his darker thoughts about the future with Raffles: "You and I belong to a special moment of time. *La Fin de Siècle* the papers call it, don't they? But it's more than just the end of any century. I have an awful fear that my nephew Willy [Kaiser Wilhelm], with his talk of Huns and Attila and inspiring fear, represents the future. I prefer my mother."[78]

Consistently, the world inhabited by both Sherlock Holmes and A. J. Raffles has been viewed through the gaslamp lens of benign retrospection, that time before the century of total wars, "that age before the world went awry." Vincent Starrett's lines for Holmes and Watson fit equally well Raffles and Bunny:

> Here, though the world explode, these two survive,
> And it is always 1895.[79]

10 SAILING TO BYZANTIUM

▼

"Well, if Armageddon's on, I suppose one should be there." RUPERT BROOKE

On August 4, 1914, England declared war against Germany. Three days later, after only five minutes of debate, Parliament passed the Defence of the Realm Act (DORA), which, among other restrictions, provided safeguards against spying, showing signals, and acts of sabotage. London was rumored to be packed with German spies, and the persecution of enemy aliens began in earnest. Forty years of scaremongering had succeeded all too well. Mobs swarmed out of control, wrecking bakers' shops and watchmakers, hunting for German grocers said to be poisoning food and barbers supposed to be cutting English throats. A *Times* reporter recorded that the trunks of German governesses were being searched for bombs and tennis courts of German nationals probed to ascertain whether they were secret artillery emplacements. In his view, "the hunting of suspected spies has become almost a popular pastime." The London *Gazette* published lists of German names anglicized—Rose for Rosenheim, Dent for Schect. Although he had been a naturalized British subject since the age of fourteen, the Prince of Battenberg resigned as first sea lord, admitting that a whispering campaign had impaired his usefulness. Even King George V saw the wisdom of downplaying his Germanic ancestry and in an official ceremony was eventually installed as the first monarch of the Windsor line. As further evidence of his Englishness, His Majesty commanded that the German emperor's name be struck from the roll of Knights of Garter and dismantled the stalls of eight Germanic knights from St. George's Chapel at Windsor.[1] (Among the literati the most notable monument to name change was Ford Madox Hueffer, who, alarmed by his Teutonic surname, became Ford Madox Ford.)

A nation weaned on lurid invasion tales accepted as canonical gospel wild rumors of the Kaiser's fleet off the east coast. At the Chelsea football ground evangelical posters ("Repent, for the time is at hand") gave way to patriotic exhortations ("Be Ready to Defend Your Home and Women from the German Hun").[2] In Essex the novelist Arnold Bennett found himself serving on the Emergency Committee of Thorpe-le-Soken, and in his diary he recorded measures taken to repel invasions. In late August eighty special constables assiduously hunted for a spy in the neighborhood; in November the major general commanding the South Midland Division, convinced that invasion was imminent, issued a proclamation forbidding civilians from sniping at Germans when they got ashore; and as late as June 1916 a staff captain told him that three German corps were practicing a landing—this information obtained by an intelligence officer who penetrated the German lines dressed as a woman. So it went on, this inability to differentiate between "rumours probable and rumours grotesque."[3]

Although few appeared aware of it, the great invasion of Great Britain had already taken place. It had featured no Germans in *Pickelhauben* goose-stepping ashore or spiderish Martians unscrewing themselves from canisters but rather a host of foreign musicians, painters, and poets allied to one or more of the cultural movements of the late Edwardian period—jazz, the Russian Ballet, Postimpressionism, vorticism, imagism, futurism, and other *isms*—that would change forever the insular and insulated way in which the English expressed themselves. These invaders flooded ashore and proceeded to bore from within, seeking nothing less than total revolution in seeing, hearing, and feeling. By the time that the Great War actually had begun, and home guards and Boy Scouts were scouring the coasts for sign of the expected German fleet, the cultural defenses of Britain had already been breached, and the invaders had become solidly entrenched in the ateliers of Kensington, the cafés of Soho, and the drawing rooms of the West End.

After a long dry season, the years immediately preceding the outbreak of the Great War were marked by a great poetic awakening. During the late Victorian period fiction had flourished, but poetry had floated on an ebbing tide. Tennyson had reigned too long, and his traditional verse approach, with his "cult of the decorated adjective,"[4] and his mood of gravity and highmindedness seemed hopelessly archaic for a restless generation whose beliefs had been undercut by radical

revelations in biology, psychology, and economics.* Beginning about
1911 a revolution got under way. In its broader outlines it consisted of
two schools which existed side by side, but which rarely touched. The
Anglophiles, who called themselves Georgians, rallied under the banner
of Edward Marsh, private secretary of Winston Churchill, and sought
to revitalize English poetry by providing fresh subjects without wrenching loose from traditional moorings. The cosmopolitans, mentored by
Ezra Pound, agreed with the Georgians on the importance of tradition
but reached out to include non-English literatures within their range of
influences. Although the future belonged to adherents of the Pound-
Eliot school, the Georgians were infinitely more popular in their day.
Between 1911 and 1922, for example, the five anthologies of *Georgian
Poetry*, edited by Marsh, sold about 73,000 copies.[5] Nor does this
number include copies of individual works sold by those writers loosely
grouped as "Georgian poets."

By far the most celebrated among this group was Rupert Brooke,
whose death in 1915 as a member of the expeditionary force against the
Turks at Gallipoli, became the collective symbol for a generation of
English youths lost in the war. Along with T. E. Lawrence, Rupert
Brooke became one of those rare legendary figures in twentieth-century
English history—"an oriflamme of the chivalry of his country."[6] The
astonishing popularity of his poems was a major cultural phenomenon
of the war years and the succeeding decade; it is probably unmatched
by any other twentieth-century poet. In 1926 his royalty figures from a
slight body of poetry and a few essays stood at an estimated 300,000
pounds.[7]

The Georgian Poetry scheme originated in a jocular exchange between Marsh and Brooke. "Eddie" Marsh, a well-connected gadfly
enthralled by poets and poetry, was entertaining Brooke in his rooms at
Gray's Inn in September 1911 when Brooke, "sitting half undressed in
his bed," as Eddie recalled the event years later, facetiously announced
he would like to prepare an anthology of experimental poetry consisting

*Tennyson was a particular target of the modernists. In outlining his requirements for
poetry to Harriet Monroe, Ezra Pound wrote: "No Tennysonianness of speech; nothing—nothing, that you couldn't, in some circumstance, in the stress of some emotion,
actually say." Another young poet, Rupert Brooke, recuperating from an illness about
this time, wrote to a friend, "I am now convalescent and can sit up and take a little warm
milk-and-Tennyson." See Robert H. Ross, *The Georgian Revolt 1910–1922: Rise and Fall
of a Poetic Ideal* (Carbondale, 1965), 21; Geoffrey Keynes (ed.), *The Letters of Rupert
Brooke* (London, 1968), 134.

of twelve pseudonymous poets in which he wrote all the poems himself.
Marsh was at once enthusiastic, but later he conceived the idea of using
real poets for the project, for he was convinced that a golden age of
poetry in England was about to dawn. He rapidly collected a stable of
poets, overcame Brooke's halfhearted objections that few of them were
really experimental, and by December had seen *Georgian Poetry 1911–
1912* through the press.* Fearing that his relationship with Churchill
might compromise the project, Marsh edited the volume anonymously.
His criteria for inclusion were never clearly defined: "interesting of
thought and feeling" and "intelligible, musical, and racy" might be
stretched to include nearly anything.[8] In effect, Marsh was a literary
chauvinist, eager to show that the "Georgian period" (King George or
St. George?—in either case, the label carries connotations of king and
country) might "take rank in due time with the several great poetic ages
of the past."[9] Whatever his literary proclivities, Marsh had the sort of
social and political connections which mattered; it is said that on the
day his anthology was published the prime minister, Herbert Asquith,
sent his chauffeur to wait outside the publisher's office for the first
available copy.[10] Marsh would take on Ezra Pound's band of invaders
by bringing the Englishness back into English poetry.

   Brooke's major contribution to this first Georgian collection was
"The Old Vicarage, Grantchester," an inventory of Cambridgeshire
pastoral delights written while he was "in exile" at Berlin earlier in
1911. The poem evolves from a contrast between things German and
things English, with the blue ribbon going to the latter. The usual
prewar stereotypes are at work: Germany is efficient, regulated, humid,
Jewish, beer-drinking, placarded with verboten signs; England is natural, unpunctual, cool, Saxon, dew-drenched, haunted by the shades of
Chaucer and Byron. Once beyond these jingoist comparisons, however,
Brooke softens his poem by comically exaggerating the dreamy satisfac-
tions of life in Grantchester, thereby playfully spoofing the attachment
of the traditional Briton to his native heath.

---

*Ezra Pound, a true experimenter, narrowly missed inclusion. Marsh requested his "The
Goodley Fere," but when Pound refused permission because it failed to illustrate any
modern tendency, Marsh did not solicit other material. D. H. Lawrence contributed
poems to this and other Georgian anthologies but withdrew from Marsh's aegis when
better opportunities for publication arose. (He later called Marsh a "policeman of poetry.") See Ross, *Georgian Revolt*, 101; Edward Marsh, *A Number of People* (New York and
London, 1939), 227.

> In Grantchester their skins are white,
> They bathe by day, they bathe by night;
> The women there do all they ought;
> The men observe the Rules of Thought.
> They love the Good; they worship Truth;
> They laugh uproariously in youth;
> (And when they get to feeling old,
> They up and shoot themselves, I'm told.)[11]

Like tissue removed for biopsy, this passage reflects the total corpus of Brooke's poetry in many ways: under the lightheartedness one sees a reliance upon abstract words (one of his greatest limitations as a poet); a distortion of reality when in conflict with nostalgia (appropriately an early title for the poem was "The Sentimental Exile"); a judgmental, even strangely puritanical, attitude reflected in his emphasis on "clean" as opposed to "dirty," adjectives which he frequently used in a moral sense; and the appearance of death thoughts, which protrude like rocky outcroppings through the surface of his mind even though the prevailing tone is intended to be humorous. Grantchester is intended to be an archaic relic of the English past rather than a real place accessible to gazetteer. In the series of questions raised in the concluding lines, Brooke seems uncertain whether his beloved village still exists (why shouldn't it, if it is a real place and he has only been away for three months?). The final lines, often quoted to evoke the leisurely ambiance of prewar England, literally stop the village clock at the declining edge of a perpetual summer afternoon: "Stands the Church clock at ten to three? / And is there honey still for tea?"*

"Grantchester," in its dreamlike absorption with bucolic and regressive English scenes, became a primary model for other Georgian poets. Essentially it is an escapist poem, written in a form which F. R. Leavis called "effete pastoralism," into which no unpleasant contemporary reminders of gasworks, colleries, or roundhouses intrude.[12] Not surprisingly it carried off the prize (thirty pounds) for the best poem of 1913 sponsored by *Poetry Review*, an organ of the traditonalists.

---

*During much of 1911 the hands of the Grantchester clock were stuck at 3:30, but Brooke changed the time to make a better rhyme. After his death some ardent Brooke fans proposed that the hands of the Grantchester clock be permanently fixed at 2:50, but local people thought the idea ridiculous. See the *New York Times* (March 9, 1986).

Among the judges were Eddie Marsh, Henry Newbolt (neither a surprise), and T. E. Hulme (who was).

Most modern readers of the poem would probably endorse George Orwell's verdict: "an enormous gush of 'country sentiment,' a sort of accumulated vomit from a stomach stuffed with place-names."[13] Yet Orwell also underlined its importance as a document for illuminating the reactionary attitudes of that rentier-professional class which served as the arbiters of taste during the prewar epoch. Other cultural historians have agreed. Brooke's life and career have been minutely examined, less for the value of his writings than for his role as living symbol of the generation of promising young Englishmen killed in the Great War.[14] In the words of F. R. Leavis, "He energized the Garden-Suburb ethos with a certain original talent and the vigour of prolonged adolescence. . . . Keats' vulgarity with a Public School accent."[15] Critical opinion is not, however, consensus. Brooke's work, so popular in its day but largely ignored in ours, provides an ideal focal point for gaining a perspective on the distinctive cast of literary taste during that period.

▼

The son of a Rugby housemaster, Rupert Brooke (1887–1915) peers from schoolboy photographs like a stoical descendant of that most famous Rugbian, Tom Brown. His record at school was exemplary, for he won his colors at rugger and cricket, authored a prize-winning poem, and served as Head of House during his last year. With his red-gold hair (which he had the courage to wear longer than the prevailing style), good public school features (blue eyes, fair complexion, well-pitted nostrils), and boyish exuberance, he was the cynosure of adoring eyes—both male and female. Awed testimonials to his physical beauty are legion, many of them couched in godlike metaphor: "exactly what Adonis must have looked like in the eyes of Aphrodite" (Leonard Woolf); "the veritable picture of a young Greek God, of Apollo himself" (a Toronto acquaintance); "a Greek god under a Japanese sunshade, reading poetry in his pyjamas, at Grantchester" (D. H. Lawrence); and most famous of all, "A Young Apollo, golden haired / Stands dreaming on the verge of strife / Magnificently unprepared / For the long littleness of life" (Frances Cornford).[16] Brooke was exactly what an English romantic poet *ought* to look like.

Older bachelors in particular relished his good looks. On hearing that

Rupert Brooke at Rugby.

Brooke was probably not a good poet, Henry James, whom Brooke entertained at Cambridge and who wrote a glowing introduction to his prose work, replied, "Thank goodness. If he looked like that and was a good poet too, I do not know what I should do."[17] In a production of the *Eumenides* at Cambridge in 1906 Brooke had only a bit part requiring only a few minutes on stage, but his appearance, clad in red wig and cardboard armor, produced a flutter among seasoned connoisseurs of young men like A. C. Benson (". . . a pretty figure, spoilt by a glassy stare") and Percy Lubbock, who remarked on the herald's "grace of a Ganymede." Eddie Marsh, who on that occasion saw Brooke for the first time, recorded eleven years later his vivid impression, not unlike that of a stagestruck lover, of "His radiant, youthful figure in gold and vivid red and blue, like a Page in the Riccardi Chapel."[18] None of them would have been pleased had they known that a characteristic Brooke bon mot of this period was "Nobody over thirty is worth talking to."[19]

His favorite play was *Peter Pan,* which he claimed to have seen at least ten times. For a time as a Cambridge undergraduate he saw the streetscapes of that city through the imagined landscapes of Barrie's play: "As I stroll through Cambridge, Trinity Street fades and I find myself walking by the shore of the Mermaid's Lagoon. King's Chapel often shrinks before my eyes, and rises, and is suddenly the House in the Tree-Tops."[20] From that play he drew (or found reinforcement for) at least two attitudes that were imprinted in his thought while still at Rugby—an infatuation with death and a deep aversion to the values of the adult world. For a poet who came to personify the spirit of English youthfulness, it is paradoxical that so many of his poems treat death directly, or in one of its guises, such as satiety in love. (To cite but one example, two of his five war sonnets—his most famous poems—are titled "The Dead" while two others either allude to or actually celebrate death in battle.) Moreover, this infatuation with death was deeply rooted in his consciousness while still a boy. In a paper on modern poetry which he read at Rugby, he concluded with a suggestion that A. E. Housman should be read "on an autumn morning when there is a brave nip of frost in the air and the year is sliding toward death."[21] "Autumn . . . frost . . . sliding . . . death"—he was only eighteen.

On his nineteenth birthday, with the lure of Cambridge immediately ahead, he wrote to a friend as though his life were nearing its end: "I am a pale ghost who has lived, and can now only dream."[22] This was a classic case of that pandemic public school malady which Cyril Con-

nolly analyzed in his "Theory of Permanent Adolescence." And to a
female confidante Brooke mused over his years at Rugby in the mood of
a latter-day Keats rhapsodizing on his terminal illness:

> As I look back at five years there, I seem to see almost every hour
> golden and radiant, and always increasing in beauty as I grew more
> conscious: and I could not, and cannot, hope for or even imagine
> such happiness elsewhere. And then I found the last days of all this
> slipping by me, and with them the faces and places and life I loved,
> and I without the power to stay them. I became for the first time
> conscious of transience, and parting, and a great many other
> things.[23]

Such thoughts, even allowing for fin de siècle attitudinizing, had a
crippling effect on his emotional development; it was as though he
visualized life beyond public school as a spiritual waste land. Of his first
year at Cambridge he confessed that his principal amusement lay in
meeting Rugby friends with whom he could "pretend we are children
again."[24]

Brooke's nostalgia for Rugby apparently did not stem from a fear of
failure at Cambridge or elsewhere, for he had already proved his mettle
in nearly every arena offering challenge to an English youth. In point of
fact, he feared just the opposite—that he might achieve "success" on
terms laid down by Philistia, which would destroy his effervescent
idealism. "There are only three things in the world," Hugh Dalton
overheard him saying at Cambridge. "One is to read poetry, another is
to write poetry, and the best of all is to *live* poetry."[25] This is the code
of a militant anti-Philistine. By the time he was twenty-one he was
already suffering anguish over the prospect of old age. His double
sonnet, "Menelaus and Helen," from the collection *Poems* (1911) contrasts Menelaus "flaming like a god" and Helen "lonely and serene" at
their reunion during the fall of Troy with the "long connubial years"
that came afterward. As an old man Menelaus waxes garrulous and
boring as he rehashes the Trojan campaign; Helen's golden voice gets
shrill as he grows deafer. The epical moment has been lost by attrition
of their shared old age:

> Often he wonders why on earth he went
>   Troyward, or why poor Paris ever came.
> Oft she weeps, gummy-eyed and impotent;
>   Her dry shanks twitch at Paris' mumbled name.

> So Menelaus nagged; and Helen cried;
> And Paris slept on by Scamander side.[26]

On this subject his imagination could run away with him. In a long
letter to a Cambridge friend he outlined what he called The SCHEME, a
way "to escape the great destroyer, to continue young" by recruiting a
select group of "the right people" who promise to meet at Basle Station
on May 1, 1933, and put whatever they have been doing behind them in
order to "be glorious at fifty . . . children seventy years, instead of
seven." In this way they would "teach the whole damn World, that
there's a better Heaven than the pale serene Anglican windless harmo-
nium-buzzing Eternity of the Christians, a Heaven in Time . . . a
Heaven of Laughter and Bodies and Flowers and Love and People and
Sun and Wind, in the only place we know or care for, ON EARTH."[27]

While on a theoretical level Brooke rhapsodically endorsed a program
of intensified living in conformity to his ideas of how a romantic poet
should perceive, little of this sensory élan found confirmation in his
poetry. His work is singularly gloomy in just those areas where poets
have traditionally been optimistic—notably in the treatment of love.
Love figures as a major subject in his *Poems* but almost invariably in
contexts of rejection, or even revulsion. In "Jealousy" the persona has
lost his former lover to a third party and exults in thoughts of their love
turning to habit and their eventual mutual decay until she must endure

> A foul sick fumbling dribbling body and old,
> When his rare lips hang flabby and can't hold
> Slobber, and you're enduring that worst thing,
> Senility's queasy furtive love-making.[28]

In the end the persona envisions their "passion dead and rotten": the
ultimate satisfaction is that "he'll be dirty, dirty!" but "Oh, when *that*
time comes, you'll be dirty too!" The little-boy nastiness of this poem
has always disturbed Brooke admirers. Yet this is only a mildly explicit
poem performance when put beside "A Channel Passage," a sonnet
which in graphic detail spells out the similarities between "A sea-sick
body, or a you-sick soul." Reviewers in England were not ready for his
sestet:

> Do I forget you? Retchings twist and tie me,
>   Old meat, good meals, brown gobbets, up I throw.
> Do I remember? Acrid return and slimy,
>   The sobs and slobber of a last year's woe.

And still the sick ship rolls. 'Tis hard, I tell ye,
To choose 'twixt love and nausea, heart and belly.[29]

Even admirers within the Marsh circle expressed annoyance at "his bad taste and at the way in which, with arrogant undergraduate bravado . . . he deliberately set out to flout long-cherished poetic conventions."[30] Marsh himself urged that this poem be deleted from the collection. Brooke refused, but he did consent to abandon the original title, "The Sea-Sick Lover."

These poems were written before, not after, Brooke's sexual relationship with Ka Cox, a fellow student at Cambridge who had long been a platonic friend. In December 1911, after learning that Ka, a prematurely matronly woman, had fallen in love with the painter Henry Lamb, whom Brooke regarded as a Bloomsbury lecher, the poet suffered "so frenzied a jealousy" that he seemed to his friends "to be almost out of his mind."[31] He precipitately left England, writing to Marsh: "I tottered, being too tired for suicide, to Cannes, not because I like the b——place, but because my mother happened to be there."[32] Following a tryst with Ka in Munich, Brooke compulsively analyzed the relationship in indiscreet letters to friends. To Virginia Stephen [Woolf] he recounted how they went to costume balls in which Ka was "disguised as a human being . . . the gay petticoats only rarely whisking aside and giving a glimpse of furry pelt beneath. She talks Deutsch now as if it were Urse." She had become comical to him, but also repulsive. To another friend he wrote (almost paraphrasing attitudes of his earlier poems): "Love her?—bless you, no. . . . The bother is I don't really *like* her, at all. There is a feeling of staleness, ugliness, trustlessness about her. I don't know. Dirt."[33] Even though they never resumed their physical relationship after the Munich interlude, Ka Cox remained the deepest female attachment of his life. Through her he may have cauterized the homoerotic tendencies which had been inculcated during his years at public school.* Thereafter he became less puritanical about sexual matters, but death thoughts continued to loom

*Brooke's complicated sexual networks have never been satisfactorily isolated or analyzed. His biographer Christopher Hassall treats the Ka Cox affair in detail but avoids discussing homosexual relationships which are touched on in John Lehmann's biography. Even though three-quarters of a century have passed, the lid remains tightly closed on many primary materials. Obscenities have been deleted from the edition of his letters. The reasons are plain—the most enduring symbol of English dead in the Great War must be kept pure.

large. Throughout his career, Death, Tragedy, and Love were con-
joined and writ large—in capital letters.

At Cambridge Brooke quickly made his mark upon university life.
Through his induction into the Society, or "Apostles," an exclusive
body of Cantabridgians selected for their intellectual promise, he was
brought into the company of distinguished writers and thinkers like
G. E. Moore, E. M. Forster, Lytton Strachey, and Maynard Keynes.
(He came to dislike their banter about the "Higher Sodomy" and
showed his disapproval by writing a paper for the Apostles, "Why Not
Try the Other Leg.")[34] He wrote reviews for the *Cambridge Review*
(including one which faulted Pound's *Personae* for obscurity and awk-
ward language while conceding originality and flashes of brilliance).[35]
He joined the Fabian Society, and rose to become its local president,
even though his political ideas were shaped more, as he said, by the
pastoral utopianism of William Morris than by direct knowledge of the
abuses of capitalism. (Beatrice Webb, who met him at Fabian summer
school, found his attitudes those of the upper-class snob.) A poor actor,
except to start a scene or two, he nevertheless co-founded the Marlowe
Dramatic Society, which produced Elizabethan plays. Meanwhile,
there were skiing parties, camping parties, boating parties, and mar-
athons of talk. A female friend recalled how it was the custom for them
"to loll in armchairs and talk wearily about art and suicide and the sex
problem . . ." all the while lambasting "the absurd prejudices of patriotism and decency."[36] Brooke's hair grew longer. Once, he was
reported by a college porter as a girl asleep on the lawn, and later a band
of London urchins assailed him with cries of "Buffalo Bill!" Great
things were expected of him as a scholar, but he did poorly in examinations. Fearing that he might fail to realize his ambition of being a
Cambridge don, with specialization in Elizabethan literature, he moved
to the isolated village of Grantchester, three miles up river, in order to
have a place for uninterrupted work. But people always had a way of
finding Rupert Brooke and making him the hub of their social wheel.
Part of the storied lore of that prewar era speaks of his declaiming and
writing poetry on the weedy lawn of the Old Vicarage, of nocturnal
plunges at Byron's pool nearby (although he always admired and found
more affinities with Keats than with Byron), and of his paddling a
canoe through the blackest night from Grantchester to Cambridge.

To prepare himself for an academic career, Brooke began spending
extended periods in Munich and Berlin. Ostensibly he was learning the

language, but his progress was poor, perhaps because of his dislike of
Germans. Years before, in a juvenile sonnet titled "Dawn" (not published in his 1911 collection) he had written of a rail trip between
Bologna and Milan in the company of two Germans, who evoked his
disgust. The windows are shut, the air is foetid, the Germans spit and
snore, and the poem concludes:

> A new day sprawls; and, inside, the foul air
> Is chill, and damp, and fouler than before. . . .
> Opposite me two Germans sweat and snore.[37]

Brooke claimed that this was the first poem based on personal experience which he ever wrote. At work was the logic of jingoism; when
cooped up in a second-class carriage, Germans smell bad—presumably
English do not. While Brooke never became a rabid Hun baiter, his
sojourns in Germany did not result in great respect for German culture.
After a three-month stint in Munich he wrote Edward Marsh: "I have
sampled and sought out German culture. It has changed all my political
views. I am wildly in favor of nineteen new Dreadnoughts. German
culture must never, never, prevail. The Germans are nice, & well-
meaning, & they try; but they are SOFT. Oh! They ARE soft."[38] At this
time the diplomatic front was heating up because of the Anglo-German
naval rivalry. No doubt Marsh was pleased to relay Brooke's patriotic
sentiments to his boss at the Admiralty.

During one of his Berlin junkets Brooke encountered T. E. Hulme,
a philosopher-poet loosely attached to the Ezra Pound group whose advocacy of classical rather than romantic norms in poetry were di-
ametrically opposed to the Georgians. For ten days they attended art
exhibitions and plays together and discussed aesthetics at the Café des
Westens. Neither man, nor "school," had any effect on the other.
Hulme came to dislike Brooke. He was annoyed by Brooke's childish
attempts to establish his superiority in German cafés by conspicuously
flaunting the *Times*. Moreover, his pragmatic streak balked at Brooke's
so-called "study" in Germany without attempting to learn the language.[39] A notorious brawler, Hulme would have been enraged had he
known of Brooke's condescending dismissal of him in a letter to Marsh:
"Hulme has arrived in Berlin. I show him round & talk to him. He's an
amiable creature, & a good talker; though I don't think much of him as
a philosophic thinker."[40] The two did not meet again; Hulme was

killed in 1917 while serving as an artillery officer on the Nieuport front.*

By 1913 Brooke had been elected a fellow of King's College, on the basis of his treatise on John Webster's plays. Marsh celebrated the occasion by giving him a dinner party in his Gray's Inn rooms, where Brooke was now spending much of his time. The guest list included William Butler Yeats, Violet Asquith, daughter of the prime minister, and Mrs. Winston Churchill. Through Marsh's connections, Brooke was moving rapidly into the power center of English cultural and political life. There were late suppers at the Ritz and dinners at 10 Downing Street. Already he had charmed arbiters of taste like Henry James and Edmund Gosse.† The German excursions had indirectly broadened his horizons and had begun to loosen some of his puritanical inhibitions. Through Marsh he met and became infatuated with Cathleen Nesbitt, a rising young actress. He wrote her impassioned but strangely noncommittal letters which she said "became inebriated with the exuberance of his own verbosity," and met her on weekends for long walks in the Chilterns or on the Downs. She always claimed that their relationship was platonic and noted the split between his "sense of sin" and his "sensual hedonistic side."[41] Certainly his letters to her were loaded with sexual innuendo even as they rested safely within the chaste conventions of Keats's Eve-of-St.-Agnes phase. His tendency to work up to a high pitch and then back off into the shadow ground of poetic rhetoric characterizes a 1913 letter, which concludes: "You are very lovely to me. I would like to put you into your quiet bed tonight, and smooth your hair, and kiss your two eyes shut, and leave you to good dreams. Perhaps my soul will do it. You'll feel a breath in the room, and hear a whisper. Goodnight, child."[42] In his crumpled grey flannel suit and blue flanneled shirt, she thought, "He really looks too beautiful to be true."[43] Yet despite his looks and his charm, some acquaintances found

---

*Despite the ideological gulf separating the two poets, they agreed that the Great War should be fought. In his series of war notes for *Cambridge Magazine* in 1916 Hulme justified the war on the basis of inculcating "heroic values" and resisting German militarism. Further, he argued that pacifists like Bertrand Russell, who had been dismissed from the Cambridge faculty for his views, placed an overvaluation on human life and adhered to a romantic notion of progress.

†Brooke plumed himself on his mastery of the art of being charming. In discussing his first meeting with James, he told a friend, "Of course I did the fresh, boyish stunt, and it was a great success." See Christopher Hassall, *The Prose of Rupert Brooke* (London, 1956), 277.

Brooke's charms only skin-deep. As one of them said, "I'm not surprised people don't fall in love with Rupert, he's so beautiful that he's scarcely human."[44] Less flattering was Norman Douglas' comparison of Brooke with "a Newfoundland puppy entering a strange room, and sniffing at all those unfamiliar objects with delighted tail-waggings."[45]

For reasons that were never made clear, Brooke suddenly booked passage to America in May 1913. In a letter to Edward Thomas he implied the cause was escape from London confinement: "London gripped me too firmly by the ankle. I have been inextricably tangled in the web of this existence—Maya, the Orientals call it, don't they?"[46] At this time his letters to Cathleen Nesbitt were getting longer and his feelings more convoluted. It was evident that in that relationship he had to either advance forcefully or withdraw altogether. The model of unrequited love—death's dimension superimposed on physical bonding—had always infatuated Brooke. What better way to guarantee its preservation than to remove the temptations altogether? Two days before departure he was engaged by the *Westminster Gazette* to prepare a series of articles based on his American tour.

Brooke seemed incapable of seeing the United States or Canada except through the heavily filtered lens of England. On arrival in New York he wrote Cathleen: "My dear, this is *not* a land for a civilized man. There are three things worth some praise; the architecture; the children's clothes; and the jokes. All else is flatulence and despair and a *living Death* [my italics]."[47] The situation briefly improved in Boston, where the natives displayed "a delicious Toryism" and a lady confessed that the trouble with America was Democracy. He was most at home at Harvard, "the Oxford and Cambridge of America, they claim," but, accustomed as he was to cricket costumes, he was offended by collegiate baseball uniforms—"dingy Knickerbockers" and "caps like hooligans." Death thoughts intruded again when he described the parade of Harvard men at Class Day. The gaps in the procession reminded him grimly of the passage of time and he took note of the empty ranks among the men of sixty—the result of the Civil War.[48]

Moving westward, he found in Niagara Falls a gigantic metaphor of "unspecified ruin." The secret to the cascade, he wrote, lay in "the feeling of colossal power and of unintelligible *disaster* [my italics] caused by the plunge of that vast body of water." Normally, Brooke brooded within the context of individual death, but at Niagara, for the first time, he touched upon the death wish concept as it related to nations. His ruminations contain the germ of his best-known single work, "The

Soldier," of 1914: "A man's life is of many flashing moments, and yet one stream; a nation's flows through all its citizens and yet is more than they. . . . Both men and nations are lured onward to their ruin or ending as inevitably as this dark flood. Some go down to it unreluctant, and meet it, like the river, not without nobility."[49]

Travel into the interior of the New World brought no comforting disquisitions upon the future of mankind—the stock in trade of most European travelers in the vast empty spaces of the West. The Indians were depressing—"swallowed by that ugliness of shops and trousers with which we enchain the earth." Their civilization had been destroyed by avatars of commerce like an American businessman, encountered on a train, who told him, "We must be a Morally Higher race than the Indians because we have Survived them. The Great Darwin proved it."[50] Yet the absence of this civilization which he wished so keenly to escape also brought forth gloomy meditations. The Rocky Mountains were a "horrid and solitary wilderness" devoid of human dimension. "The maple and the birch conceal no dryads, and Pan has never been heard amongst these reed-beds." It was "a godless place"— godless not because the gods had forsaken it, but because they had never entered it at all. It was only topography not yet humanized into region. Wrenching logic to conform to his personal melancholia, Brooke argued that without human deaths there could be no history, and without history there could be no civilization. "There walk, as yet, no ghosts of lovers in Canadian lanes. This is the essence of the grey freshness and brisk melancholy of the land. And for all the charm of these qualities, it is also the secret of a European's discontent. For it is possible, at a price to do without gods. But one misses the dead."[51]

His writing assignment for the *Westminster Gazette* expired in San Francisco, but Brooke was lured into the South Pacific. As he explained to his mother: "I want to see [Robert Louis] Stevenson's place, and I want to hunt up traces of Gauguin, the painter."[52] Hawaii proved to be a spoiled horror, but among the Samoans and Fijians he found a zone threatened but not yet destroyed by Europeans. These people were "far nearer the Kingdom of Heaven—or the Garden of Eden . . . than oneself or one's friends," even though it was inevitable that in time their islands would become "indistinguishable from Denver and Birmingham and Stuttgart."[53] In Samoa he watched a native dance, which he compared for Cathleen to a performance by Nijinsky. "Much of it I could not understand; some of it I felt it my duty, as an English gentleman, not to." Bronze girls and men, naked to the waist and glistening with coconut palm oil, went through convulsive rhythmic movements until, at the crisis, the movement grew slighter and "more exciting." At the end Brooke felt "strange ancient raucous jungle cries awaking within me."[54] The distance from Rugby and Cambridge was no longer a matter of miles. He was having illuminations that peeled away outer layers of civilized skin and brought him, at rare but intense moments, near a prelapsarian consciousness. Yet even while he would write a friend in England about how "these people are nearer Earth & the joy of things than we snivelling city-dwellers," he was busily jotting down poems, most of them in conventional sonnet form, and packing them off to Eddie Marsh by registered mail.[55]

Most of the South Pacific poems are eminently forgettable. Inspired by chaste memories of Cathleen, they overlap in subject and tone the mildly anguished poems written before his departure from England. Opening lines like "Not with vain tears, when we're beyond the sun," or "I have peace to weigh your worth, now all is over," or "When she sleeps, her soul, I know, / Goes a wanderer on the air" serve as finger-posts pointing backward to Victorian piano pieces of a flagrantly senti-mental sort. Few of these efforts would ever have been seen had they not appeared in the company of Brooke's war sonnets in the posthum-ous editions of his *Collected Poems*, for they communicate little beyond the mannered sighs of a vibrating ego in doubt of itself. On the other hand, when not agonizing in the manner of a latter-day Keats, he could display his genius for outrageous comedy that had always delighted his friends. After visiting among Fiji cannibals, he wrote Violet Asquith that he was meditating on a sonnet which would contain the lines "Broiled are the arms in which you clung/and devilled is the angelic tongue," and "The ear that heard your whispered vow / Is one of many *entrees* now."[56]

Yet there was a phase, toward the end of his tour, when Brooke might have succeeded in making a mad plunge into a world Victoria never knew. January of 1914 found him in Tahiti en route home. He found a pension, with a veranda overlooking the sea, and remained for three months in a remote native village. Always prone to blood poison-ing, he cut his leg on coral while swimming, and the multiple infections put him to bed, where he was nursed by Taatamata, a native girl. She was slim, very dark, and provided Brooke with the only deep nonverbal communication of his life. He alluded to her in a letter to Marsh: "I have been nursed & waited on by a girl with wonderful eyes, the walk of a goddess, & the heart of an angel, who is, luckily, devoted to me. She gives her time to ministering to me, I mine to probing her queer mind. I think I shall write a book about her—Only I fear I'm too fond of her."[57]

There was little danger that Brooke would grow too fond of her or any other woman, but he did introduce her as Mamua in "Tiare Tahiti," a poem which lightly contrasts delights of sensory reality with life after death, heavily tinctured with platonic ideals.

> Oh, Heaven's Heaven!—but we'll be missing
> The palms, and sunlight, and the south;
> And there's an end, I think, of kissing,
> When our mouths are one with Mouth.[58]

The contrast is resolved by Mamua's capacity for being able to "wash the mind of foolishness" by snaring flowers, kissing, and "floating lazy, half-asleep" in the awaiting lagoon. She is less a real woman than a bland imitation of one of Gauguin's Tahitian women.* Brooke admirers have usually drawn forth this octosyllabic inventory of exotic imagery as evidence that the poet had at last graduated from public schoolboy to man of the world. But investing so-called primitive people, particularly women, with richer emotional lives and greater physical vitality than creatures of civilization was a weary romantic convention already ancient when used by Chateaubriand, Wordsworth, and others over a century before. Brooke's letters home clearly show that he underwent no psychic transfiguration through his affair with Taata. While he enjoyed referring to himself as having become "a minor character in a Kipling story" whose experiences "with Conrad characters in a Gauguin *entourage*" had left him "Quite, quite hard," he always wrote of the South Pacific with the detachment of a literary tourist whose real world was defined by the things back in England that he missed: "theatres and supper parties & arguments & hedges & roast beef & beer & misty half-colours."[59] Exit Tahiti—enter Grantchester. A few weeks later Brooke was hurrying back to the civilization that he affected to despise and to the war that would kill him. Earlier, in a letter outlining his plans for Cambridge lectures, he had prophesied: "Won't 1914 be fun!"[60]

---

*Taatamata proved to be all too real for Brooke's literary executors. Among Brooke's papers there are photographs of her, but none were reproduced in either his official biography or in the edition of his letters. Moreover, a photo of her naked to the waist has mysteriously disappeared from the papers. For a picture of Taatamata, see Michael Hastings, *The Handsomest Young Man in England: Rupert Brooke* (London, 1967), 161.

▼

Returning by way of the United States, Brooke reached England in June 1914 to be met at Euston Station by Cathleen and Marsh. After thirteen months as *Wandervogel* he resumed the old way of life as though the interim had not existed. Now twenty-six, Brooke still gave off his Apollonian glow. A Chicago acquaintance had recorded how "every woman who passes—and every other man—stops, turns round, to look at that lithe and radiant figure."[61] During the month that remained before the outbreak of war, Brooke led a frenetic existence among the London literati. At a homecoming party at Gray's Inn he demonstrated a Samoan fertility dance at dawn under plane trees. There were breakfasts with Siegfried Sassoon, D. H. Lawrence, and other recruits to Marsh's Georgian troop; lunches with Henry James and other notables; dinners at 10 Downing Street with the Asquiths and Churchills; and poetry readings and Stravinsky concerts. But this round of social events failed to conceal his deep dissatisfaction with life. To an old Cambridge intimate he bared his distress in one of the most anguished letters he ever wrote:

> I have no respect for young women. I have as little as a sick man has for that gruel which he has to take to keep him alive. I know *all* about them. And I hate them. . . . I *must* marry soon. . . . It seems such an important step. Perhaps there's a better choice in Samoa. . . . I pray continually. Twelve hours a day, that I may, sometime, fall in love with somebody. Twelve hours a day that I may *never* fall in love with anybody. Either alternative seems too Hellish to bear.[62]

He yearned for marriage but not a wife. Relationships with women seemed to flourish when fanned by passionate letters and to lapse when the distance closed. Friends noted that he was becoming a die-hard antifeminist, likely to argue that mixing the sexes was a calamity and that "manliness in men was the one hope of the world."[63] There were diatribes against "lean & vicious people, dirty, hermaphrodites and eunuchs, Stracheys, moral vagabonds, pitiable scum."[64] This was an unhappy time for English males with dreams of patriarchy or with expectations that their women would match Tahitian women in adoring subservience.* Cathleen was especially threatening to him because she

*So subservient that they committed suicide when their lovers left them. This was the substance of a dream which Brooke had about Taatamata a few months later. In it he returned to Tahiti and learned that she had killed herself just after he left the island.

was a successful actress with her own career and with neither interest in
nor aptitude for playing Wendy to his Peter Pan. It was at this time that
he met, through Eddie's network, Eileen Wellesley, daughter of the
duke of Wellington, and once again Brooke commenced an ardent
epistolary courtship.

External events were soon to put an end to Brooke's erotic frustra-
tion. When Austria declared war on Serbia, the Whitehall set smelled a
general war, and the spoor drifted down from Churchill to Marsh to
Brooke. To a friend he wrote: "Everyone in the governing classes
seems to think we shall all be at war. . . . France and England are the
only countries that ought to have any power. Prussia is a devil. And
Russia means he end of Europe and any decency."[65] He was stimu-
lated by the prospect of England at war and wondered whether others
had, like himself, "a Brussels-before-Waterloo feeling."[66] The first
week in August found him with his mother at Rugby, where a note
reached him from Lady Eileen. In his reply, a letter brimming with
topographical patriotism, he expatiated on a recent excursion to
Hampden-in-Arden:

> It's the sort of country I adore. I'm a Warwickshire man. Don't
> talk to me of Dartmoor or Snowdon or the Thames or the Lakes. I
> know the *heart* of England. . . . It is perpetually June in War-
> wickshire, and always six o'clock of a warm afternoon. . . . Here
> the flowers smell of heaven; there are no such larks as ours, & no
> such nightingales; the men pay more than they owe; & the women
> have very great & wonderful virtue, & that, mind you, by no
> means through the mere absence of trial. . . . Shakespeare & I are
> Warwickshire yokels. What a county![67]

The landscape he describes owes more to musty books than to fresh
observation, filled as it is with allusions to nightingales, honest yeomen,
and virtuous women—with Shakespeare thrown in as a boon companion. As usual, when he was excited (and he seemed always to have been
afflicted with manic peaks of excitement alternating with troughs of
depression) he became so drunk on romantic rhetoric that he had difficulty in separating what he felt from what he thought he ought to feel.
(There is also the possibility that he felt nothing at all but was able to

---

Trying to account for his dream he noted, "Perhaps it was my evil heart. I think the
dream was true." See Hassall, *Prose*, 476. For a sorrowful romantic always disturbed by
heterosexual contact what could have been more satisfying as a conclusion to the Taatamata affair than her suicide?

cover his emptiness with a mellifluous flow of words.) In glorifying bucolic places like Grantchester and Warwickshire, for example, he affected to locate them at the holy center of his affections, and almost to make them sacred shrines, yet the unvarnished truth is that he preferred to spend his time in London, a place which he pretended to despise.

The theory has been offered that Brooke was in love with England and that the war brought him an opportunity to "marry England and flee into the fellowship of men and the waiting embrace of death."[68] In a general way, this is what happened—not only to Brooke but to countless other young men of the 1914 generation. Disgusted with the crass materialism which belittled their youthful aspirations, they sprang to the defense of an abstraction signed and sealed ENGLAND. If imperial Germany had not existed, it would have been politic to have invented her. Shortly after the declaration of war Brooke wrote an essay for the *New Statesman* which describes the explosive impact of a newly found patriotism on a fictionalized English Everyman contemplating a possible German invasion:

> As he thought "England and Germany," the word "England" seemed to flash like a line of foam. With a sudden tightening of his heart, he realised that there might be a raid on the English coast. He didn't image any possibility of it *succeeding*, but only of enemies and warfare on English soil. The idea sickened him. He was immensely surprised to perceive that the actual earth of England held for him a quality which he found in A——[a female friend], and in a friend's honour, and scarcely anywhere else, a quality which, if he'd ever been sentimental enough to use the word, he'd have called "holiness." His astonishment grew as the full flood of "England" swept him on from thought to thought. He felt the triumphant helplessness of a lover. Grey, uneven little fields, and small ancient hedges rushed before him, wild flowers, elms and beeches, gentleness, sedate houses of red brick, proudly unassuming, a countryside of rambling hills and friendly copses.[69]

It was but a step from here to his famous war sonnets. He was in love—but with an abstraction of preindustrial England dotted with sandbox objects like "sedate" cottages and "ancient" hedges and "friendly" copses. He was having as much difficulty communicating his love of country as he had earlier had with love of women. When seized by the patriotic afflatus, the best he could do was to resort to recruiting poster stereotype and cliché. The passage is important, however, in mirroring states of mind of countless young men during the summer of 1914 as they responded to the threat from imperial Germany.*

In a hawkish mood but undecided how he wished to serve, Brooke wrote Cathleen Nesbitt of a "less creditable period" of his life when he was "enmeshed with intellectuals." They were "dehumanized, disgusting people . . . mostly pacifists and pro-Germans."[70] In mid-September, after Marsh pulled strings with Churchill, he received his commission as sublieutenant of the Royal Naval Volunteer Reserve, which had been organized as a special force to protect the Channel ports. In command of thirty men, many of them stokers from remote areas, Brooke wrote Eileen Wellesley—he was now writing both women alternately—that once he would have found "incredible beauty" in watching "rows of naked, superb men bathing in a September sun," but no longer—"I am a warrior."[71]

Within three weeks of his appointment orders came to cross the Channel for the relief of Antwerp. Brooke found it glorious. Belgians cheered as they marched through the street and flung chocolates and kisses at them. After a night on the grounds of a chateau, they repaired some trenches, watched some shrapnel exploding at a distance ("like a German wood-cut, very quaint and graceful and unreal"), and then withdrew after "very nearly" walking into a German ambush.[72] On their retreat they passed lakes of burning petrol and thousands of desperate refugees—"a Dantesque Hell, terrible"[73]—but were safely returned to England, with no casualties except blistered feet, after less than seventy-four hours in the war zone. This was the closest Rupert Brooke ever came to experiencing the horror of modern warfare. On arrival in London, he and Arthur Asquith (the prime minister's son) hurried to the Admiralty to report personally to Churchill. It was like

---

*Wilfred Owen, who would shortly become England's most powerful antiwar poet, was teaching English at Bordeaux when the war began. Although he distanced himself from the excessive war fever of the first months, he was aroused by the threat that Germany posed to the English language and its literature. To his mother he wrote: "If once my fears are roused for the perpetuity and supremacy of my mother-tongue, in the world—I would not hesitate, as I hesitate now—to enlist" (September 23, 1914) and "Do you know what would hold me together on a battlefield? The sense that I was perpetuating the language in which Keats and the rest of them wrote! I do not know in what else England is greatly superior, or dearer to me, than another land and people" (December 2, 1914). See Harold Owen (ed.), *Wilfred Owen: Collected Letters* (London, 1967), 285,300.

talking over a match with one's housemaster. Brooke had now found "a central purpose" for his life, as he explained to Cathleen, "the thing God wants of me is to get good at beating Germans."[74]

During the long, cold winter of 1914–15 the Hood Battalion underwent training in Dorset, where Brooke worked on the five poems which became celebrated as the "war sonnets." They were first published in the December 1914 issue of *New Numbers*, an obscure literary journal founded to publish the work of four Georgian poets—Brooke, Lascelles Abercrombie, Wilfred Gibson, and John Drinkwater. They made no special impression when they appeared; it was only *after* Brooke's death that they became institutionalized. (*New Numbers* promptly collapsed, because in trying to meet the public demand for the issue containing Brooke's sonnets, the editor used up his entire wartime quota of paper.)

The first, inappropriately titled "Peace," is a song of praise to God for having given the young men of Brooke's generation the gift of war.

> Now, God be thanked Who has matched us with His hour,
> And caught our youth, and wakened us from sleeping,
> With hand made sure, clear eye, and sharpened power,
> To turn, as swimmers into cleanness leaping,
> Glad from a world grown old and cold and weary,
> Leave the sick hearts that honour could not move,
> And half-men, and their dirty songs and dreary,
> And all the little emptiness of love![75]

The idea here is proto-Orwellian: war is peace because it provides youths with an opportunity to escape the tedium and boredom of conventional existence by purifying them in the destructive element of battle. By definition men are those who fight; those who refuse are half-men with nothing better to do than to make dirty love poems. The poem reflects Brooke's self-hatred, for what has he been but a maker of love poems? While the baptism metaphor—swimmers leaping into cleanness—comes from his earlier observation of bathing soldiers, it also brings to mind the appalling image of lemmings making a genocidal plunge into the sea. Too much immersion in the water, or for too long, is to drown. The sonnet concludes with an argument that youths "who have known shame" find a release in war, which at its worst can destroy nothing except the body, in which case agony is ended. The final line—"And the worst friend and enemy is but Death"—leans heavily upon John Donne. The difference is that while Donne employed paradox effectively because his poems were premised upon the certitude of Christian immortality, Brooke's vision is gaudily funereal and necrophilic. ("Necrophilia" is used here in the characterological rather than the sexual sense.) Death on his terms is to be welcomed not because it allows for the continuation of life, but because it is an agent of annihilation.

Two of the war sonnets are titled "The Dead"—which is consistent with Brooke's habit of mind. "Blow out, you bugles, over the rich Dead!" began as an elegy for a school friend but in its final form develops the theme of war as a means of returning to an heroic age. The logic of the poem propounds that those who "poured out the red / Sweet wine of youth" make us "rarer gifts than gold" because they have rediscovered lost verities. Because of the war, according to the poem's concluding lines,

> Honour has come back, as a king, to earth,
> And paid his subjects with a royal wage;
> And Nobleness walks in our ways again;
> And we have come into our heritage.[76]

In a 1912 notebook Brooke had started a poem with the line "And I am come into my heritage," which is presumed to have referred to his relationship with Ka Cox. It may seem incongruous to find a line from a love poem used in a death poem, but Brooke had no trouble with the borrowing. Death and Love—abstract entities for him—had always been his major subjects. Now, in his final poems, they had become almost interchangeable.

The fifth sonnet, "The Soldier," stands as the centerpiece of Brooke's work because it embalmed as if in amber how so many non-combatants wished to remember that lost generation of English youth who perished in the Great War. It is one of the most famous poems in the English language, as wildly admired during the war years as it was abused during the peace decades that followed.

> If I should die, think only this of me:
>   That there's some corner of a foreign field
> That is for ever England. There shall be
>   In that rich earth a richer dust concealed;
> A dust whom England bore, shaped, made aware,
>   Gave, once, her flowers to love, her ways to roam
> A body of England's, breathing English air,
>   Washed by the rivers, blest by suns of home.

And think, this heart, all evil shed away
  A pulse in the eternal mind, no less
    Gives somewhere back the thoughts by England given;
Her sights and sounds; dreams happy as her day;
  And laughter, learnt of friends; and gentleness,
    In hearts at peace, under an English heaven.[77]

It is hard to imagine a poem more superciliously nationalistic. The British Empire will expand, not by the robust presence of Kipling's Tommy Atkins putting up a good fight for the Union Jack, but by the proliferation of English corpses around the world. The superiority of the English extended even to their dead soldiers. One wishes to know what qualities the Englishman has which account for this superiority, but as usual Brooke relies upon the imagery so generalized—happy dreams, peaceful hearts, and friends' laughter—that a careful reader must wonder why they are endemic only to England. The poem is lightly washed with a pallid Church of England tincture of Christian faith (though elsewhere, as in his poem "Heaven," Brooke had lightly satirized the notion of human immortality by demonstrating that for a fish the idea of God would be Fish). Through death, evil has been filtered out, and the heart has become "a pulse in the eternal mind" somehow bouncing back the reverberations of the dead soldier's exclusively *English* experiences.

The phenomenal popularity of "The Soldier" during the war years can only be explained by assuming that admirers merely skimmed over its glib surfaces. (In a letter to Robert Frost trying to account for Brooke's éclat, Edward Thomas astutely noted that he was "a rhetorician, dressing things up better than they needed.")[78] In its attempt to make death attractive, this poem is the crowning achievement of Brooke's long love affair with death. However, for a reader not persuaded by his specious reasoning, the poem seems an exercise in morbidity, with its grotesque implication that as fertilizer the English soldier is top drawer.

During the winter of 1914–15 while the Hood Battalion continued its training in Dorset, Brooke experienced some bouts with illness which impaired his immune system, but he recuperated after nine days as guest of the Asquiths, where he was a favorite of the prime minister's daughter. When news leaked of Churchill's master plan for the invasion of Turkey through the Gallipoli peninsula, Brooke was exultant. Like other public school men brought up on tales of the Trojan war and the Crusaders, he viewed the approaching campaign through the romantic lens of myth and legend. Although the expedition was a top secret, Brooke could not resist informing friends (and mother) of his good luck. To Dudley Ward, a Cambridge crony who had long played Horatio to his Hamlet soliloquies, he wrote: "It's too wonderful . . . and the best expedition of the war. Figure me celebrating the first Holy Mass in St. Sophia since 1453."[79]* More revealing was a letter to Violet Asquith. After boyish speculations about fighting on the plains of Troy and bombarding Hero's tower with fifteen-inch guns, Brooke glowingly analyzed his present mood:

> I've never been quite so happy in my life, I think. Not quite so *pervasively* happy; like a stream flowing entirely to one end. I suddenly realize that the ambition of my life has been—since I was two—to go on a military expedition against Constantinople. And when I *thought* I was hungry, or sleepy, or falling in love, or aching to write a poem—*that* was what I really, blindly, wanted.[80]

Here was an honest cri de coeur without the dissimulation and conventional rhetoric of his poems—not, of course, about Constantinople in particular, but about the concentration of his energies toward war, a long-buried, newly discovered ambition far more powerful than activities like writing poems or making love, which he had done only halfheartedly because he was *supposed* to do them. Yet his confession contains the death wish that saturates his mode of thinking; his allusion to "a stream flowing entirely to one end" must refer, on an unconscious level, to the stream of life, the "one end" of which can only be nonlife, or death.

In late February Brooke sailed from England aboard the *Grantully Castle*, a liner converted into a troopship but with most of its amenities intact. On board he jotted in his notebook ideas and scraps for a long

---

*Ward had disappointed Brooke by his failure to enlist. In a letter to a mutual friend, Brooke spoke of Ward affectionately but echoed sentiments found in his poem, "The Soldier": "I wish he'd enlist. I'd like to enter the Hereafter with him. He would be sensible about God: if we met him. He's English." See Keynes, *Letters*, 656. The test of friendship had become the willingness to die together. (Whether it was God who was English, or just Ward, is not clear.)

poem on England which may have been intended to capture the epical nature of the expedition by superimposing contemporary events upon episodes of classical legend, but only fragments exist:

> And Priam and his fifty sons
> Wake all amazed, and hear the guns,
> And shake for Troy again.[81]

Rumors swept the ship that there were a quarter of a million Turks waiting on Gallipoli peninsula for ten thousand British troops, but morale among the Hood officers, chosen from among the elite of the empire, was unimpeachable. Nearly all were public school men; they carried Herodotus as guidebooks and circumvented the censor by using classical allusions in letters home. By mid-March they had anchored off Lemnos. Allusions to death crop up everywhere in Brooke's letters home, but never in a self-pitying or regretful tone. He wrote Ka Cox as though he were already dead, telling her that she was "the best thing" he had found in life, but concluding, "It's a good thing I die."[82] To Dudley Ward he gave instructions for destroying certain letters, especially those from Eileen Wellesley, urged him to inform Taata of his death, and wrote, as though it were an addendum, "It's odd, being dead."[83] To Cathleen Nesbitt he reported amusingly that although some on board had sworn they had seen Olympus, he had directed his field glasses toward shore but had failed to see gods. Yet he added, "My eyes fell on the holy land of Attica. So I can die."[84]

From Lemnos the expedition made a feint toward Gallipoli, then inexplicably turned south for Egypt. They saw no Turks, but Brooke reported that one man thought he spotted a camel through his field glasses. Outside Port Said the Hood Battalion camped on dirty sand near the Arab quarter and a few days later Brooke came down with sunstroke and dysentery. Sir Ian Hamilton, commander of the expedition, visited Brooke in his tent and offered him a place on his staff, which was declined. (Caught up in Crusader zeal, like the others, Sir Ian noted in his diary Brooke's "knightly presence.") Brooke made light of his illness and composed a dysentery poem (which Marsh did not include in his collected works):

> My first was in the night, at 1,
> At half-past 5 I had to run,
> At 8.15 I fairly flew;
> At noon a swift compulsion grew,

I ran a dead-heat all the way.
I lost by yards at ten to 2.
This is the seventh time today.

Prince, did the brandy fail you, too?
You dreamt that arrowroot would stay?
My opium fairly galloped through.
This is my seventh time today.[85]

While meant to be amusing and unconventionally "unpoetic," like his famous "Channel Passage," this poem—one of the last he wrote—describes the body disordered and rotten. The theme of death is here sublimated by meticulous attention to his anal dysfunction. Since anal compulsions are a prominent symptom of necrophilia, this poem is an appropriate terminus for Brooke's career. Much more menacing, though no one recognized it at the time, was a swelling of his upper lip, presumably the result of an insect bite.

Though still weak from dysentery and sunstroke and advised to remain behind, Brooke insisted upon sailing with the *Grantully Castle* on April 10. A week later, as they anchored off Skyros, an island of the Sporades, a letter from Marsh arrived enclosing an April 5 cutting from the *Times* telling how the dean of St. Paul's had quoted Brooke's fifth war sonnet in his Easter sermon, commending its "pure and elevated patriotism" while regretting that it fell short of Isaiah's vision and Christian hope. (Brooke wryly remarked to a companion that he was sorry that the dean did not think he was as good as Isaiah.)[86] Through the dean's plug the poem became an instant success in England—its fourteen lines becoming a national elegy.

Meanwhile Brooke's lip continued to swell. By April 22 pain had spread to his chest and back, and the surgeon aboard became alarmed. The condition was diagnosed as acute blood poisoning. Moved to a nearby French hospital ship, Brooke died on April 23. Because the expedition was scheduled to sail for Gallipoli the next morning, the funeral took place that night. One of the burial party, with remarkable prescience, recorded in his journal, "It was as though one were involved in the origin of some classical myth."[87] "Oc" Asquith reported "everywhere the smell of thyme (or is it sage? or wild mint?)"[88] They carried the coffin a mile inland to a grove on Skyros, heaped lumps of pink and white marble onto the cairn, while a Greek interpreter wrote an epitaph on a wooden cross.

Here lies
The Servant of God
Sub-lieutenant in the
English Navy
Who died for the
Deliverance of Constantinople from
the Turks

There were multiple ironies. None of the Hood officers, nearly all of them public school classical scholars, could read the inscription because it was in modern, not ancient Greek, and the site was the personal property of a Greek shepherd, who subsequently protested this invasion of his dominion—famous English poet be damned. Moreover, anticlimax hung about the event: the most celebrated victim of the Gallipoli campaign—and perhaps of the entire war—had been brought to his death not by human adversary but by septicemia resulting from an insect bite.

The facts of the case had nothing whatever to do with the processes of media mythmaking, which began at once—so rapidly, in fact, that one almost suspects that Rupert Brooke was the first poet in history to be created by the exigencies of governmental propaganda. Winston Churchill announced Brooke's death in the *Times* of April 26 with a eulogy thrilling to anyone willing to credit its self-serving rhetoric. "Rupert Brooke is dead . . . simple force of genius . . . willing to die for the dear England whose beauty and majesty he knew . . . advanced to the brink in perfect serenity . . . incomparable war sonnets . . . shared by thousands of young men . . . revelation of Brooke himself . . . all that one would wish England's noblest sons to be . . . etc."[89] Brooke's sonnets and his timely death had a greater positive impact upon civilian morale than any other event in the entire Gallipoli campaign, which Churchill had engineered. Churchill beat the Georgians to the draw. But apologetics perhaps reached their zenith with Lascelles Abercrombie's eulogy in the *Morning Post* of April 27. As a major Georgian voice—and eventually one of Brooke's heirs—Abercrombie pulled out all the stops as he compared Brooke's life to Tom Brown's at Rugby as ideal public schoolboy and his death to Sir Philip Sidney's as exemplum of poet-soldier. He singled out for highest praise Brooke's "mastering passion, the most elemental of passions, the passion for life." Obviously disturbed by Brooke's infatuation with death, he explained it away by a broad stroke of circumlocution: "Like all lovers of life, he had pleased himself with the thought of death and after death; not insincerely by any means, but simply because this gave a finer relish to the sense of being alive."[90] Other hagiographers hastened to point out that Brooke had died on "the day of Shakespeare and St. George."[91] (It had also been on a Friday—but Easter had inconveniently passed.) Within seven weeks Marsh had brought out his edition of the *Collected Poems*, which contained a 159-page memoir of Brooke, whose death was "the worst blow I have ever had."[92] This book, a runaway best-seller in Britain and America, launched the Brooke cult and fueled the explosion of war poets, a major phenomenon of those years.*

Efforts to deify Rupert Brooke did not end in 1915. After the war, when the country was in mourning for the tragic loss of nearly a million British dead, Brooke was trotted out to uphold the tarnished *dulce et decorum est . . .* tradition. At the dedication of a plaque in Rugby Chapel (near a similar memorial to Thomas Hughes) Sir Ian Hamilton gave the keynote address, telling how Brooke entered a room "like a prince unconscious of his own royalty, and by that mere act put a spell upon everyone around him."[93] In the audience was an officer of the Hood battalion. (Of the four commanding officers in Brooke's company, only one survived the war). A prewar friend remarked that the ceremony "had absolutely no relation to Rupert at all. It was someone else they were commemorating."[94] *Something* else would be closer to the mark, for Brooke had become, except for personal friends, a hallowed symbol—a counterweight against blasphemers who cried that British soldiers had died in vain. The crowning achievement in this mythologizing came in 1931 when a statue—a bronze nude symbolizing Youth—was unveiled overlooking Skyros town. The figure, a neutered abstraction, resembles neither Rupert Brooke nor any other human who ever lived.

From the beginning there were apostates who knew that the Brooke cult owed more to his role as pied piper for the juggernaut (though this was never his intention) than to any sincere regard for his poetry. Virginia Woolf, who had known and liked him, thought that if he had

---

*Edmund Gosse claimed that the boom in war poetry was absolutely unprecedented in English history and that one had to return to the *chansons de geste* of the eleventh century to find an equivalent period in European literature. He estimated that 500 volumes of war poetry were published in England during the war. An index prepared by the British Museum lists 239 volumes under the heading "British." See Edmund Gosse, *Some Diversions of a Man of Letters* (London, 1919), 264; *Subject Index of the Books Relating to the European War, 1914–1918* (London, 1970).

lived he would have made a fine prime minister because of his gift with people. But as for his war poems, they were "mere barrel-organ music," while his earlier pieces "were all adjectives and contortions, weren't they?"[95] Ezra Pound's poem "Our Contemporaries" caused a mild furor when it appeared in Wyndham Lewis' vorticist journal in July:

> When the Taihaitian princess
> Heard that he had decided
> She rushed out into the sunlight and swarmed up a
>   cocoanut palm tree,
>
> But he returned to this island
> And wrote ninety Petrarchan sonnets.[96]

Although his intention had been to criticize the whole Georgian movement for their timidity and traditionalism, his poem was hailed as a flagrant breach of good taste, especially by Edward Marsh. Pound, however, claimed that no malice had been intended and that Brooke would have been entertained by his lines. The argument he had was not with Brooke, who had "perhaps a certain amount of poetry in life," but with "literary hen-coops like Lascelles Abercrombie," who stank of the past.[97] The fracas clearly showed how far apart were the two major "schools" of poetry in England, with the "invaders"—captained by Pound, Lewis, and Eliot—demanding objectivity and detachment and the Georgians leaning upon nostalgia and involvement. Even D. H. Lawrence, who contributed to the Georgian anthologies and had once marveled at Brooke's personal magnetism, sensed through the war sonnets that Brooke was a "deader." Writing to Cynthia Asquith, the prime minister's daughter-in-law, he went on to say: "One can smell death in Rupert; thank heaven, not really here: only the sniff of curiosity, not the great inhalation of desire."[98]

Later generations have generally repudiated Brooke's poetry as they have questioned the judgment and integrity of the leaders of that generation who carried Britain into the Great War. There was nothing in his work which had not been done before and nothing which needed to be done again. Auden's poem "Letter to Lord Byron" dismisses Brooke in a single couplet:

> For gasworks and dried tubers I forsook
> The clock at Grantchester, the English rook.

Less mercifully, by the 1920s many Eton boys had become so bored with the cloying sentimentality of the Brooke cult that they had developed their own chant: "Ow boo-hoo boo-hoo, stands the church clock at ten to bloody three and is there honey still for bloody tea?"[99]

The clock had truly stopped. By the thirties the modernist movement in poetry had left Brooke far behind—a curiosity of the war years, a romantic relic who spoke for a lost, prewar generation when English poets were not expected to work for a living and when it was perfectly natural for their work to be read by prime ministers and first sea lords. Brooke's extraordinary popularity resulted from his being the right man with the right voice at the right moment. Quite fortuitously he had become the rallying center of a cult savagely determined to preserve the faith, his comparatively slender oeuvre buttressed by Christopher Hassall's quarter-million-word biography and Geoffrey Keynes' even longer edition of the letters, both of them models of scholarly craftsmanship. But, with the demise of the original cultists, the gospel faded, and the great structure showed signs of collapse until it could be written of Rupert Brooke what no good citizen dared to think in 1915: "as a poet he is not immortal—he is only dead."[100]

II NINETEEN-FOURTEEN

▼

Those who do not know how to live must make a merit of dying.
GEORGE BERNARD SHAW, *preface to Heartbreak House*

It is the summer of 1914. Picture a schoolboy of seventeen in a country vicarage. He lies in a hammock eating plums in a garden full of delphiniums. He has just been involved in an offensive against wasps' nests and has not been very brave. He is also afraid of "creepy" country lanes after dark. On August 4 he meets a sweating soldier on a bicycle looking for his colonel's house. Late that night a notice at the post office announces that England is at war. So begins the memoir of a subaltern who will shortly be engaged in two of the bloodiest battles of the war—the Somme and Third Ypres.[1] Sunlight, summer gardens, along with lawn parties, cricket pavilions—these are the recurring patterns woven into tapestries of memory during that summer before Europe took the plunge. Working retrospectively, the mind simplifies complex experiences too painful to contemplate as wholes. "Before the war it was always summer—a delusion, as I've remarked before, but that's how I remember it," laments the protagonist of George Orwell's novel *Coming Up for Air* (1939).[2]

Memoirs of well-to-do English men and women repeatedly allude to the summer of 1914 as a dreamy Neverland which preceded the war. For the London smart set the season was memorable for its artistic extravaganzas. Foreign sounds captivated the capital. From America came jazz in the long-running revue *Hullo Ragtime*. The Russian ballet and opera companies brought exotic spectacles which broke abruptly with "the Viking world of bearded warriors drinking blood out of skull" that had been dictated by German musicians.[3] Nijinsky conveyed a struggle for human freedom as he danced the puppet to life in *Petrouchka*. Osbert Sitwell recalled how *Le Coq d'Or* was "laden with omen and prophet," with King Dodan as the symbol of youth of the world and the Astrologer as reactionary evils.[4] At Drury Lane Richard Strauss teamed with Diaghilev in a sumptuous production of his *La Legende de Joseph*, heavy with seduction and framed by a massive Babylonian set. During the third week of July, Siegfried Sassoon, after joining the queue and jostling up the narrow stairs every night to watch the extraordinary Russians, would return home to Kent with piano scores of *Prince Igor* and *Boris Goudonov*, which he played on his piano in candlelight. All of this belonged, in the words of Vera Brittain, to "a long-vanished and half-forgotten world—in which only the sinking of the *Titanic* had quite temporarily reminded its inhabitants of the vanity of human calculation."[5]

August 3, a Monday, was Bank Holiday. Germany and France were at war. Crowds in a holiday mood cheered M.P.s as they arrived at Parliament Square. The floor of the House of Commons was packed when Sir Edward Grey, the foreign secretary, with finely chiseled and pale face, rose and explained the commitment of 1839 which pledged England to guarantee Belgian independence. Conservatives showed their support of national unity by applauding the Liberal party decision, and when John Redmond, leader of the Irish Nationalists, rose and pledged the cooperation of the Irish race to the British cause, the members broke into cheers. The threat of war with Germany had at one stroke resolved the nettlesome "Irish Problem," which earlier had brought the nation to the brink of civil war. In the Foreign Office later that evening, as he watched lamplighters from his window, Sir Edward made the most memorable remark of his life, "The lamps are going out all over Europe; we shall not see them lit again in our life-time."[6]

On the following day, August 4, Prime Minister Herbert Asquith, with hands shaking and voice almost broken, notified the Commons that an ultimatum had been sent to Germany. Unless Germany guaranteed the neutrality of Belgium by midnight (11 P.M. London time), England would go to war. Then the Speaker read a message from the King calling for mobilization of the army. (The navy had already been mobilized.) These announcements were received in silence by the House.[7]

By late afternoon crowds carrying signs "Rule Brittania" and "The Marseillaise" milled through Whitehall and Trafalgar Square. At the Nelson column there were demonstrations against and for the war, as the rival groups glared at each other. High above, the effigy of Nelson gazed steadily toward the southeast—toward England's traditional enemy, not the country of Wilhelm of Germany but of William of Normandy. Cries of "The King!" herded the crowds to Buckingham Palace, where His Majesty, dressed in uniform of an admiral of the fleet and joined by the Queen and the Prince of Wales, came to a balcony and waved to the massed throng, which sang "For He's a Jolly Good Fellow." At eleven in the evening thousands pressed into Parliament Square and counted the strokes of Big Ben. There were no proclamations or official appearances, and the crowd dispersed in a holiday mood shouting "War! War!"[8] The mood of this mob had been caught many times before by William Le Queux and company.

Popular enthusiasm for war appeared to be boundless. On August 6 Asquith issued a call for 500,000 men. Within thirteen months 2,257,521 had volunteered.[9] In the mad rush of volunteering, regiments had to establish waiting lists, and many recruiting sergeants required money under the table before they would sign up a young enthusiast. Old soldiers on the retired list did a brisk business—for pounds and shillings—instructing eager civilians privately in the mysteries of close-order drill. The drill field became a kind of ballroom where one mastered a complicated and rhythmic series of movements not unlike the tango. "It was rather fun for adults to be able to play at such things without being laughed at," wrote a 1914 recruit.[10] Disenchantment lay ahead, but not in this year of visionary gleam when crusaders again walked the earth.

Dissent either went underground or was drowned out by the hurlyburly. It was a time of brutal revelation for rationalists like Bertrand Russell, who had always believed that war was foisted on reluctant populations by despotic governments. Watching the exultant crowds in the streets, he discovered, to his amazement, that "average men and women were delighted at the prospect of war."[11] But what of exceptional men and women—surely they would oppose it? To his further amazement he would soon discover that the bulk of his colleagues at Cambridge regarded him as a mad dog when he wrote and spoke against the government's role in declaring and prosecuting the war. Removed from his Trinity College lectureship and eventually jailed in 1918 for his seditious writings, Russell singled out 1914 as a watershed year in the history of mankind: "For the next 1000 years people will look back to the time before 1914 as they did in the Dark Ages to the time when the Gauls sacked Rome."[12]

Another rationalist rubbing against the grain, George Bernard Shaw watched the floodtide of jingoism with equal disgust but with less surprise. Exposing human folly had long been his chief trade, and the present war was of no more moral consequence than "an engagement between two pirate fleets."[13] Both England and Germany had been duped by their Junkers—which he defined as squirearchs and country noblemen—who had joined with Militarists in order to jump at this opportunity to smash the other and establish their own dominant oligarchy. His manifesto *Common Sense about the War,* which appeared in November, argued that the proper remedy was for both armies to "shoot their officers and go home to gather in their harvests in the villages and make a revolution in the towns."[14] (The Russians would do just that in 1917.)

While the English fingered the writing of von Bernhardi as proof of German belligerence, Shaw went farther back to *The Battle of Dorking* as evidence that for forty years the message of English policy had been "To Arms; or the Germans will besiege London, as they besieged Paris." He went on to cite, as further evidences of English jingoism, the outcry against the Channel tunnel, Lord Roberts' campaign for national service, and the celebrations of the warrior ethos in the work of Henry Newbolt, Rudyard Kipling, and H. G. Wells—particularly *The War in the Air*. Moreover, the present newspaper denunciations of Germans as barbarians for damaging Rheims cathedral was sham sentimentality, for "If Rheims cathedral were taken from the Church tomorrow and given to an English or French joint stock company, everything transportable in it would presently be sold to American collectors, and the site cleared and let out in building sites."[15] Having examined the relevant Foreign Office correspondence, Shaw had not the slightest doubt that England could have prevented the war in the West by making it clear to both France and Germany that she would join either power in the event of an attack by the other. The public outcry against his treatise can be imagined. He was libeled as "Bernhardi" Shaw; the prime minister privately said that he should have been shot; Henry James expressed revulsion at Shaw's "descending into the arena at the present crisis and playing the clown"; and H. G. Wells compared him to "an idiot child screaming in a hospital."[16] When the rumor grew that portions of his manifesto were being distributed as German propaganda in neutral countries, Shaw felt his support among friendly labor pressmen begin to erode.

With England under the bootheel of carmagnoles and corroborees, Shaw, convulsed with rage at the collapse of common sense, concluded that serious playwriting during the war years was impossible. As he said, when men are dying you cannot tell wives and mothers how they are "being sacrificed to the blunders of boobies, the cupidity of capitalists, the ambition of conquerors, the electioneering of demagogues."[17] *Heartbreak House,* his definitive reconstruction of "cultured, leisured Europe before the war," was not published until 1919, when exhaustion had replaced fulmination as the dominant mood of the country.[18]

▼

One immediate casualty of the war was the trusty old invasion narrative, which languished and then died—probably because there was enough lurid matter in the morning paper to satisfy the public appetite for apocalyptic fare. Since the primary purpose of those stories had been to warn the populace of an approaching war and to scare up support for the defense establishment, the need for such works became superfluous once England was up to the hilt in a real war.* (In view of the massive hunt for spies and traitors during the war years when DORA reigned supreme, it is likely that a publisher focusing on alarmist narratives of any sort would have been regarded as "defeatist" or pro-German and promptly shut down.)[19] It was a time of "one virtue, pugnacity; one vice, pacifism," or so Shaw characterized the prevailing mood.[20]

Proclamations explaining what to do in the event of a German invasion circulated throughout the country. (Because of its Dorking and War of the Worlds connection, Surrey was particularly prone to invasion fears; stories of Germans being dropped from hovering zeppelins circulated until well into 1916.)[21] Straight out of Le Queux was the night in Berkhamstead when Graham Greene's uncle was called out to help block the Great North Road down which German armored cars were said to be advancing toward London. No Germans were found but at least some townspeople stoned a dachshund in High Street.[22]

Like the rest of the nation, English poets immediately enlisted in the crusade. On August 5 the *Times* printed on its editorial page Henry Newbolt's 1897 poem "The Vigil," with its rousing final stanza:

*One interesting war-time mutation, which shows the flexibility of the genre as a vehicle for propaganda, is "Baron von Kartoffel's" *The Germans in Cork: Being the Letters of His Excellency, the Military Governor of Cork in the Year 1918* (1917), which was written to show the Irish that the Germans, far from being the liberators they pretended to be, intended to annex Ireland to the Reich. See the bibliography of I. F. Clarke, *The Tale of the Future* (London, 1961). Clarke lists only two other invasion narratives—both featuring Germans as invaders, of course—published during the war years.

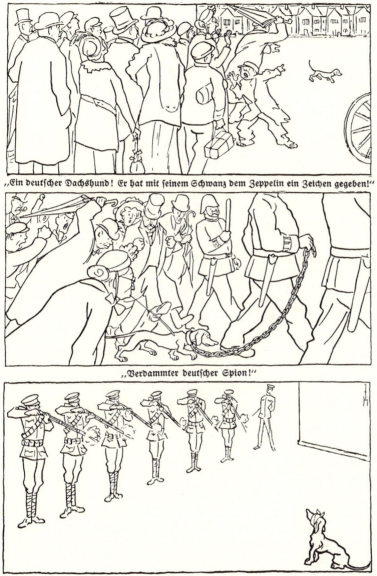

"The spy furor in London." *Top:* "A German dachshund. He has signaled a Zeppelin with his tail!" *Middle:* "Damned German spy!" *Bottom:* "Fire!" From *Gott Strafe England!*

> So shalt thou when morning comes
>   Rise to conquer or to fall,
> Joyful hear the rolling drums,
>   Joyful hear the trumpets call.
> Then let Memory tell thy heart;
>   "England! what thou wert, thou art!
> Gird thee with thine ancient might,
>   Faith! and God defend the Right!"

This poem, Newbolt reported four days later, was "being quoted, sung, recited and reprinted from one end of the country to the other."[23] During the succeeding week, the *Times* printed other exhortatory verse by William Watson, R. E. Vernède, Robert Bridges (the poet laureate), Lawrence Binyon, and Maurice Hewlett, but none of these effusions quite caught the public ear. Other poems followed, including two of the most popular of the war: Rudyard Kipling's "For All We Have and Are" (September 2) with its no-nonsense "Stand up and meet the war. / The Hun is at the Gate," and Thomas Hardy's "Men Who March Away" (September 9), in which the poet's pessimism breaks through his patriotic veneer. The fact that so many of these early war poems attempted to demonstrate that England's course had been stamped with God's seal of approval coupled with the hunch that similar works were being produced by poets among the enemy nations inspired poetaster J. C. Squire to write:

> God heard the embattled nations sing and shout:
> 'Gott strafe England'—'God save the King'—,
> 'God this'—'God that'—and 'God the other thing'.
> 'My God', said God, 'I've got my work cut out.'[24]

Needless to add, this was not published in Lord Northcliffe's *Times*— nor did the war poems of Siegfried Sassoon, Isaac Rosenberg, or Wilfred Owen ever find a place in his pages.

The government moved swiftly to mobilize English writers into a special propaganda section, designed originally to counter German propaganda in the United States which might persuade Congress to cut off munitions sales to Britain. Early in September C. F. G. Masterman called a conference attended by such luminaries as James Matthew Barrie ("small and insignificant"), Arnold Bennett ("looking every inch a cad"), Robert Bridges ("calmly indifferent"), G. K. Chesterton ("enormous, streaming with sweat"), Arthur Conan Doyle ("solid and good-humoured"), John Galsworthy ("bald and solemn"), Thomas Hardy ("very old and faded"), H. G. Wells ("with cockney accent"), Henry Newbolt, E. V. Lucas, John Masefield, and many others.[25] All promised to aid the cause by writing or lecturing, but while they waited to be mustered into service the government decided that publishers and newsmen made better propagandists and placed the litterateurs on indefinite hold.* Undaunted, Barrie and A. E. W. Mason (ex-marine, former secret service officer in Morocco, and author of *The Four Feathers*, a best-selling novel of 1902 about a reclaimed coward) sailed at once to America to initiate their own private propaganda campaign, but they were headed off and silenced by the British Embassy in Washington, which feared that their appearance would spark a counterdemonstration by German-Americans. (The British were particularly worried about pro-German blocs in the American Middle West.) The government had scrapped the frontal approach in disseminating propaganda in favor of a covert strategy which entailed "nursing" American correspondents in London and subsidizing American publishers (such as George Doran of New York) to publish pro-British books and pamphlets.[26] It was just as well, for most of the patriotic efforts penned by the stay-at-homes have proved to be retrospective embarrassments at best. E. V. Lucas, a gracious travel writer in normal times, obligingly produced *In Gentlest Germany* (1915), which, after digs at Goethe and Beethoven for no better reason except that they were Germans, features a grotesque Kaiser in bathing costume and Iron Cross praying "God punish England," and Count Zeppelin speaking of a sky full of airships raining death on England, "Would not that be a glorious justification of German culture and the sacred Emperor's lifelong devotion to peace?"[27] Such bottled-in-bile works are better forgotten.

Efforts to impose proper literary standards upon the men in the ranks proved to be more difficult. Arthur C. Ainger, a forty-year assistant master at Eton, supplied the *Times* on September 29 with his own hand-tooled marching songs for the British army. A fair sample was this drubbing of the Kaiser:

*By 1918 Masterman's operation had evolved into the Ministry of Information, lodged at Wellington House, with Lord Beaverbrook in charge of an annual budget of 1,300,000 pounds. But in those lean years for literature, novelists and poets were in less demand for public display than disabled British officers in full uniform. See Public Records Office (Kew), INF 4 (Ministry of Information Files, 1914–18), File 1A.

He shot the wives and children,
The wives and little children,
He shot the wives and children,
And laughed to see them die.

(chorus)

So now we're off to Berlin,
To Berlin, to Berlin,
So now we're off to Berlin,
To ask the reason why.

In a more benign mood Ainger offered this marching song:

Here's to Lord Kitchener, brown with the sun,
Gentle, persuasive, and balmy,
Giving his orders and getting them done,
All that we want for the Army—
Give him a shout, etc.

This provoked a reader of the *Times* to comment on the inappropriate-
ness of calling Lord Kitchener "balmy." Did the poet not know that
this word in common usage was synonymous with "barmy"—half-
witted or lunatic? When other letters deepened the controversy, pointing out that actual marching songs tended to be an illogical mélange of
music hall tags, obscenities, nonsense rimes, blasphemy, and foot soldier fatalism, Ainger abandoned his enterprise plaintively: "It is clearly
useless for any sane person to try to write marching songs for him [the
soldier]: his only laureate must be the village idiot."[28]

Dramatic pieces suitable for supercharged patriotic consumption
were conspicuously absent during 1914, but almost immediately expec-
tant heads turned westward toward Wessex country. As early as August
18 Thomas Hardy began to receive pleas that his verse drama *The
Dynasts* be brought up to date so that the Kaiser could join Napoleon as
bête noire of democracy and enlightenment. To these enthusiasts
Hardy replied pessimistically that others were free to continue his
saga—at least into the twenty-first century when it was likely that "all
dynasties [would be] likely to be finished by that time." The best that
one could do in the present age, with hope and chivalry eroded, was to
sit in apathy "and watch the clock spinning backwards."[29] However, in
September, when Harley Granville Barker approached him about a
production at the Kingsway theater, Hardy consented, wisely leaving

the abridgment to Barker. To his publisher Hardy explained that the actors worked for half salary; with jingoes and censors looking over one's shoulders, it was "a question of producing something martial, bearing on English victories; or shutting the theatre altogether."[30] The play ran from November 14 to January 15. By this time Hardy was too highly revered to be subjected to damaging criticism, but there is no record of anyone sitting through *The Dynasts* a second time. More in tune with the mood of the country was Horatio Bottomley's production of *England Expects* at the London Opera House, in which a cockney female wailed for the benefit of those males who had not yet enlisted, "Ow wee dount wornt—te le-oose yew—bat we thinkew orter gow"— to borrow Shaw's transliteration of this song so indelibly associated with the fall and winter of 1914–15.[31]

The war spirit promptly percolated down to the public school, that great incubator of conformity and militancy. Schoolboys mounted guard at railway bridges, raised money for the Red Cross by selling empty jam jars, and cut up linoleum to make slippers for wounded soldiers. Niggardly housemasters used the "shortage" dodge to raise prices and cut boys' rations to near-famine levels in some schools, and if there were complaints they could shame their charges with Harry Lauder's lurid reminder that there was a war on: "When you cut yourself another slice of bread, look at the knife. There's blood on it. The blood of a British soldier you have stabbed in the back." Evelyn Waugh remembered that at Lancing, "We were cold, shabby and hungry in the ethos, not of free Sparta, but of some beleaguered, enervated and forgotten garrison."[32] Many boys were confused by the conflicting creeds taught at school. At Rugby William Plomer harbored "powerful feelings of resentment" at his seniors because at one moment they might be explaining the Sermon on the Mount and at another cheering on boys in khaki stabbing sacks of straw painted with a likeness of the Kaiser.[33] At Anthony Powell's preparatory school the headmaster used boys as "slave-laborers" in chopping wood for his house, always telling them that "life was worse in the trenches."[34] A debatable point, that.

During the first months of the war students all over England were exposed to a poem of John Oxenham's which opened with

> What can a little chap do,
> For his Country, and for you?
> What *can* a little chap do?[35]

What, the reader might ask, did John Oxenham do? He went to the front, very late in the war—not as soldier but as a visiting literary gentleman. His contribution to the defeat of Hunnery was a travel book with the elevated title *High Altars: The Battlefields of France and Flanders As I Saw Them*. Oxenham almost makes Kipling sound like a pacifist. The war is fought against a "Mongrel German Empire" with whom reason is no more possible than "with a mad dog or a maniac . . . or a volcanic eruption."[36] He travels in style—at the expense of the Ministry of Information. At a requisitioned chateau bedecked with family portraits dating back to the seventeenth century there are wide hearths with blazing logs, and the bath water arrives early. Outside, placid cows graze in the well-groomed park—a contrast, had Oxenham bothered to note it, with the filthy middens and barnyards inhabited by thousands of British Tommies back from the trenches. At Arras he admires an "athletic figure of Christ" looking down on the ruins; farther on, at Vimy Ridge, the landscape of red poppies "like little clots of blood" reminds the author that without the sacrifice of all those brave men the Germans might have overrun Suffolk, Essex, Kent, and Surrey.[37] At General Haig's headquarters he is told—and believes—that even before the Germans sank the *Lusitania* they had struck a medal celebrating the atrocity and that the nightingales at Kemmel during a bombardment increased the volume of their song in order to be heard over the big guns. The staff must have enjoyed Oxenham's visit, for he believed everything they told him and he had nothing good to say about the enemy. "The Boche," he wrote, "is no *sportsman* [my italics]."[38] Presumably Oxenham was.

"Sportsman" was one of those key words like "amateur" which loomed so large in the psyche of Englishmen of the Great War period. When kept within the bounds of lawn and field games they were innocuous enough, but when metamorphosed into the context of martial arts or racial destiny they could become lethal indeed. One of the lexical peculiarities of that period is the affinity which existed between words denoting games and those connoting war—and vice versa. A vivid example is provided by the memoir of General Sir Beauvoir de Lisle, an aristocrat and career soldier who commanded the Twenty-ninth Division on the Western Front. His book is appropriately titled *Reminiscences of Sport and War*, for in the general's view the two activities are inseparable. This is no book for a bleeding heart. When a "nigger" in Egypt laughs while being beaten with a leather strap, Sir Beauvoir orders use of the buckle end. It probably comes as no surprise that there is a chapter titled "Horses I Have Known" and that he regards "shell-shock" as poppycock. In his division in France men using the "shell-shock" dodge are promptly "cured" by tying them with wire to the top of a trench parapet at night for half an hour; more stubborn cases can be brought around by putting them on wire mattresses and turning on an electric current. Like all good soldiers the general dislikes war "in principle" but confesses that "no sport can equal the excitement of war, no other occupation can be half as interesting."[39] Generals do not necessarily die in bed, for he recalls a corps commander dying of heart failure on the way to the front in 1914 due to excitement and another major general who shot himself because he was unable to join the first force that sailed for France. The concluding lines of the memoir—for the benefit of a reader who might have missed his message—is "Yes, sport and war are closely allied. The man who excels in sport always excels in war. To me both are great games and the greater is War."[40]

Lest one conclude that this sporting attitude toward war was peculiar to rear line commanders, there is the memoir of the youth lying in a vicarage garden cited earlier in this chapter. Charles Carrington, who had enlisted as a private in Kitchener's New Army, found himself posted to France as an nineteen-year-old subaltern in time for the Somme battle. No hero, but eager to do his duty, he compared his first experience in battle with the closest correlative in civilian life—his first day at public school. "It was the same feeling that I had on my first day at school—a blankness, a numbness of intellect." He was torn by competing anxieties—fear of being killed versus dread of losing face—and it was difficult to know which was greater. When he came under his first massive bombardment at La Boisselle, his real self was "smitten helpless with fear," yet when the order came to attack, his public self took command and he went over the top "no more afraid than if it were all a game." In the heat of battle, when his servant thrust a half-full water bottle in his hands, Carrington, though tempted, replies, "Stanley, you're a sportsman, but I can't take it off you. I've drunk up all my own." Then he adds, probably subconsciously echoing Sir Philip Sidney's dying words at Zutphen, "If you're sure you can spare some, give it to the wounded. They're wanting it pretty badly." Finally, after a hard fight when the crest is taken by the English and the fragmented battalion is unified again, his commander "came up and greeted me with the enthusiasm of a boy who meets a friend at a very exciting football match."[41] For a "new-boy" at the end of the game it was exactly like being slapped on the back by the house captain and hearing those cherished words of acceptance, "well played!" Any schoolboy would have instantly recognized the connection between lobbing a grenade and bowling a cricket ball—or being on the receiving end of the pitch—as he would imagine kicking a football toward the enemy lines when going over the top.[42] Whether on playing field or battlefield the proper English sportsman had no doubt that his kind were more than a match for those German professionals.

Though the English upper classes were loath to abandon their faith in the invincibility of the amateur sportsman, certain recent historical events had suggested that the type might be nearing extinction. The famous race to the South Pole in 1912 between England and Norway was a case in point, for the outcome should have served as a warning that clinging stubbornly to the British way of doing things could lead not only to failure but also to tragedy. Robert Falcon Scott placed his trust in machines and horses, neither of them suited for the bitter climate of Antarctica; Roald Amundsen won the race handily because he had planned to use—and then to eat—dogs, which no English gentleman would have thought of, much less dared to do. After two centuries of outdistancing other European nations in exploration and colonization, England came up ignominiously short. Scott failed and died; Amundsen succeeded and lived. The reason, Amundsen always believed, was because Scott's efforts were pathetically amateurish.[43] As might have been expected, the British were enraged that a Norwegian had beaten them to the Pole: the secretary of the Royal Geographical Society told the Norwegian ambassador that he "regretted that the South Pole had first been attained by a *professional* [my italics]."[44] The British proceeded to salvage what they could out of failure. Scott was promptly canonized as a martyred hero, schoolchildren for a generation afterward were taught that the British discovered the Pole, and a line from one of Scott's final letters was wildly admired: "We have been to the Pole and we shall die like gentlemen."[45] For Englishmen, dying well had become the best revenge.*

Essentially, the mind-set of Scott belonged to the nation as a whole, for England, despite its industrial prominence, in many ways looked backward to a preindustrial world where problems were solved by

---

*Another letter found on Scott's frozen body was addressed to his friend James Matthew Barrie, asking for financial help for his widow and son. Scott's son, Peter (b. 1909), had been named for Peter Pan. See Elspeth Huxley, *Scott of the Antartica* (London, 1977), 255.

sinew and nerve, in the manner of Tom Brown at Rugby. Despite the
attention given to the literature of Athens, the model for the British
Empire was rigorously Spartan. The Great War would be fought in
Europe, Asia, Africa, and on the high seas by English males whose
attitudes, as reflected in their popular culture, included a profound
distrust of behavior or ideas not conforming to insular norms, a preoccupation with games and physical action at the expense of intellectual
activity, and a conviction that individual improvisation—coupled with
God's obligation to "Defend the Right"—would outweigh central planning and control.

In the end, England would muddle through the Great War and
emerge as a bedraggled pyrrhic victor not because of greater wisdom or
virtue but because she was fortunate enough to draw powerful allies in
the diplomatic lottery of 1914–18. (The outcome would have been
radically altered if Germany had not been engaged in a two-front war,
or if the German Navy had restricted its U-boat attacks on neutral
shipping, or if the English language had not been the dominant tongue
in the United States, or if. . . .) For the truth was that England, the
birthplace of the industrial revolution, had degenerated by 1914 into
what Correlli Barnett has called "a working museum of industrial ar-
chaeology."[46] For example, England produced only half as much steel
as Germany—steel being a primary indicator of industrial might. Moreover, in 1914 there were no aircraft engines of British design—France
had to loan these. Only one ball bearing factory existed in the entire
country. England relied on the United States for precision tools like
calipers and micrometers, on Switzerland for clock mechanisms used in
artillery fuses and pressure gauges, and on Germany for most of its
optical glass and chemical products. (During the war England averted
catastrophe by illegally appropriating German patents for high explosives, dyes, photographic materials, paint, and drugs.)[47] Not until
June of 1915 did the government finally assume responsibility for man-
aging the industrial output of the country, when Lloyd George assumed
control of the newly created Ministry of Munitions. Up to that time
contracts for munitions were put up for bids on the same competitive
basis as those for plum jam and tissue paper. What England did have
was the largest stockpile of gold reserves in the world, which allowed
her to buy materials and talent she could not produce.

Meanwhile, there was a war to be fought. At the end of it there loomed
a statistical nightmare beyond the calculation of anyone, jingo or pacifist.
In 1914, the number of British casualties stood at 908,371 dead (702,410

"May God punish England!" John Bull is unable to buy off the devil. From the cover of a wartime German book of anti-British cartoons.

from the British Isles). The wounded totaled 2,090,212—a deceptive number since many of these men were wounded more than once.[48] (However, it should be noted that a larger number of British nationals escaped without injury or excessive inconvenience and that conspicuous among this group were those whose decisions had brought about the deaths of others—Whitehall officials, scaremongering writers, and military staff.) Some 229,434 British soldiers (an undetermined but goodly number of whom had never seen a battle) received medals, which amounts to a ratio of almost one medal for every four dead soldiers.[49] (In the British army a soldier does not receive a medal just for being wounded or killed, as is the custom with the Americans.) The financial cost of the Great War cannot be estimated, but expenditure for the British army alone during the period between April 1914 and April 1919 came to 2,905,464,351 pounds.[50] Whoever needed it could take comfort in the fact that Germany and France suffered even more.

Perhaps an even greater loss than flesh and money, which are expendable resources in any case, was the gnawing sense that human problems had grown too complex to admit of solution. The great Edwardian writers—Galsworthy, Wells, and Shaw—had struggled with the problems of mankind, while the postwar writers would disappear into the womblike recesses of the self. The change can be traced in E. M. Forster, whose career spanned two epochs. In looking backward from late middle age, he wrote that when he was young, "problems lay about like sheets torn out of Euclid, all waiting to be solved," but that this attitude "was scotched then killed by the first world war." In the 1920s, the realization dawned that "solutions were hydras who produced more heads than had been decapitated." The result, Forster predicted, was that the world "has passed out of our control" and the human race "is powerless to avert its own destruction."[51] With that inductive leap one lands squarely into the modern age—into a time of ever more sophisticated techniques for manipulating nationalistic prejudices—where the possibilities for resolving political conflicts appear even less promising than they were in the period before the Great War.

NOTES

▼

1 INTRODUCTION

1 *The Crown of Wild Olive* (Boston, n.d.), 67.

2 Ibid., 74.

3 Brian Bond, *War and Society in Europe, 1870–1970* (Leicester, 1983), 53.

4 Ibid., 56.

5 John Gooch, *The Prospect of War: Studies in British Defence Policy* (London, 1981), 42.

6 John M. Mackenzie, *Propaganda and Empire: The Manipulation of British Public Opinion, 1880–1960* (Manchester, 1984), 2–4.

7 Eric Hobsbawm, "Mass Producing Traditions: Europe, 1870–1914," in Eric Hobsbawm and Terence Ranger, *The Invention of Tradition* (Cambridge, 1983), 282.

8 Arnold Toynbee, *Experiences* (New York, 1969), 214; Attlee quoted in Mackenzie, 194.

9 Mackenzie, 17–18.

10 Ibid., 26.

11 Ibid., 58.

12 *The Psychology of Jingoism* (London, 1901), 3.

13 Mackenzie, 31.

14 Maurice Frest (ed.), *Historical Compendium to Hymns Ancient and Modern* (London, 1962).

15 J. S. Bratton, *The Impact of Victorian Children's Fiction* (London, 1981), 14.

16 Guy Arnold, *Held Fast for England: G. A. Henty, Imperialist Boys' Writer* (London, 1980), 63.

17 Mackenzie, 205.

18 (London, 1890), viii.

19 The poem is Sir Edwin Arnold's "Berlin—the Sixteenth of March."

2 PAPER INVASIONS

1   Thomas Hardy, *The Dynasts* (London, 1934), I, 197.
2   For brief descriptions of invasion narratives of this period see the comprehensive bibliography of I. F. Clarke, *The Tale of the Future* (London, 1961).
3   Hugh Cunningham, *The Volunteer Force: A Social and Political History, 1859–1908* (London, 1975), 92.
4   *The Battle of Dorking* (Edinburgh and London, 1871), 57.
5   Ibid., 64.
6   Ibid.
7   I. F. Clarke, *Voices Prophesying War 1763–1984* (London, 1966), 41.
8   The illustration is reproduced in Clarke, *Voices*, 42.
9   Ibid., 39.
10 *Punch, or the London Charivari* (September 23, 1871), 125. In the same issue, however, editors could not resist poking fun at some directives issued by the militia, such as "One hospital orderly per regiment will carry a medical companion" (124).
11 Gooch, 2.
12 The London *Times* (May 9, 1859). Tennyson later proudly noted that three days after the publication of his poem, permission was granted for formation of the Volunteer Force. Published under the byline "T," it was mistaken for the handiwork of Martin Tupper, a popular poetaster whose muse had long been warning against the French menace and urging rifle clubs as a palliative. Derek Hudson, *Martin Tupper, His Rise and Fall* (London, 1949), 189–90.
13 The Volunteers are treated definitively in Hugh Cunningham. For the elephant episode, see 71.
14 Ibid., 89.
15 For the Territorials, see chapter 4 below.
16 Raymond L. Schults, *Crusader in Babylon: W. T. Stead and the* Pall Mall Gazette (Lincoln, Nebraska, 1972), 94.
17 *The Battle off Worthing* (London, 1887), 7.
18 Ibid., 11.
19 Ibid., 49.
20 Ibid., 53.
21 Clarke, *Voices*, 111.
22 Ibid., 112.
23 Collected in *Life's Little Ironies* (London, 1894), 182.
24 Robert Gittings, *Young Thomas Hardy* (London, 1975), 132.
25 *The Taking of Dover* (Bristol, 1888), 5.
26 Philip Colomb et al., *The Great War of 189–, A Forecast* (London, 1893), 1.
27 Ibid., 80.
28 Clarke, *Voices*, 67.
29 Colomb, 298.
30 William Le Queux, *The Great War in England in 1897,* (London, 1894), 43.
31 Ibid., 46–47.
32 Ibid., 54–55.
33 Ibid., 325.
34 A. J. A. Morris, *The Scaremongers: The Advocacy of War and Rearmament, 1896–1914* (London, 1984), 96.

35 Ibid., 98.
36 Burke Wilkinson, *The Zeal of the Convert* (Washington, 1976), 65.
37 Andrew Boyle, *The Riddle of Erskine Childers* (London, 1977), 108.
38 Ibid., 113.
39 Ibid., 197.
40 Ibid., 109.
41 *The Riddle of the Sands* (New York, 1915), 94.
42 Ibid., 108.
43 Ibid., 104–5.
44 Gooch, 10.
45 Boyle, 25.
46 Morris, 157.
47 Clarke, *Voices*, 145.
48 William Le Queux, *The Invasion of 1910* (London, 1906), 5.
49 N. St. Barbe Sladen, *The Real Le Queux* (London, 1938), 197.
50 Le Queux, *The Invasion of 1910*, 356.
51 Ibid., 529.
52 Ibid., 546.
53 Morris, 158.
54 Ibid., 98.
55 *Journals and Letters of Reginald Viscount Esher* (London, 1934), II, 379.
56 Morris, 161.
57 Ibid., 99.
58 Sladen.
59 *The Ministry of Fear* (London, 1943), 71.
60 Ibid., 72.

3 THE COLLIDING WORLDS OF H. G. WELLS

 1 From *Evolution and Ethics* (1894); quoted in Mark R. Hillegas, "Cosmic Pessimism
    in H. G. Wells's Scientific Romances," *Papers of the Michigan Academy*, XLVI
    (1961), 657.
 2 H. G. Wells, *Experiment in Autobiography* (New York, 1934), 159.
 3 Gooch, 36.
 4 H. G. Wells, *The War of the Worlds* (London, 1924; Atlantic edition), III, 213.
 5 *Pall Mall Gazette* (September 25, 1894).
 6 Norman and Jeanne Mackenzie, *The Time Traveler: The Life of H. G. Wells* (Lon-
    don, 1973), 113.
 7 *War of the Worlds*, p. 379.
 8 Ibid., 302.
 9 Ibid.
10 *War of the Worlds*, 421.
11 Ibid.
12 Frank McConnell, *The Science Fiction of H. G. Wells* (New York, 1981), 140.
13 *War of the Worlds*, 449.
14 Ibid., 451.
15 Bernard Bergonzi, *The Early H. G. Wells* (Manchester, 1961), 138.
16 Nordau, quoted in Ibid., 5.

17 *War of the Worlds*, 445.
18 Ibid., 265–66.
19 Mackenzie, 101.
20 W. T. Stead, quoted in Patrick Parrinder (ed.), *H. G. Wells: The Critical Heritage* (London, 1972), 61.
21 Wells, *Experiment in Autobiography*, 549; Mackenzie, 192.
22 H. G. Wells, *Anticipations and Other Papers* (London, 1924; Atlantic edition), 178, 183.
23 Ibid., 171.
24 Ibid., 184.
25 Ibid., 182.
26 Ibid., 264.
27 Parrinder, 13.
28 Wells' introduction to 1914 edition of *Anticipations* in 1924 edition, 279.
29 *Experiment in Autobiography*, 650ff.
30 Collected in *The War in the Air and Other War Forebodings* (London, 1926), 385ff.
31 Ibid.
32 H. G. Wells, *The War in the Air* (London, 1908), 62, 66.
33 Ibid., 115.
34 Ibid., 222.
35 Originally published in Lord Northcliffe's *Daily Mail*; collected in *The War in the Air*, 465.
36 *Experiment in Autobiography*, 72.
37 Collected in *The War in the Air*, 475.
38 *Experiment in Autobiography*, 72–74.
39 Mackenzie, 231.
40 H. G. Wells, *Little Wars: A Game for Boys* (London, 1913), 97, 100.
41 H. G. Wells, *The World Set Free and Other War Papers* (London, 1926; Atlantic edition, XXI), 129.
42 Ibid., 212.
43 *Experiment in Autobiography*, 45, 70.
44 Ibid., 143.
45 Ibid., 590.
46 Ibid., 571.
47 Mackenzie, 297.
48 H. G. Wells, *The War That Will End War* (New York, 1914), 16.
49 *War That Will End*, 12, 14.
50 W. Warren Wagar, *H. G. Wells and the World State* (New Haven, 1961), 33.
51 Bergonzi, 171.
52 Orwell, 145.
53 Wagar, 48.
54 *After London; or, Wild England* (London, 1885), 68.
55 Ibid., 33.
56 Ibid., 26.
57 D. G. Hogarth, *The Life of Charles M. Doughty* (London, 1928), 170.
58 Ibid., 7.
59 Ibid., 148.
60 *The Cliffs* (London, 1909), 44, 22, 32.

61   Ibid., 60.
62   Ibid., 267.
63   Hogarth, 172.
64   Ibid.
65   Stephen Tobachnick, *Charles Doughty* (Boston, 1981), 157.
66   *The Clouds* (London, 1912), 67.
67   Robert Graves, *Good-bye to All That* (London, 1960), 244.
68   Anne Treneer, *Charles M. Doughty* (London, 1935), 278.
69   Tobachnick, 156.
70   Wilfred Scawen Blunt, *My Diaries, 1888–1914* (New York, 1932), 624.
71   Ibid., 812.
72   Ibid., 846.

4 BOY SCOUTS TO THE RESCUE

1   Thomas Packenham, *The Boer War* (New York, 1979), 419.
2   Ibid.
3   Ibid., 424–25.
4   (London, 1907), 45.
5   Packenham, 423–25.
6   Ibid., 441.
7   Sir Robert Baden-Powell, *Pig-Sticking or Hog-Hunting* (London, 1924), 21.
8   William Hillcourt, *Baden-Powell: The Two Lives of a Hero* (London, 1964), 237.
9   John Springhall, *Youth, Empire and Society: British Youth Movements, 1883–1940* (London, 1977), 17.
10   Hillcourt, 48.
11   Ibid., 248.
12   Field Marshal Earl Roberts, *A Nation in Arms* (London, 1907), 27.
13   Ibid., 51.
14   Ibid., 82.
15   The Brownsea Island encampment is treated in detail by Hillcourt, 267ff., and by Reynolds, 141ff.
16   Springhall, 68.
17   Hillcourt, 286.
18   Ibid., 287.
19   Ibid., 294.
20   Samuel Hynes, *The Edwardian Turn of Mind* (Princeton, 1968), 29.
21   Hillcourt, 296.
22   Reynolds, 128.
23   Hillcourt, 296.
24   Ibid., 298.
25   Hillcourt, 302.
26   Reynolds, 115.
27   Hillcourt, 314.
28   Springhall, 62.
29   *My Adventures as a Spy* (London, 1915), 131.
30   Hillcourt, 346.

31 F. Haydn Dimmock (ed.), *The Scouts' Book of Heroes: A Record of Scouts' Work in the Great War* (London, 1919), 10.
32 Ibid., 60.
33 Hillcourt, 392.
34 E. S. Turner, *Boys Will Be Boys* (London, 1957), 178.
35 Ibid., 176.
36 Ibid., 179.
37 Ibid., 181.
38 Guy Arnold, *Held Fast for England: G. A. Henty, Imperialist Boys' Writer* (London, 1980), 63.
39 Ibid., 22.
40 Ibid., 180.
41 "Boys' Weeklies," *The Collected Essays, Journalism and Letters of George Orwell* (New York, 1968), I, 465.
42 Reynolds, 157. As commander of the South African Constabulary as early as January 1901, B-P regularly closed letters with "Be Prepared"; ibid., 121.
43 Turner, 176.
44 *Punch* (March 17, 1909), 188.
45 *The Swoop! or How Clarence Saved England. A Tale of the Great Invasion* (New York, 1979), passim.
46 George Orwell, *The Collected Essays, Journalism and Letters of George Orwell*, (New York, 1968), III, 342.
47 Ibid.
48 Hector H. Munro, *The Westminster Alice* (London, 1902), 4.
49 Ibid., 10.
50 Ibid., 44.
51 A. J. Langguth, *Saki: A Life of Hector Hugh Munro* (London, 1981), 248.
52 H. H. Munro, *The Complete Works of Saki* (Garden City, 1976), 767.
53 Langguth, 251.
54 *Complete Works*, 786.
55 Ibid., 765.
56 Ibid., 761.
57 Ibid., 814.
58 Langguth, 235.
59 *Complete Works*, 398.
60 (August 8, 1914); quoted in Langguth, 248.
61 Rothay Reynolds, preface to *The Toys of Peace* (London, 1929), xxv.
62 *Fortnightly Gazette* (May 10, 1915); quoted in Langguth, 261.
63 Ibid., 272.
64 Ibid., 277.
65 Munro, *Toys of Peace*, 223.

5 PLAYING THE GAME

1 General Sir Ian Hamilton, *When I Was a Boy* (London, 1939), 89, 126.
2 John Betjeman, *Summoned by Bells* (London, 1960), 69.
3 Jonathan Gathorne-Hardy, *The Old School Tie: The Phenomenon of the English Public School* (New York, 1977), 152.

4   Ibid., 153.
5   Leonard Woolf, *Sowing* (London, 1960), 75.
6   L. E. Jones, *A Victorian Boyhood* (London, 1955), 231, 201.
7   Ibid., 190.
8   Shane Leslie, *The Oppidan* (New York, 1922), 30.
9   Ibid., 31.
10 Gathorne-Hardy, 141.
11 E. L. Grant Watson, "Pioneers," in Graham Greene (ed.), *The Old School* (London, 1934), 221.
12 Ibid.
13 Arnold Toynbee, *Experiences* (New York, 1969), 5.
14 W. H. Auden, "Honour," in Greene (ed.), 17.
15 Gathorne-Hardy, 50.
16 Richard Perceval Graves, *A. E. Housman, The Scholar-Poet* (London, 1979), 23.
17 Betjeman, 68.
18 Gathorne-Hardy, 62.
19 Jones, 220.
20 Evelyn Waugh, *A Little Learning: An Autobiography* (Boston, 1964), 103; Milne quoted in J. R. Honey, *Tom Brown's Universe: The Development of the Victorian Public School* (London, 1977), 215.
21 Hamilton, 91.
22 "Such, Such Were the Joys," *The Collected Essays, Journalism and Letters of George Orwell* (New York, 1968), IV, 347–48.
23 Gathorne-Hardy, 166.
24 Cyril Connolly, *Enemies of Promise* (Boston, 1939), 281.
25 Stuart Cloethe, *A Victorian Son* (London, 1972), 161.
26 Jones, 153.
27 Cyril Alington, *Things Ancient and Modern* (London, 1936), 228.
28 Gathorne-Hardy, 89.
29 Guy Chapman, *A Kind of Survivor* (London, 1975), 30.
30 Vivian de Sola Pinto, *The City That Shone: An Autobiography* (London, 1969), 131.
31 Lytton Strachey, "Dr. Arnold," *Eminent Victorians* (New York, 1963), 202.
32 Ibid., 214.
33 Ibid., 213.
34 (New York, 1958), 127.
35 Thomas Hughes, *Tom Brown's School Days* (New York, 1880), 2.
36 Ibid., 72.
37 Ibid., 7.
38 Ibid., 142.
39 Ibid., 221.
40 Toynbee, 7.
41 Hughes, 311.
42 Ibid., 375.
43 Edward C. Mack, *British Schools and British Opinion, 1780 to 1860* (London, 1938), 255.
44 Edward C. Mack, *Public Schools and British Opinion Since 1860* (New York, 1941), 135.
45 Correlli Barnett, *The Collapse of British Power* (London, 1972), 100.

46 Ibid., 101.
47 E. C. Beon, *The Schoolmaster* (New York, 1908), 106.
48 David Newsome, *On the Edge of Paradise: A. C. Benson, The Diarist* (London, 1980), 77.
49 Ibid., 68.
50 Ibid., 69.
51 Ibid., 70.
52 Patrick Howarth, *Play Up and Play the Game: The Heroes of Popular Fiction* (London, 1973), 14.
53 Patric Dickinson (ed.), *Selected Poems of Henry Newbolt* (London, 1981), 14. For biographical matter on Newbolt, see Dickinson and Margaret Newbolt (ed.), *The Later Life and Letters of Sir Henry Newbolt* (London, 1942), passim.
54 Henry Newbolt, *The Twymans: A Tale of Youth* (Edinburgh, 1911), 82.
55 W. E. Leonard and S. B. Smith (eds.), *De Rerum Natura* (Madison, 1965), 320.
56 *Selected Poems*, 37.
57 Howarth, 1.
58 Dickinson, 18.
59 Ibid., 35.
60 Ibid., 61–62.
61 Ibid., 44.
62 Margaret Newbolt, 232.
63 Ibid., 227.
64 Ibid.
65 Henry Newbolt, *The Book of the Happy Warrior* (London, 1917), ii.
66 Ibid., 283.
67 Ibid., 270.
68 Ibid., 275.
69 Ibid., 277.
70 *The Happy Warrior*, 284.
71 Margaret Newbolt, 315.
72 *Selected Poems*, 151.
73 Canto 74, *Cantos of Ezra Pound* (New York, 1970), 433.
74 Connolly, 325.
75 (London, 1970), 37.
76 Quoted in I. F. Clarke, *Voices Prophesying War, 1763–1884* (London, 1966), 132.
77 Gathorne-Hardy, 200.
78 (Garden City, 1929), 10.

6 AT THE WICKET

1 Shane Leslie, *The Oppidan* (New York, 1922), 30.
2 Ibid., 80.
3 Connolly, 180. Both G. A. Henty and Robert Graves took up boxing as a cool calculation to ward off bullies at their schools, Westminster and Charterhouse, respectively.
4 Leslie, 12.
5 Esme Wingfield-Stratford, *The Victorian Sunset* (New York, 1932), 348.
6 Leslie, 61.

7 Ibid., 49.
8 Ibid., 22.
9 Ibid., 23.
10 Ibid., 22.
11 Ibid., 53.
12 Ibid., 103.
13 Ibid., 211.
14 Ibid., 214.
15 Ibid., 216.
16 Ibid., 341.
17 The fire is discussed in David Newsome, *On the Edge of Paradise: A. C. Benson, the Diarist* (London, 1980), 78ff, and L. E. Jones, *A Victorian Boyhood* (London, 1955), 175ff.
18 Ibid., 362.
19 Ibid., 365.
20 "Mr. Bennett and Mrs. Brown," *The Captain's Death Bed and Other Essays* (London, 1950), 91.
21 Arthur Ponsonby, *The Decline of Aristocracy* (London, 1912), 18.
22 Ibid., 136.
23 Ibid., 200.
24 Ibid., 222.
25 J. A. Mangan, *Athleticism in the Victorian and Edwardian Public School* (Cambridge, 1977), 28.
26 J. R. S. Honey, *Tom Brown's Universe: The Development of the Victorian Public School* (London, 1977), 175.
27 Mangan, 29.
28 Ibid., 71.
29 Ibid., 144.
30 Ibid.
31 Esme Wingfield-Stratford, *Before the Lamps Went Out* (London, 1945), 123.
32 Republished as *Mike at Wrykyn* (New York, 1953), 4.
33 Mangan, 128.
34 Honey, 229.
35 Mangan, 129.
36 Honey, 227.
37 Mack, 295.
38 Arnold Lunn, *The Harrovian* (London, 1913), 3.
39 Ibid., 33.
40 Lunn, 48.
41 Ibid., 44.
42 Ibid., 67.
43 Ibid., 140.
44 Ibid., 222.
45 Ibid., 109.
46 Ibid., 81.
47 Arnold Lunn, *Come What May: An Autobiography* (London, 1940), 114.
48 Ibid., 139.
49 Alec Waugh, preface to the new edition, *The Loom of Youth* (London, 1955), 11.

50   *A Little Learning, An Autobiography* (Boston, 1964), 93.

51   Preface to the first edition, 13.

52   No exact figures are available for the public schools, but of the 838 Balliol College (Oxford) men serving in the British forces during the Great War, 183 were killed—a 22 percent mortality rate. (This is exactly twice the national figure of 11 percent killed of those who served.) There is every reason to suspect that the figures for other colleges and for public schools would be close to that of Balliol. See J. M. Winter, "Balliol's 'Lost Generation,'" *Balliol College Annual Record* (1975), 23.

53   *Loom*, 21.

54   Ibid., 28.

55   Ibid., 126.

56   Ibid., 87.

57   Ibid., 191.

58   Ibid., 154.

59   Ibid., 228.

60   For Brooke, see chapter 10, below.

61   *Loom*, 228.

62   Ibid., 261.

63   Ibid., 263.

64   Ibid., 287.

65   Martin Browne, *A Dream of Youth: An Etonian's reply to "The Loom of Youth"* (London, 1918), passim. Another objector was Jack Hood, but his *Heart of a Schoolboy* (London, 1919) inadvertently reinforced Waugh's thesis about games obsession.

66   Lyttleton reviewed Waugh in *Contemporary Review* (December, 1917); Mack, *Public Schools Since 1860*, 354.

67   Honey, 114.

68   (July, 1925); Mack, *Public Schools Since 1860*, 354.

69   Ian Hay, *The Lighter Side of School Life* (Boston, 1915), 209.

70   Ibid., 211.

71   Ibid., 208.

72   Ibid.

73   Ibid., 87.

74   Ibid., 33.

75   Ibid., 189.

76   Ibid., 227.

77   Hamilton, 130; Shaw is quoted in Mack, *Public Schools Since 1860*, 266.

78   Mangan, 195.

79   Esme Wingfield-Stratford, *Before the Lamps Went Out* (London, 1945), 113.

7   PETER PAN'S ENGLAND

1   Andrew Birkin, *J. M. Barrie and the Lost Boys* (London, 1979), 69.

2   Five of these photographs are reproduced in Birkin, 89–91, but over the years Barrie took hundreds of snapshots of the five Davies boys.

3   *The Little White Bird, or Adventures in Kensington Gardens* (New York, 1902), 256.

4   Ibid., 258.

5   Ibid., 158.

6 Roger L. Green, *Fifty Years of Peter Pan* (London, 1954), 89. Shaw then wrote *Androcles and the Lion* to show Barrie how a play for children should be written.
7 *Peter Pan, or the Boy Who Would Not Grow Up* (London, 1928), 17.
8 Ibid.
9 Ibid., 31.
10 Ibid., 91.
11 Birkin, 118.
12 *Peter Pan*, 61.
13 Ibid., 143.
14 Birkin, 289.
15 *Peter Pan*, 17.
16 Birkin, 196.
17 Ibid., 286.
18 *Peter Pan*, 128.
19 *Peter Pan*, 139.
20 Anthony Powell, *To Keep the Ball Rolling* (London, 1976), I, 43.
21 Graham Greene, *A Sort of Life* (London, 1971), 56.
22 "Bookshop Memories," *The Collected Essays* (New York, 1968), I, 244.
23 M. V. Brett (ed.), *Journals and Letters of Viscount Esher* (London, 1934), II, 367.
24 Denis Mackail, *The Story of J. M. B.* (London, 1941), 408.
25 A Patriot [Guy du Maurier], *An Englishman's Home* (London, 1909), 50.
26 Ibid., 56.
27 Ibid., 95.
28 Birkin, 172.
29 Clarke, 184.
30 Morris, 413.
31 Hynes, 48.
32 Birkin, 172.
33 Mackail, 408.
34 Katherine Mansfield, *In a German Pension* (New York, 1935), 19.
35 Stanley Casson, *Steady Drummer* (London, 1935), 13.
36 Ibid., 17.
37 Birkin, 192.
38 From Peter Davies's memoir, Birkin, 223.
39 Birkin, 237.
40 *"Der Tag"* (New York, 1914), 4.
41 Ibid., 11.
42 Ibid., 20.
43 "The New Word," *Echoes of War* (New York, 1918), 92.
44 Ibid., 106.
45 Birkin, 236.
46 Dunbar, 273–74.
47 Birkin, 246.
48 Ibid., 243.
49 Dunbar, 275.
50 Birkin, 247.
51 "A Well-Remembered Voice," 181.

52 Birkin, 367.
53 Ibid., 293.
54 Ibid., 293.
55 Ibid., 296. The version in Dunbar is inaccurate, 360.
56 Birkin, 282.
57 Ibid., 286–88.

8 MISSIONARY OF EMPIRE

1   Quoted in Roger L. Green, *Kipling: The Critical Heritage* (London, 1971), 202.
2   From Robert Buchanan's scathing review in *Contemporary Review* (1899), quoted in ibid, 236.
3   Rudyard Kipling, *Mine Own People* (New York, 1891), 12.
4   James's remarks about Kipling's work are from private letters quoted in Green, 68–69. James seems to have been particularly confounded by Kipling's story "The Ship That Found Herself" (1894), in which the mechanical parts of a ship talk to each other. (Cast iron says little, but steel plates are loquacious.)
5   *A Room of One's Own* (New York, 1957), 106.
6   David Cecil, *Max: A Biography* (London, 1964), 251.
7   Quoted in C. E. Carrington, *The Life of Rudyard Kipling* (Garden City, 1955), 263.
8   Quoted in J. I. M. Stewart, "Kipling's Reputation," in John Gross (ed.), *The Age of Kipling* (New York, 1972), 157.
9   *Rudyard Kipling's Verse* (Garden City, 1943), 223.
10 Dickinson, 17.
11 Quoted in Green, 305.
12 *A Soldier's Memories in Peace and War* (London, 1917), 187.
13 Ibid., 189.
14 *Good-bye to All That* (London, 1960), 63.
15 *Verse*, 415.
16 Ibid., 200.
17 "An English School," *Land and Sea Tales for Scouts and Guards* (London, 1923), 262.
18 *Stalky & Co.* (Garden City, 1914), 153.
19 Robert Buchanan in *Contemporary Review;* quoted in Green, 245.
20 *Stalky*, 194.
21 Ibid., 197.
22 Ibid., 246.
23 Review in *Academy;* quoted in Green, 232.
24 Lord Birkenhead, *Rudyard Kipling* (New York, 1978), 208.
25 Ibid., 215.
26 Ibid., 235.
27 Ibid., 184.
28 Ibid., 252.
29 *Verse*, 300.
30 *Verse*, 487.
31 *Puck of Pook's Hill* (Garden City, 1915), 125.
32 Carrington, 296.

33 Richard Faber, *The Vision and the Need: Late Victorian Imperialist Aims* (London, 1966), 99.

34 Lord Birkenhead, 256.

35 *A History of England* (Oxford, 1911), 16, 22, 39, 162, 244, 241.

36 *Verse*, 715.

37 Ibid., 718.

38 Ibid., 727.

39 Carrington, 317.

40 "An English School," *Land and Sea Tales for Scouts and Guards*, 258.

41 *Verse*, 169.

42 Orwell, *The Collected Essays*, I, 160.

43 Quoted in Green, 338.

44 Ibid., 295.

45 Eliot L. Gilbert (ed.), *O Beloved Kids: Rudyard Kipling's Letters to His Children* (London, 1983), 113.

46 *A Diversity of Creatures* (Garden City, 1917), 266.

47 Carrington, 329. In "The Captive," a story collected in *Traffics and Discoveries* (1904), a general remarks of the Boer War, "It's a first class dress parade for Armageddon."

48 *Verse*, 328.

49 Gilbert, 178.

50 So labeled by Stanley Baldwin's son Oliver; Lord Birkenhead, 316. Carrington notes that this story was being written six months prior to the death of his son in France, not after the event, as has sometimes been claimed.

51 *A Diversity of Creatures* (London, 1917), 429.

52 *Debits and Credits*, 40.

53 Carrington, 348.

54 Quoted in Morton Cohen (ed.), *Rudyard Kipling to Rider Haggard* (London, 1965), 81.

55 Gilbert, 14.

56 Carrington, 338.

57 Rider Haggard interviewed several soldiers who had been nearby and pieced together this account. See Cohen, 86.

58 Carrington, 341.

59 Angus Wilson, *The Strange Ride of Rudyard Kipling* (New York, 1977), 300.

60 Lord Birkenhead, 271.

61 *The Fringes of the Fleet* (New York, 1916), 119. Most of Kipling's journalism during the war years was promptly reprinted in the United States in order to encourage American intervention.

62 Lord Birkenhead, 273.

63 John Gross (ed.), *The Age of Kipling* (New York, 1972), 147.

64 T. S. Eliot, introduction to *A Choice of Kipling's Verse* (London, 1942), 21.

65 *Verse*, 386.

66 Ibid., 387.

67 Ibid., 388.

68 D. S. Higgins (ed.), *The Private Diaries of Sir H. Rider Haggard* (London, 1980), 180.

69 Ibid., 142.

9 GENTLEMEN SPORTSMEN

1 Sir Arthur Conan Doyle, *A Study in Scarlet* (1888).
2 Ibid.
3 Sir Arthur Conan Doyle, "The Red-Headed League" (1891).
4 Holmes' publications have been compiled by Vincent Starrett, *The Private Life of Sherlock Holmes* (New York, 1933), 113–17.
5 *A Study in Scarlet.*
6 Sir Arthur Conan Doyle, "The Adventure of the Norwood Builder" (1903).
7 Sir Arthur Conan Doyle, "The Adventures of the Speckled Band" (1892).
8 Sir Arthur Conan Doyle, *The Hound of the Baskervilles* (1902).
9 Sir Arthur Conan Doyle, *The Valley of Fear* (Garden City, 1930), 181.
10 Sir Arthur Conan Doyle, "The Adventure of the Solitary Cyclist" (1904).
11 Sir Arthur Conan Doyle, "The Adventure of the Missing Three-Quarters" (1904).
12 Sir Arthur Conan Doyle, *Memories and Adventures* (Boston, 1924), 273.
13 Ibid., 75.
14 Sir Arthur Conan Doyle, "The Adventure of the Final Problem" (1893).
15 George Lukács, *Realism in Our Time* (New York, 1962), 47.
16 *Memories,* 11.
17 Pierre Nordon, *Conan Doyle* (New York, 1967), 300.
18 Sir Arthur Conan Doyle, *The Great Boer War* (New York, 1902), 1.
19 Ibid., 425.
20 (October, 1900), 433–46.
21 Sir Arthur Conan Doyle, *The War in South Africa: Its Cause and Conduct* (New York, 1902), 3.
22 Ibid., 21.
23 Ibid., 32.
24 Ibid., 53.
25 Ibid., 109.
26 Ibid., 84.
27 Ibid., 85.
28 Ibid., 93.
29 Ibid., 132.
30 Nordon, 74.
31 *Memories,* 308.
32 Ibid., 238.
33 General Friedrich von Bernhardi, *Germany and the Next War* (New York, 1914), 14.
34 Ibid., 10.
35 Ibid., 106.
36 (Boston, 1914), 33.
37 "Danger," *The Stark Munro Letters* (New York, 1930), 256.
38 Ibid., 256.
39 Nordon, 88.
40 Sir Arthur Conan Doyle, *The Poison Belt* (Garden City, 1930), 264.
41 Ibid., 267.
42 Ibid., 309.
43 Nordon, 90.
44 Ibid., 91.

45 Richard L. Green and John M. Gibson, *A Bibliography of A. Conan Doyle* (Oxford, 1983), 296.
46 Ibid., 93.
47 Ibid., 97.
48 *Memories*, 339.
49 Ibid., 384.
50 Ibid., 340.
51 Ibid., 348.
52 *The British Campaign in France and Flanders* (London, 1918), III, 50.
53 Ibid., 101.
54 *The British Campaign in France and Flanders* (London, 1917), II, 43–44.
55 Green and Gibson, 183.
56 Sir Arthur Conan Doyle, "His Last Bow."
57 Nordon, 106.
58 *Memories*, 394.
59 Charles Higham, *The Adventures of Conan Doyle* (New York, 1976), 265; Dan Richard Cox, *Arthur Conan Doyle* (New York, 1985), 225.
60 Higham, 330.
61 Sir Arthur Conan Doyle, *The History of Spiritualism* (London, 1926), II, 278.
62 *Memories*, 283.
63 Anthony Curtis' introduction to E. W. Hornung, *Raffles the Amateur Cracksman* (London, 1972), n.p.
64 Orwell, "Raffles and Miss Blandish," in *The Collected Essays*, III, 213.
65 Esme Wingfield-Stratford, *The Victorian Sunset* (New York, 1932), 346.
66 Hornung, "The Gift of the Emperor," *Raffles*, 145.
67 Hornung, "A Jubilee Gift," in ibid., 176.
68 E. W. Hornung, *Notes of a Camp-Follower on the Western Front* (New York, 1919), 221.
69 Ibid., 153.
70 Ibid., 154.
71 Ibid., 2.
72 Ibid., 169, 163.
73 Ibid., 96.
74 Ibid., 152.
75 Ibid., 206.
76 Ernest Hemingway, *A Farewell to Arms,* chapter 27.
77 Graham Greene, *The Return of A. J. Raffles* (London, 1975), 79.
78 Ibid., 46.
79 Vincent Starrett, "221B," quoted in Basil Rathbone, *In and Out of Character* (New York, 1962), 183.

10 SAILING TO BYZANTIUM

1 Michael MacDonagh, *In London During the Great War* (1935), 15, 33, 65.
2 Ibid., 40.
3 *The Journal of Arnold Bennett, 1896–1928* (New York, 1933), 542, 593.
4 Attributed to Richard Aldington by Robert H. Ross, *The Georgian Revolt, 1910–1922: Rise and Fall of a Poetic Ideal* (Carbondale, 1965), 50.

5   Edward Marsh, *A Number of People* (New York and London, 1939), 329.

6   Edmund Gosse, *Some Diversions of a Man of Letters* (London, 1919), 268.

7   Christopher Hassall, *Rupert Brooke: A Biography* (London, 1964), 528. A Brooke
    publicist estimates sales of the poetry totalling 700,000 copies; see Michael Hast-
    ings, *The Handsomest Young Man in England: Rupert Brooke* (London, 1967), 58.
    Another Brooke scholar puts the sales figure at 600,000 by 1954; see Robert B.
    Pearsall, *Rupert Brooke: The Man and Poet* (Amsterdam, 1954), 167.

8   Marsh, 322–23.

9   Marsh's prefatory note to *Georgian Poetry, 1911–1912* (London, 1912), n.p.

10 John Lehmann, *Rupert Brooke His Life and His Legend* (London, 1980), 70.

11 *Collected Poems* (London, 1918), 56.

12 *New Bearings in English Poetry* (London, 1952), 28.

13 "Inside the Whale," *The Collected Essays*, I 503.

14 Brooke is treated as a major emblematic figure in Robert Wohl's *The Generation of
    1914* (Cambridge, 1979), in George Dangerfield's *The Strange Death of Liberal
    England* (New York, 1935), and in Reginald Pound's *The Lost Generation of 1914*
    (New York, 1965).

15 *New Bearings*, 27.

16 Lehmann, 4; Christopher Hassall (ed.), *The Prose of Rupert Brooke* (London, 1956),
    406; Samuel Hynes, *Edwardian Occasions* (London, 1972), 147; Marsh memoir in
    The Collected Poems of Rupert Brooke (London, 1918), xxvii.

17 Hassall, 187.

18 Ibid., 107; Marsh memoir in *Collected Poems*, xxiv.

19 Hassall, 108.

20 Ibid., 117.

21 Ibid., 95.

22 Letter to Geoffrey Keynes in *The Letters of Rupert Brooke*, edited by Geoffrey
    Keynes (London, 1968), 59.

23 Letter to Frances Darwin, in Hastings, 71.

24 Marsh memoir, xxiv.

25 Hassall, 143.

26 *Collected Poems*, 93.

27 Letter to Jacques Raverat, in Keynes, 192–95.

28 *Collected Poems*, 92.

29 Ibid., 109.

30 Arundel De Re, quoted in Ross, 93.

31 Keynes, 331.

32 Marsh memoir, lxxii.

33 Ibid., 364, 379.

34 Paul Levy Moore, *G. E. Moore and the Cambridge Apostles* (London, 1979), 261.

35 Reprinted in Eric Hamberger (ed.), *Ezra Pound: The Critical Heritage* (London,
    1972), 59.

36 Hassall, 190.

37 *Collected Poems*, 142.

38 Keynes, 300.

39 Alun R. Jones, *The Life and Opinions of T. E. Hulme* (London, 1938), 99. Curi-
    ously, Hulme was one of the judges awarding a prize to Brooke's "Grantchester,"
    but he was probably overruled by Marsh and Newbolt.

40 Keynes, 408.
41 Cathleen Nesbitt, *A Little Love and Good Company*, (London, 1975), 74.
42 Keynes, 418.
43 Nesbitt, 92.
44 Hassall, 258. This conforms to E. M. Forster's evaluation of Brooke as "humorous intelligent and beautiful" but "essentially hard . . . and I don't envy anyone who applied to him for sympathy." *Selected Letters of E. M. Forster* (Cambridge, Mass., 1983), I, 227.
45 Norman Douglas, *Looking Back* (New York, 1933), 327.
46 Keynes, 459.
47 Ibid., 469.
48 Rupert Brooke, *Letters from America* (London, 1916), 38 and passim.
49 Ibid., 96. In writing to a Cambridge friend about Niagara, Brooke was capable of self-mockery: "I sit and stare at the thing and have the purest Nineteenth Century grandiose thoughts, about the Destiny of Man, the Irresistibility of Fate, the Doom of Nations, the fact that Death awaits us All, and so forth. Wordsworth Redivivius. Oh dear! oh dear!"; Keynes, 491.
50 *Letters from America*, 143, 139.
51 Ibid., 155.
52 Keynes, 523.
53 Ibid., 544.
54 Ibid., 522.
55 Ibid., 534.
56 Ibid., 541.
57 Ibid., 565.
58 *Collected Poems*, 14.
59 Ibid., 568, 573.
60 Ibid., 540.
61 Hassall, 441–42.
62 Keynes, 596.
63 Hassall, 442.
64 Keynes, 572.
65 Keynes, 602.
66 Hassall, 456.
67 Ibid., 599.
68 Wohl, *The Generation of 1914*, 88.
69 *The Prose of Rupert Brooke* (London, 1956), 199.
70 Keynes, 613.
71 Hassall, 465.
72 Keynes, 624.
73 Ibid., 632.
74 Hassall, 471.
75 *Collected Poems*, 5.
76 Ibid., 7.
77 Ibid., 9.
78 Jon Silkin, *Out of Battle: The Poetry of the Great War* (Oxford, 1978), 68.
79 Keynes, 660.
80 Ibid., 662.

81 Marsh memoir, cliii.
82 Ibid., 670.
83 Ibid., 672.
84 Ibid., 670.
85 Hassall, 497–98.
86 Keynes, 684.
87 Hassall, 512.
88 Lehmann, 144.
89 Marsh memoir, clviii–clix.
90 Printed in Hastings, 185.
91 Marsh memoir, cliii.
92 Marsh, *A Number of People*, 247.
93 Lehmann, 155.
94 Hassall, 527.
95 Ibid., 529.
96 *Blast* (July, 1915), 21. He attached a footnote to the poem which read, in part: "Malheureusement ses poèmes ne sont rempli que de ses propres subjectivités, style Victorien de la 'Georgian Anthology.'"
97 Charles Norman, *Ezra Pound* (New York, 1960), 161.
98 Quoted in Stephen Spender, *Love-Hate Relations: English and American Sensibilities* (New York, 1974), 164.
99 Auden, *Collected Poems*, ed. Edward Mendelson (London, 1976; New York, 1976); Connolly, 193.
100 *Edwardian Occasions*, 152.

11 NINETEEN-FOURTEEN

1   Charles Edmonds [Charles Edmund Carrington], *A Subaltern's War* (New York, 1930), 15–16.
2   (New York, 1950), 120.
3   Osbert Sitwell, *Great Morning!* (Boston, 1947), 263.
4   Ibid.
5   *Testament of Youth: An Autobiographical Study of the Years, 1900–1925* (New York, 1935), 51.
6   Viscount Grey of Fallodon, *Twenty-Five Years 1892–1916*, II (New York, 1925), 20. The quotation may not be accurate, and it may never have occurred. In his memoir, Grey reports what a friend says that he said, not what he remembered having said.
7   Michael MacDonagh, *In London During the Great War* (London, 1935), 4–6. MacDonagh was a *Times* correspondent specializing in political affairs.
8   Ibid., 8–10.
9   John Terraine, *Impacts of War, 1914 & 1918* (London, 1970), 47.
10 C. E. Montague, *Disenchantment* (London, 1922), 11.
11 *The Autobiography of Bertrand Russell, 1914–1944* (Boston, 1968), 4.
12 Ibid., 115. The enthusiastic response of European intellectuals to the war receives definitive treatment in Roland N. Stromberg, *Redemption by War: The Intellectuals and 1914* (Lawrence, Kansas 1982).
13 Stanley Weintraub, *Journey to Heartbreak: The Crucible Years of B. Shaw, 1914–1918* (New York, 1971), 30.

14 *The New Statesman* IV (November 14, 1914), "Special War Supplement," 3.

15 Ibid., 4.

16 Weintraub, 61, 63, 78.

17 George Bernard Shaw, preface to *Hearbreak House* (New York, 1919), liv.

18 Ibid., ix.

19 For a meticulous case study of how an English writer with German wife was harassed, see Paul Delany, *D. H. Lawrence's Nightmare; The Writer and His Circle in the Years of the Great War* (New York, 1978).

20 Preface to *Heartbreak House*, xxii.

21 MacDonagh, 105.

22 *A Sort of Life*, 64.

23 Patric Dickinson (ed.), *Selected Poems of Henry Newbolt* (London, 1981), 48.

24 Jon Silkin, *Out of Battle: The Poetry of the Great War* (Oxford, 1978), 140. Only five days after the outbreak of the war Thomas Hardy wrote in a letter, "Among the ironies of the time is the fact that all the nations are praying to the same God. There was a gleam of reason in the old nations when they prayed for deliverance each to his own god, but that reasonableness is gone." Richard Little Purdy and Michael Millgate (eds.), *The Collected Letters of Thomas Hardy,* (Oxford, 1985), 41.

25 The characterizations are supplied by A. C. Benson, a participant. Quoted in David Newsome, *On the Edge of Paradise: A. C. Benson, The Diarist* (London, 1980), 313.

26 Public Records Office (Kew), INF 4 (Ministry of Information Files, 1914–18), file 4A.

27 (London, 1915), 74.

28 These nuggets of fools' gold were dug out of the files of the *Times* by John Terraine, 72, 215.

29 *Collected Letters*, 42, 45.

30 Ibid., 59.

31 Weintraub, 54.

32 *A Little Learning: An Autobiography* (Boston, 1964), 99, 116.

33 "The Gothic Arch," in Graham Greene (ed.), *The Old School* (London, 1934), 133.

34 "The Wat'ry Glade," in Greene, 150.

35 Anthony Powell, *To Keep the Ball Rolling: The Memoirs of Anthony Powell,* (London, 1976), I 34.

36 *High Altars* (London, 1918), 8.

37 Ibid., 21, 27.

38 Ibid., 38.

39 (London, 1939), 168.

40 Ibid., 272.

41 Carrington, 34, 64, 71, 98, 104.

42 For various accounts of the football stunt, see Paul Fussell, *The Great War and Modern Memory* (Oxford, 1975), 27–28.

43 "I felt sure he had chosen the wrong means of locomotion, and I gravely doubted his ability to make the round trip successfully." Raoul Amundsen, *My Life as an Explorer* (New York, 1927), 261. Amundsen diplomatically refrained from listing other flagrant British oversights, among them inappropriate or inadequate clothing, goggles, food, tents, sledges, paraffin tins, and skis—to mention only the most obvious examples.

44 Roland Huntford, *Scott and Amundsen* (London, 1979), 548.

45 Mark Girouard, *Return to Camelot: Chivalry and the English Gentleman* (New York, 1981), 4.
46 *The Collapse of British Power* (London, 1972), 88.
47 Ibid., 84ff.
48 *Statistics of the Military Effort of the British Empire during the Great War, 1914–1920* (London, 1922), 237.
49 Ibid., 554.
50 Ibid., 561.
51 *Edwardian Occasions*, 107.

Index

▼

Library of Congress Cataloging-in-Publication Data
Eby, Cecil D.
The road to Armageddon.
Includes index.
1. English literature—19th century—History and criticism. 2. English literature—20th century—History and
criticism. 3. Military art and science in literature.
4. Popular literature—Great Britain—History and
criticism. I. Title.
PR469.M55E2   1987   820′.9′358   87-9212
ISBN 0-8223-0775-8